D1328396

WITHDRAWN

SYRIA

DAWN CHATTY

Syria

The Making and Unmaking of a Refuge State

OXFORD
UNIVERSITY PRESS

OXFORD
UNIVERSITY PRESS

Oxford University Press is a department of the
University of Oxford. It furthers the University's objective
of excellence in research, scholarship, and education
by publishing worldwide.

Oxford   New York

Auckland   Cape Town   Dar es Salaam   Hong Kong   Karachi
Kuala Lumpur   Madrid   Melbourne   Mexico City   Nairobi
New Delhi   Shanghai   Taipei   Toronto

With offices in

Argentina   Austria   Brazil   Chile   Czech Republic   France   Greece
Guatemala   Hungary   Italy   Japan   Poland   Portugal   Singapore
South Korea   Switzerland   Thailand   Turkey   Ukraine   Vietnam

Oxford is a registered trade mark of Oxford University Press
in the UK and certain other countries.

Published in the United States of America by
Oxford University Press
198 Madison Avenue, New York, NY 10016

Copyright © Dawn Chatty 2018

All rights reserved. No part of this publication may be reproduced,
stored in a retrieval system, or transmitted, in any form or by any means,
without the prior permission in writing of Oxford University Press,
or as expressly permitted by law, by license, or under terms agreed with
the appropriate reproduction rights organization. Inquiries concerning
reproduction outside the scope of the above should be sent to the
Rights Department, Oxford University Press, at the address above.

You must not circulate this work in any other form
and you must impose this same condition on any acquirer.

Library of Congress Cataloging-in-Publication Data is available
Dawn Chatty.
Syria: The Making and Unmaking of a Refuge State.
ISBN: 9780190876067

Printed in the United Kingdom by Bell and Bain Ltd, Glasgow

CONTENTS

To Lucy and Charles de Burgh

ACKNOWLEDGEMENTS

This book has several beginnings: my early childhood fascination with the diversity of peoples I saw walking the streets of old Damascus; my later discovery of its outlying Cretan, Circassian, and Kurdish quarters made up of refugees from the end of the Ottoman Empire, and my academic study of forced migration in the modern states of the Levant. It was a conversation with Alasdair Craig, a commissioning editor at Hurst Publishers, that persuaded me that this book needed to be written. Syria's long history as a place of refuge needed to be retold, especially now with the horror of Syria's violent conflict and humanitarian catastrophe part of our daily news.

The interviews that are quoted in this book were collected over nearly a decade between 2005 and 2015 in Syria, Turkey, Lebanon, and Jordan thanks to, first, a Major Research Fellowship from the Leverhulme Foundation and later grants from the British Academy and the Council for British Research in the Levant. Often working with local research associates, I was able to gain access to many key informants though their good offices. I need to thank Sarab Atassi, the former scientific director at the French Institute for Near Eastern Studies in Damascus (IFPO) as well as Jihad Darwaza and her sister Watfa Darwaza in Damascus for all their help in hosting me, arranging interviews, transcribing them, and discussing meanings and various interpretations with me—often over long evenings on balconies in Damascus drinking coffee or herbal teas. Tawfik Al Asadi also led me to key informants and assisted in the conduct of interviews and in transcriptions. In Turkey, Onver Cetrez, the deputy director of the Swedish Institute in Istanbul,

ACKNOWLEDGEMENTS

provided me with accommodation and made many useful suggestions regarding possible key informants. I had the assistance of Mazen Gharibah and his team of Syrian researchers in Istanbul as well as Kirsten Biehl, a doctoral student from Oxford fluent in Turkish and English. In Gaziantep I was particularly grateful for the support I received from Urs Fruehauf at the Deutsche Gesellschaft für Internationale Zusammenarbeit (GIZ) and also from Zeina Bali in assisting with my interviews with displaced Syrians. I was fortunate to have the support of Dr Ali Zafer Sagiroglu from Beyazit University in accessing displaced Syrians in the Turkish-run refugee camps near Nizip. In Lebanon I had the help of Lena Al-Habash and Maha El Helou, as well as the staff of the Amel Association in reaching out to displaced Syrians. The Jordanian Hashemite Fund for Human Development (JOHUD) facilitated my entry into Za'tari refugee camp, and Maha Al-Asil worked closely with me in identifying key informants and co-interviewing with me.

I owe a great debt to Nigel James, Michel Athanson, and Sebastian Ballard for preparing the maps in this book. I would also like to thank Margaret Okole, and Mary Starkey for editing and searching out of inconsistencies that I could no longer see. My thanks also go to Jon de Peyer, senior editor at Hurst Publishers, for viewing hundreds of photographs until he finally located the image for the front cover.

My greatest thanks go to my husband, Nicholas Mylne, for his acceptance of a very distracted companion for over a year. His patience and kindness saw me through the writing of a story which is full of dark shadows and sadness. In the end, it is the hope of a return to Syria some day which many of those I interviewed still hold that I must applaud. It is the light at the end of a very dark tunnel.

Some of the material in this book appeared originally in the following article and book, and is used here with permission: 'The Making of a Cosmopolitan Quarter: Sha'laan in the 20th Century', *Syria Studies* 6 (2) (2014): 29–54 and *Displacement and Dispossession in the Modern Middle East*, Cambridge: Cambridge University Press, 2010.

INTRODUCTION

That land known as Syria has long fired the Western imagination. For much of the nineteenth century its cities, particularly Aleppo and Damascus, were part of the itinerary of the more adventurous Europeans making their 'Grand Tours' to the relics of ancient civilizations. These two cities vied for the accolade of being the longest continuously inhabited cities in the world, and over the centuries both hosted groups seeking refuge. Damascus, furthermore, had strong links to Christian and Muslim tradition: Saul is known to have had a revelation—called his Damascene moment—as he approached the city, leading him to convert from Judaism to Christianity and take the name Paul. Muhammad is said to have approached the 'fragrant city' from the desert and been so overcome by the luxuriant and fertile gardens before him that he turned back, saying he was not yet ready to enter paradise.

Much of ancient Greek tradition is supposed to have been preserved and then passed on to the West via the keen husbandry of the early Muslim Umayyad dynasty based in Damascus. The seven centuries of Muslim rule in Spain and Portugal also traced their heritage and roots back to the Damascene caliphate. During these centuries many diverse social groups maintained their ethno-religious character, secure in a widespread tolerance of these various syncretic religious and social communities, some tucked away in the mountainous coastal region of Syria and others comfortably established in suburbs of Damascus and other cities. Only once was this local conviviality shattered, in response to the 1860 civil war in Mount Lebanon between the Maronite Christians and the local Druze community. Many Druze from Mount

Lebanon sought refuge in Syria, primarily in the Hauran region of South Syria. But in Damascus and also Aleppo riots erupted, only to be quelled several days later, by Abdul Qadir al-Jaza'iri, the exiled Algerian national 'freedom fighter' whom Napoleon III had permitted to leave his house arrest in France to take up open residence in Damascus along with a few hundred of his men.

Wherever one turned in Syria one came across stories—some underplayed and others exaggerated—of exile, refuge, and asylum. My story was no exception. I had just accepted my first teaching post at the American University of Beirut (AUB) in September 1975. Upon arrival at the airport, I learned that the country was under curfew, and, though it was unacknowledged at the time, was facing a civil war. After a few terrifying days getting used to the sound of rocket fire and semi-automatic weapons, I was granted faculty accommodation on a back street connected to the University Hospital. My sense of safety, however, was shattered when I discovered that numerous armed militias were competing to control the street, moving their snipers from one rooftop to another on the street behind my flat. Often during these clashes I felt the need to lie flat on the floor of my bedroom in case any flying bullets pierced the walls. Street fighting in the city put an end to any thought of starting the teaching term on time, and for two months we awaited instructions to commence our courses. During this time I began to look for escape from the city, which was tearing itself apart. Often I negotiated trips to Damascus by taxi for myself and some of the other new faculty. Taking back roads over the mountains, we generally made the trip in three or four hours instead of the usual two. Beirut and Damascus are the two closest capital cities in the world.

At such times, arriving in Damascus was a release, a haven, and a refuge. It was also an opportunity to relax, meet up with many other Lebanese and American faculty from AUB, and join the large swarm of other Lebanese also seeking respite from the civil war in their country. Days were spent enjoying the charms of the old city with its mix of Aramean, Greek, Roman, and early Muslim monuments. Were it not for the fact that we had no idea what the next day would bring and that, having travelled light, were also vaguely concerned about our property—rented, borrowed, or owned—back in Lebanon, we might have passed for tourists rather than refugees from a civil war in a neighbouring country.

INTRODUCTION

In November 1975 I was standing in the middle of a wide round-about in Damascus's Baramki quarter looking for a shared taxi to travel to Amman. Taxis were easily the most comfortable way to travel, and taxi drivers hung about waiting for passengers, generally five, before setting off on their regular routes between cities in the region. I could hear the shouts 'Beirut, Beirut', 'Halab, Halab' (Aleppo), 'Baghdad, Baghdad', 'Amman, Amman'. I was just about to turn to the taxi driver to grab a seat in the Amman taxi when I heard 'Grozny, Grozny'. I stopped in my tracks. Why would anyone be going to Chechnya from Damascus, I thought. The call for passengers to Grozny stayed in my mind over the entire trip to Amman. At one point I engaged my taxi driver in conversation. 'Do you get many taxi drivers to Grozny?' I asked. 'Yes, enough', he said. 'There are many Cherkass [Circassians] and Sheyshan [Chechnyans] in Syria and Jordan.' This pronouncement intrigued me, and for the next few decades I began—rather unsystematically at first—to map out areas in Damascus, and Syria as a whole, where communities who did not identify solely as Syrian could be found, to explore how and why they happened to be there.

People have moved throughout history. It is part of our heritage as human beings. It explains our distribution across the face of the earth, and it is captured not only in genome research but also in literature—secular as well as sacred. Texts dating back to the Bible and before, to Homer's *Iliad* and to Virgil's *Aeneid*, tell of forced migration of peoples as well as individual exiles and refuge. Some migrations appear to have been voluntary and opportunistic, taking place over centuries and millennia: the migration of neolithic farmers from the Fertile Crescent via Anatolia and the Balkan land mass; other pioneering sea-faring colonization through Cyprus and the Aegean, bringing agricultural and husbandry practices to Europe around 8000 BCE (Fernández et al. 2014). Other migrations were dramatic and violent: the expulsion of the Israelites to Babylon in 586 BCE and their release from servitude by Cyrus the Great when he took Babylon in 538 BCE. Yet others were mysterious, such as the movement of the 'Sea Peoples' in the twelfth and thirteenth centuries BCE, who appeared suddenly along the Mediterranean's eastern coastline, wreaking havoc wherever they went. Although migrations have occurred all over the globe, Syria and the Fertile Crescent have been at the heart of migrations of people, ideas, and goods for millennia. It has been a crossroads for trade; the famous Silk Route from China to Europe ran through Aleppo and Damascus. It has also been an important stopping place on religious pilgrimages both within Christianity and Islam.

The name Syria conjures up several geographical places with fuzzy boundaries: the Fertile Crescent, the Near East, the Levant. Somehow Syria—Greater Syria in the era before Sykes–Picot—means many things to many peoples. For centuries, particularly the past 200 years, it has been a destination for people who have been forced to move from their homes and homelands because of war, conquest, and religious coercion. The mixing of numerous people came to create a special tolerance of others; a trait that many visiting modern Syria have found both surprising and pleasing. A wander around the streets of the old city of Damascus in the first decade of the twenty-first century would have been marked by the sound of numerous languages being spoken on the street: Arabic, Kurdish, Persian, Turkish, perhaps some French and English, too. The side streets and neighbourhoods would have been occupied by families of Syrian Arabs, Armenians, Druze, Palestinians, Circassians, Albanians, Kosovars, and a few Sephardic and Mizrahi Jews. Damascus was renowned for its plurality of ethno-religious and other minority groups. It had one of the first housing complexes in the world for forced migrants: the Muhajiriin quarter on Mount Kassioun, built under the direction of the Ottoman sultan Abdul Hamid II to house the Muslims fleeing from Crete after the Greco-Turkish War of 1897 which led to the union of Crete with Greece. Damascus, and Syria as a whole, was marked by a local conviviality, a cosmopolitanism which tolerated and sometimes celebrated those of other ethnicities and regions.

We know that Syria, the modern truncated state so tragically in the news for most of the second decade of the twenty-first century, has now seen more than 50 per cent of its people dispossessed, attacked, barrel bombed and displaced, either internally within the borders of the country or externally across frontiers with its neighbouring countries. As those host states have become full and welcomes less enthusiastic—nearly 30 per cent of the population of Lebanon is now made up of Syrian refugees—Syrians are seeking safety further afield in North Africa, the Balkans, and Europe. It is, the United Nations High

Commission for Refugees (UNHCR) admits, the greatest displacement and refugee crisis since the Second World War.

Although there had been several international refugee organizations working to provide emergency assistance—and in some cases resettlement—to the dispossessed since the First World War, it was at the close of the Second World War that the 'international community vowed never again to allow atrocities like those of that conflict to happen again'. As a complement to the United Nations Charter (1945), the Universal Declaration of Human Rights (UNDHR) was elaborated over a period of two years under the chairmanship of Eleanor Roosevelt, and was presented to the UN General Assembly for ratification on 10 December 1948. Article 13 of the UNDHR stated that everyone has the right to seek and enjoy in other countries asylum from persecution. Upon its adoption by the UN General Assembly, it inspired a rich body of legally binding international human rights treaties addressing injustices, in times of conflicts, in societies suffering repression. It set out, for the first time in modern history, fundamental human rights to be universally protected. At about the same time, and also as an outcome of the crisis in Europe of the millions of European— particularly Jewish—refugees, the international community set up the International Refugee Organization in 1947 to assist in the return or resettlement of this displaced population. By 1949 this organization had fallen out of favour and a new agency, the UNHCR, a subsidiary organization of the General Assembly, was adopted by Resolution 319 (IV) in December 1949. As many of the UN member states disagreed over the implications of a permanent body, the UNHCR was given a three-year mandate from January 1951 'to provide, on a non-political and humanitarian basis, international protection to refugees and to seek permanent solutions for them' (UNHCR 2005). After the signing of the 1951 Convention relating to the Status of Refugees it became clear that refugees were not solely restricted to Europe and that a wider, global mandate in refugee protection and humanitarian assistance was necessary. The rest, one might say, is history, with the UNHCR now claiming more than 60 million people worldwide as people of concern, with over 20 million of them regarded formally as refugees. Of these last, 5 million or 25 per cent of the UNHCR's recognized refugees are from Syria.

This book aims to contextualize the current mass migration from the modern nation-state of Syria and re-situate it within the past 150 years of involuntary movement of populations which has indelibly marked the region, starting from the closing decades of the Ottoman Empire. It seeks to establish the displacement of peoples into and out of Greater Syria as part of the policy of empire, carried further by the colonial encounter, then revitalized in the Arab socialist awakening of the mid-twentieth century, and finally the disintegration of that socialist contract in the early 2000s when the modern nation-state turned on its citizens—labelling them terrorists. Beginning in 2012 and reaching a peak in 2015, nearly 5 million Syrians sought safety outside their country, while a further 7 million looked for refuge within its borders. The dispossessed were not exclusively Arab or Muslim, but comprised many social groups of mixed ethnicities and religious backgrounds. No one minority community has been targeted, and no reports of 'ethnic cleansing' have emerged. Rather, people have been fleeing the country on the basis of perceived and actual insecurity and challenges to life identified on an individual basis. By grappling with these sociological phenomena, an understanding of the nature of identity and of belonging in Syria will be sought, as well as an understanding of how individual and community generosity to the displaced is later reflected in notions of civic community action. Such an understanding, grounded in an anthropological perspective, can help us better comprehend the individual and social tragedies that are the played out when communities are dispossessed, displaced, and forced to move.

Using an anthropological perspective and, whenever possible, in-depth interviews conducted in Aleppo, Beirut, Damascus, Amman, Gaziantep, and Istanbul, the book aims to examine the way in which dispossession and forced migration has come to be a defining feature of life in Syria in the twenty-first century. It strives to illuminate the ethnographic, the individual lived experience within separate ethnic and minority communities as well as the mixed, modern communities that emerged after the demise of the Ottoman Empire. Coping strategies and mechanisms of individuals and groups in integrating strangers and guests at the community level and at the level of society as a whole will be interrogated. Neither solely victims nor totally political actors, the lives of the dispossessed and often marginal forced migrants in Syria, and from Syria, will be drawn out to give a full-bodied portrayal of the individuals and communities that have shaped modern Syria both as a refuge state and as a displaced and dispossessed community.

Following the significant out-migrations of people from Iraq and Syria in the twenty-first century, the question must surely be asked, what will the modern state of Syria be like once the civil war has ended? Will its largely professional and highly skilled population return? Will the pullback be strong enough to bring back those who have successfully found refuge outside the region? In other words, will a 'brain drain' have occurred, wiping out an entire sector of Syrian society, as has happened in twenty-first-century Iraq (Sassoon 2009)? The book seeks to lay bare the past and present contexts of refuge, asylum, dispossession, statelessness, and forced migration, in Syria, specifically, and the Levant, in general. It attempts to explore the social, political, and environmental costs which such displacement throws up. Although some groups of self-defined communities who were forced to move within the region succeeded in physically inte-grating and creating new identities as minorities (Armenians, Circassians, Chechnyans, Assyrians, Albanians, Druze), one must ask what has hap-pened to them now, in this second wave of forced migration and exile. Others had been left stateless in the Syrian state (Palestinians; Kurdish refugees from the 1920s Republic of Turkey); what has happened to them as they seek safety without the aid of any identity documents to smooth their journey into exile a second time in less than a century? Still others have found themselves internally displaced with little recourse to international protection of their human or cultural rights, while a minority have managed to escape the region altogether, joining the ranks of refugees and émigrés resettled in Europe and North America and giving the term 'diaspora' new meanings (Palestinians, Armenians, Assyrians, Yazidis, Kurds, Maronites).

This study seeks to understand the individual and community life experience within which modern Syria, as a state which provided ref-uge, came into being. It sets out to illuminate how local sentiments of empathy resulted in extended generosity as a duty. It also seeks to make sense of the current outflow of people from Syria to neighbour-ing states and further afield, as individuals and families seek survival with dignity. We know that more than 1.1 million Syrians have crossed over into Lebanon, a nation of only 4.4 million. Another 2.9 million have crossed into Turkey, which has a population of 76 million. And at least 620,000 have sought refuge in Jordan among its population of less than 6.4 million. Why have some sought refuge across national borders, and why have others remained in Syria even when fighting has destroyed their homes and neighbourhoods? Why have some chosen Turkey, others Lebanon, and still others Jordan to ask for asylum? Why have some who fled returned? And finally, why have so few of Syria's Christian minorities fled? Current figures show that they are leaving at the same rate as Muslim Sunni groups; hence a mass expulsion of Christians does not seem to be occurring, unlike what we observed in Iraq a decade earlier.

Understanding these movements means taking a bird's-eye view of the ethnic composition of Syria both in the late Ottoman era and in the modern state carved out of the general Ottoman region known as *Bilad al-Sham* (Greater Syria or the Levant). *Bilad al-Sham* in the late nineteenth century was a region of surprising ethnic and religious complexity. In large measure this was an outcome of the mid-nineteenth-century Ottoman reforms which gave a form of self-government to the separate ethno-religious communities of the Levant, such as the Greek Orthodox, the Nestorian Christians, the Assyrians, the Catholics, the Apostolic Armenians, and the Jews. Adding to this mix of peoples were the nearly 4 million forced migrants from the borders of the Ottoman, Russian, and Austro-Hungarian Empires who eventually settled in eastern Anatolia and the Levant itself. These included Tatars, Abkhaz, Circassians, Chechnyans, and Dagestanis. Existing tensions in this part of Anatolia were exacerbated by the influx of these Muslim forced migrants and contributed to the justification for local massacres that saw Armenians and other Christian minority groups seek asylum in Syria.

By the time of the Paris Peace Conference and the Treaty of Sèvres at the end of the First World War, the establishment of the League of Nations Mandates, and the later Treaty of Lausanne in 1923, *Bilad al-Sham* had been divided up between the British Mandate, which the British almost immediately further subdivided into Transjordan (east of the River Jordan) and Palestine, and the French Mandate covering much of the rest of Syria. Under their League of Nations Mandate to bring Syria to 'full independence', the French authorities quickly proceeded to divide Syria into a Greater Lebanon and an Alawite state along the northern Mediterranean, a Druze state just north of Transjordan, a Bedouin 'state' in the semi-arid desert (*Badia*) of Syria and two further statelets composed of Aleppo and Damascus and their hinterlands. This French policy of 'divide and rule' was deeply unpopular and opposed by most nationals who felt they belonged to Greater Syria, *Bilad al-Sham*. After more than a decade of open revolt, the Syrian people were able partially to persuade the French to formally reunite them under their League of Nations Mandate into one territorially much smaller nation-state in 1936. This modern state excluded the new state of Greater Lebanon and, of course, the former territories which had been part of Greater Syria but under British Mandate.

The sense of unity in diversity which the Syrian peoples in the truncated modern state displayed during their twenty years under French Mandate continues to have resonance today. This book focuses, whenever possible, on individual narratives of migration into the modern state of Syria, the pathways to integration, adaptation, and compromise to create a local cosmopolitanism or conviviality. It also seeks to lay bare the experience of more contemporary displacement across the borders to Turkey, Jordan, and Lebanon. It seeks to humanize and acknowledge the significance of these experiences of moving both into and out of Syria, while also celebrating the unique adaptive quality of human social life. It seeks to address the ongoing struggles of marginal societies—minority groups, ethnic and religious communities, and non-sedentary societies—to preserve their own traditions and cultures in the face of pressure to change and conform to the practices and identifying features of mainstream communities.

With the recent transformation of a widespread social movement demanding greater freedoms from an authoritarian state into an armed uprising, and a profoundly vicious regime response targeting innocent civilians, Syria's people have reluctantly poured out of the country, seeking refuge and asylum in neighbouring states and in Europe. Their journeys remain 'temporary' and, perhaps wishfully, a short-term displacement in the minds of many Syrians. An understanding of these new journeys into near and far exile may go some distance in helping to understand the relationship between politics, forced migration, and identity formation in the Middle East. As such this work contributes to our understanding of important conceptual and substantive issues of community cohesion and sustainability in the face of significant regional insecurity and conflict.

The modern Syrian nation has been the core focal point for refuge for the displaced and dispossessed from the Balkans, the eastern Mediterranean, and the Caucasus for nearly 150 years. Its many formerly refugee communities are citizens of one single state. The people of this nation are now being forced to disperse along the Mediterranean rim and to the north. Its close social, economic, and kin-based contacts in the region have meant that many Syrians had social networks and capital to assist them in their early exile. Their historical humane tolerance and local appreciation of the pain of displacement and dispossession has also assisted them, and has been reciprocated to a significant degree by their neighbours in the region. However, as these places filled up and doors closed, some Syrians began to look to Europe for safety. Instead of finding succour in their desperate journeys, they found themselves identified as illegals. The motivating force behind the UNDHR and the 1951 Convention on the Status of Refugees was a desire to ensure that never again would there be such suffering as that experienced in the wake of the Second World War. Unfortunately that is exactly what is happening now.

Like pieces in a puzzle each chapter of this book adds a layer to understanding the intricate process of refuge and local integration into the modern state of Syria and then, ironically, the mass outflow with the violent war being fought in country. Each chapter may be read in isolation as a vignette, with a historical background summary of dispossession and displacement followed by the contemporary responses of individual forced migrants who found refuge and sanctuary in Syria. The last chapter addressing Syrian displacement across its borders then grapples with the irony of a state that provided refuge for so many over a century and more now experiencing nearly half of its own population displaced and searching for safety and sanctuary. As a whole the chapters follow a central thread that providing refuge and seeking refuge—as in Marcel Mauss's seminal essay *The Gift*—is a duty (to provide hospitality) which brings with it an obligation to return a gift (Mauss 2016 [1925]). In the late Ottoman period providing refuge and asylum to the waves of forced migrants entering the empire could be seen through a political economy lens, with the newcomers contributing significantly to the economies of the regions where they were settled. But on an ideational level, I argue, these forced migrants were integral to the emergence of an acceptance of the 'Other' and a local conviviality and tolerance of difference which particularly characterized the modern state of Syria. As Syrians have had to flee their country in massive numbers these same sentiments are being played out in their neighbouring states. Without any international rights-based legislation to rely on, Syrians have found safety and asylum across the near frontiers of their state. For how long is another matter.

Chapter 1 gives a brief history and overview of Greater Syria, *Bilad al-Sham*, from the middle of the nineteenth century to the end of the First World War, when the region was carved up following the secret agreement of the victorious European allies (Britain, France, and Russia). It was a period when the first waves of mass expulsions from the borderlands of the Russian and Ottoman Empires began to reach Greater Syria. It delineates the particular features of the late Ottoman reforms which encouraged and fed the continued local cosmopolitanism that characterized the Levant. It also highlights the deep social traditions of hospitality to the stranger as a duty and identifies the transformation of this social responsibility into a religious and moral duty in the later years of the Ottoman Empire (e.g. the Sufi *tekiyye*—accommodation and soup kitchens for students, migrants, and the poor). The chapter sets the stage for the chronologically arranged chapters that follow. Beginning with the earliest wave of Crimean Muslims—the Tatars, and the Circassians from the Caucuses—it moves forward, presenting the Armenian, Kurdish, Palestinian, and Iraqi forced migrations into Syria, and closes with the Syrian displacement to its neighbouring states.

Chapter 2 looks at the Circassian, Chechnyan, and other Muslim communities expelled from the Caucasus and Balkans in the late nineteenth century who found their way to Syria. They were the earliest groups to be forced out of their homelands on the borderlands of the Ottoman and Tsarist Russian Empires. Some were attracted to the land packages provided by the Ottoman Refugee Commission to establish frontier settlements to fight off Bedouin incursions. Others gathered around the orchards of Damascus on land grants from the sultan or on the Jaulan (Golan) Heights. These European Muslims maintained their unique cultural heritage while achieving significant economic successes in their new homeland as farmers, military officers, and gendarmerie. From a reputation for banditry and brigandage, they came to be regarded as model subjects and later good citizens of the modern Syrian nation-state.

Chapter 3 looks at the formerly protected Christian minorities of the Ottoman Empire: the Armenians, along with the Copts, Greek Orthodox, and Nestorians. These special communities (the *dhimmi* communities of the empire) were recognized by the French Mandate authorities in the inter-war years and granted citizenship along with other non-Arab social groups. Originally experiencing some social discrimination, they were largely successfully integrated into the new Syrian nation-state as important minorities. This chapter focuses on the oral testimonies and narratives of members of the Armenian communities exiled from Anatolian Armenia who found refuge and asylum with co-religionists in Aleppo and Damascus.

Chapter 4 examines the Kurdish forced migration of the 1920s into Syria. If one can measure suffering, then perhaps one can say that the Kurds suffered most from the fall of the Ottomans. Kurdistan had once been an integral part of the empire, and Kurds themselves were often the backbone of Ottoman military adventures against Tsarist Russia. Kurds were also the last of the Ottoman subjects to look to creating a national homeland. They were, however, dramatically undermined by the drawing of four state boundaries—those of Turkey, Iran, Syria, and Iraq—through the middle of their homelands. Their struggle for self-determination, and in Syria, for restoration of the mere rights of citizenship which had been withdrawn in the early 1960s, is the focus of this chapter. Despite the lack of citizenship, these Kurds have continued to maintain their cultural, social, and linguistic heritage, and have managed, in this current crisis, to maintain a 'neutrality' as a borderland people which may provide them with numerous political options in the future.

Chapter 5 looks at Palestinian forced migration into Syria in the 1930s and later with the *Nakba* (Disaster) of 1948. The chapter focuses on the life stories of Palestinians, some refugees, some exiles living in the middle-class neighbourhoods of Damascus, as well as some residents of the UN refugee camps scattered around the country. It integrates the stories of the landless Palestinian labourers, the nationalist elite reformers, and the members of the Palestinian middle classes in an effort to understand the resilience, cultural survival, and coping strategies of a people still wishing to return to their homes in the towns and villages of Palestine, often less than 100 miles away. With the current humanitarian disaster, it examines how the lessons learned over the last few generations help or hinder Palestinian refugees from Syria in finding refuge outside the country.

Chapter 6 examines Sha'laan, a modern cosmopolitan quarter in Damascus. During the Mandate period the French authorities planned out a new city outside the walls of 'Old Damascus' and beyond the Ottoman garrison quarter of Souq Sarouja. Sha'laan was that 'new city', halfway between the old city and the suburb of Salahiyya on Mount Kassioun. Originally an area of fruit orchards watered by tributaries of the Barada, it became the locus of settlement for numerous exiles (from the Russian Bolshevik Revolution), Syrian professionals returning from training abroad with foreign wives, Armenians, Druze, Circassians, Palestinian revolutionary leaders, and European expatriates. Its location and cosmopolitan make-up made it an ideal intermediary space for social groups and political organizations to mix in safety and in silent resistance to the French occupation.

Chapter 7 examines first the trickle and then the flood of refugees from Iraq into Syria, beginning in the 1980s. A largely professional middle-class community with long-established social and economic links in Syria, Iraqis displaced by the 2003 Anglo-American attack to dislodge Saddam Hussein came to Syria and rejected efforts by the international community to label them as refugees. With strong social networks and social capital they bypassed UN camps set up to provide emergency assistance and made their way to the major cities: Aleppo, Damascus, Homs, and Hama. In a short period of time their integration was largely complete; they found work or invested in businesses and began to engage in circular movements which puzzled UNHCR. Their regular migration back into Iraq and out again to check on businesses, or family members left behind, called into question the notion that refugeeness was a one-directional flow: out but never back.

Chapter 8 examines the flight of Syrians from majority and minority communities. Drawing on interviews with Syrians in Turkey, Lebanon, and Jordan, it examines the perceptions of refugees, host communities, and policymakers and practitioners. It draws out the historical anteced-ents and connections that have aided Syrians in their flight and exile. It seeks to explain how, for example, a refugee-receiving country such as Lebanon could accept a 30 per cent rise in its population over less than two years and not collapse under the weight of such in-migration. It addresses the disparity in understandings between host communities and Syrians, and seeks to position the regional social traditions of the duty of hospitality (*karam*) to the stranger up against the international norm of the right to asylum as the principal motivation for providing sanctuary. And finally, it suggests that the overwhelming regional response of 'duty' as the primary impulse for providing sanctuary bodes well for the future return and rebuilding of Syria and its society when conditions permit.

1

FORCED MIGRATION AND REFUGE
IN LATE OTTOMAN SYRIA

Ayşe, a graduate student at the University of California in Los Angeles (UCLA), presented herself as a Syrian national with a Turkish mother, hence the unusual—to me—spelling of her name. In conversation with her one afternoon in 1976 outside the UCLA Social Science library, my father asked her about her last name. He had noticed that it placed her somewhere outside Syria, and so he pressed her: 'Where are your grandparents from?' he asked politely. Ayşe replied, 'From Crete. My family was driven out when Crete was given to Greece at the beginning of the twentieth century. Some of my family went directly to Anatolia but others, like my grandparents, settled in Syria.'

The twenty-first century is rapidly coming to be known as the 'century of displacement', with as many people crossing international borders and becoming refugees as those who remain internally displaced in their countries (Colson 2003: 2). The previous century was often labelled the 'century of the refugee', with the establishment of not one but two United Nations agencies for refugees: the United Nations Relief and Works Agency (UNRWA), with a mandate to carry out relief and works programmes for Palestinian refugees, currently numbering nearly 5 million, and the United Nations High Commission for Refugees (UNHCR) to oversee the protection of all the world's other refugees, whose mandate currently extends to nearly 35 million refugees and other people of concern (especially stateless people and internally displaced people). Looking back further, the nineteenth century, then, must be considered the century of refuge for the masses expelled from the borderlands between imperial Russia, Europe, and the Ottoman Empire. How did this come about, and what was its impact on the modern nation-state of Syria?

'Greater Syria', or the region commonly known as the Levant, has been the focus of movements of people since ancient times. Invaders from close at hand (Sumerians, Babylonians, Assyrians, Egyptians) or further afield (Romans, later Byzantines, Sassanians, Mongols, Turks) have all fought to control Greater Syria, or as Arabs commonly refer to it, *Bilad al-Sham*. Greater Syria, and more specifically the modern truncated nation-state of Syria at the heart of the Fertile Crescent, has seen wave after wave of conquerors turned collaborators and converts. Our story can best be told by reaching back to the early period of the rise of Islam, when mounted fighting forces from the Arabian heartland carried the message of the Prophet Muhammad out across the Middle East and beyond. Following the Prophet's death in 632 CE, his successors (caliphs) established an Islamic empire centred on Damascus, which became known as the Umayyad Caliphate, and would eventually extend to Transoxiana and Sind in the east, the Caucasus to the north, and across North Africa (the Maghreb) to the west, to include Andalusia in Spain. At its height, this Damascus-based caliphate covered more than 15 million square kilometres and was home to 62 million people (nearly 29 per cent of the world's population at that time), making it the fifth-largest empire in history in both area and proportion of the world's population. The Umayyad caliphate was known for its unique synthesis of art and architecture, its blending of crafts and craftsmen from Eastern and Western origins. When the caliphate was overthrown by the Abbasids of Baghdad in 750, one branch of the Umayyad dynasty escaped to Spain and set up the Umayyad Caliphate of Cordoba, which lasted until 1031.

The Umayyads based in Damascus ruled for eighty-nine years, and during that time established a tradition of incorporating existing social and administrative practices into their bureaucracy. The majority Christian and Jewish populations of the time maintained relative autonomy, and their judicial matters were dealt with in accordance with their own laws and by their own religious leaders. Educated and skilled professionals—Christian and Jewish—were integrated into Umayyad state structures and provided enormously important services, as well as acting as bridges to the knowledge systems of the Greek Byzantines and the Sassanian Persians. This was perhaps the origin of the cosmopolitanism and conviviality which was to re-emerge in heightened character during the closing century of the Ottoman Empire, and the final days of the Muslim Caliphate in the twentieth century.

This chapter will examine the historical background to much of the movement of peoples into Greater Syria, and will focus on the modern rump state of Syria which emerged in 1946. After a brief examination of the rise of the Ottoman Empire in the Arab heartland and the establishment of the *millet* system of managing its ethno-religious minorities, it will then focus on the last century of Ottoman rule and the largely internal displacement of peoples within the empire as its borders began to cave in. It will look for clues to explain the by-and-large successful 're-rooting' of these dispossessed and forced migrant communities from the northern frontiers of the empire, who continued to maintain a separateness of identity and sense of social cohesion in the truncated, modern Syria while promoting a commonality of political aspirations within the state.

The Ottoman Empire and its Approach to Government

The Ottomans were the last of the Turkic tribes to move west into Anatolia from Central Asia and Iran. They did so within the framework of the Seljuk Turkish Empire, which had its capital in Isfahan, and promoted the development of military emirates along the borders with Byzantium. The most successful of these was the emirate ruled by Osman, the Ottoman founder. From its power base in Anatolia, the Osmanli ruling family defeated the Byzantines and embarked on its own empire-building project. The Ottoman Empire expanded steadily from 1300 to 1699, extending across the western region of the Middle East including northern Arabia, North Africa, and much of south-east Europe, and held sway over most of this vast territory until the beginning of the twentieth century (Shaw and Shaw 1977). It was perhaps one of the most successful of the cosmopolitan sultanates to emerge in the Islamic world (Lindholm 2002). The Ottoman rulers were able to maintain their supremacy over the centuries by warfare and military expansion rather than by trade. By maintaining a war-based economy, they found it possible to advance into Europe over an extended period, thereby building an internal sense of unity on martial successes. The highpoint of their expansion north came in 1529 with the siege of Vienna, which however failed to capture the city. It was 150 years later, in 1683, that they suffered their first major defeat at the battle of Vienna.

Mass Expulsion in Ottoman Lands

The expulsion of religious minorities was a common feature of the European landscape, going back five hundred years or more. Much of this policy of 'removals' was part of early European efforts to build nation-states with a common ethno-religious background. Minorities that were deemed threatening to the dominant group in a territory, and religious communities that did not subscribe to the established majority religion, were driven out. The first large-scale expulsion of religious minorities took place in Andalusian Spain in the late fifteenth century. In 1492 Catholic Spain, finally united under Isabella and Ferdinand, succeeded in defeating the Moorish King Boabdil and taking the last Moorish stronghold of Granada. This ended 700 years of Islamic rule in the peninsula, starting with the Umayyad Caliphate at Cordoba established in 756 by Abdul-Rahman I, the only survivor of the Abbasid massacre of his family in Damascus in 750 (Fletcher 1992; Harvey 1990). Approximately 200,000 people—Jews and Muslims— left Spain in 1492 and sought refuge mainly along the southern Mediterranean rim, settling in a wide arc of towns and cities from Tangiers and Oujda (Morocco), Cairo (Egypt), Damascus and Aleppo (Syria), Constantinople (Turkey) and Thessalonica (Greece).[1] Between 1609 and 1614 another 275,000, mainly Muslim converts to Christianity (Moriscos) and Jews, were expelled and deported (Harvey 1992; Mackay 1992).

By the mid-nineteenth century a new political crisis developed as the Austro-Hungarian, Russian, and Ottoman Empires were facing campaigns for national self-determination by their subject peoples, while the individual German states were moving towards unification under the leadership of Prussia. The result of this activity was the creation and recognition of new nation-states along the borderlands of

Europe, Russia, and the Ottoman Empire. The first to emerge was Greece in 1832, after decades of meddling and interference by Russia. Greece then became a client state of Russia and Britain, both of which were intent on reducing Ottoman power in the Balkans. Christian Orthodox Greece steadily encroached on Ottoman territory, and each of its gains precipitated the flight of part of the local Muslim population. Greece acquired Thessaly in 1881, Crete in 1908, and Macedonia in 1913. As these territories were fairly evenly divided between Greek Orthodox and Muslims, their annexation to Greece resulted in massive flight by the Muslims to the remaining Ottoman territories. There followed the establishment of Bulgaria, Serbia, and Montenegro. Each new state sought to 'unmix' their nationalities as the minority ethno-religious groups came to be regarded as obstacles to state building. As a result of the Western-inspired nationalist movements of the nineteenth century, and the 'unmixing' of peoples, Greek, Bulgarian, Romanian, and Turkish minorities generally moved from territory that had become a new state in which they constituted a minority, to another where their ethno-religious identity was dominant. The Muslims in these territories largely resettled in Asia Minor and in *Bilad al-Sham*. They numbered in the millions, and either fled or were expelled, moving south and seeking refuge in the Ottoman heartlands and in Syria.

Refuge in the Ottoman Lands

The 400 years of social and political transformation in Europe between 1500 and 1900 which resulted in more or less homogeneous nation-states also witnessed the rise and fall of Ottoman hegemony over the Muslim Caliphate of the Balkans, the Middle East, and North Africa. Throughout this period the dispossession and forced migration of peoples within the Ottoman Empire did not emerge as a drive to 'homogenize' its lands, but rather in response to international pressures resulting from lost expansionist bids or failed attempts to repulse competing claims to Ottoman border lands.

What was remarkable about the Ottoman Empire was how its organizing ethos was not based on ideas of ethnic superiority of one community over another, but rather on the superiority of Islam. Its tolerance

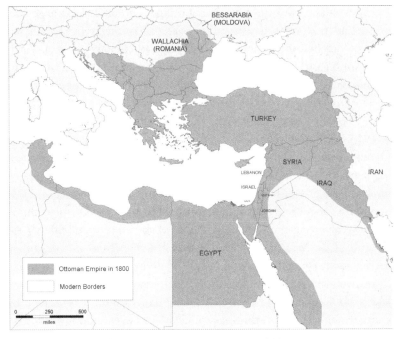

Map 1: Ottoman Empire in 1800s

of its Jewish and Christian communities was based on religious tenets as well as economic and political realism. European interests in their co-religionists in the Middle East as well as Ottoman principles of self-governance for these ethno-religious groups resulted in the establishment of protected community *millets*, whose religious and social affairs were organized from within the structured and specific mechanisms of the church or synagogue. It was the legacy of these *millets* that shaped the way in which the great forced migrations of the late nineteenth and early twentieth centuries were absorbed into the fabric of the societies and cultures of the Middle East, and in our case, Syria.

As the three great empires of Europe—the Austro-Hungarian, the Tsarist Russian, and the Ottoman Empires—fell at the beginning of the twentieth century, the mass movement of people into and within the Middle East far surpassed that of those fleeing the region. The history of Ottoman tolerance for minorities is part of the explanation for this great inflow. However, the fact that Muslim refugees from the border lands of the three great empires had no welcome either in Europe or in the new Soviet Union also determined that the first—or perhaps only—choice of movement was south.

The Millet (*Religious Community*) *Governing the non-Muslim* (Dhimmi) *Peoples*

The Ottoman administration adapted and formalized the protected status of non-Muslim peoples within the empire through the Islamic concept of the *dhimmi* (the free, non-Muslim subject living in a Muslim society). The *dhimma* contract, by extension, was the covenant of protection and safety awarded to the non-Muslim in return for paying certain taxes. This covenant was extended to Christians and Jews as *Ahl al-Kitab* ('people of the book', e.g. the Old Testament or the Torah) and later to Sikhs, Zoroastrians, and Mandaeans. The origin of this practice was attributed to Muhammad as he conquered Arabia and extended the first Islamic empire into North Africa and south-west Asia. It was said that he offered those he was about to fight three options: to convert to Islam, to pay tribute, or to fight. The first to accept the second option of keeping their religion but paying tribute were the Jews of Khaybar, in the Hijaz. In the early Ottoman era *dhimmi* communities were found throughout the empire living side by side with other *dhimmi*s as well as Muslims; in some places they made up entire neighbourhoods, in others whole villages. Governing such widely scattered and intermingled peoples was an administrative challenge.

The Ottomans established the institution of the *millet* (which comes from the Arabic *milla*, religious community or denomination) as a way of managing the internal affairs of their empire. Ottoman law did not recognize notions of ethnicity or citizenship. A Muslim, of any ethnic background, enjoyed precisely the same rights and privileges as any other Muslim. The various sects of Islam such as Sunni, Shi'a, and Alawi had no official status, and were all considered to be part of the Muslim *millet*. Only the 'syncretic' Druze of the Syrian Jebel Druze and Lebanon enjoyed a type of autonomy. They were often regarded as heretics by both Sunni and Shi'a Muslims, as they had their own sacred book and law. Christian and Jewish minority groups of all denominations and sects were spread across the empire, with significant minorities in most of the major cities. Even as late as the nineteenth century, Constantinople, for example, was 56 per cent Muslim, 22 per cent Greek Orthodox, 15 per cent Apostolic Armenian, and 4 per cent Jewish (A. Levy 2002). While Muslims were a large majority in the Asiatic provinces, and a significant one in the European areas of the empire, most regions had substantial Christian and Jewish minorities.

The term *millet* originally meant both a religion and a religious community. Although it had its origins in the earlier Umayyad and Abbasid Empires, the Ottomans regulated and institutionalized it, setting up mechanisms for its proper operation. All Ottoman population records were by religion, not ethnic or linguistic categories. Thus, Muslims, for example, could be ethnically and linguistically, Turks, Arabs, Kurds, Albanians, Bosnians, Circassians, and others. Jews, especially in the northern provinces, were mainly Sephardic, the descendants of those who had been given refuge after being expelled from Spain and Portugal. But there were also many Mizrahi (Oriental) Jews. The Christians were mainly Orthodox and comprised Greeks, Serbs, and Bulgarians in the Balkans and Arabs in Palestine and Syria (McCarthy 2001: 3). The actual patterns of residence varied widely. In some areas ethnic groups were fairly homogeneous. Few non-Albanians, for example, lived in Albania. But there were Muslim, Catholic, and Orthodox Albanians. Most of west and central Anatolia was ethnically Turkish; the south-east was Kurdish, while in the Levant or Greater Syria they were mainly Arab. Yet these regions also had significant Christian and Jewish as well as Muslim populations. In many other areas, especially in Ottoman Europe, there was a thorough mix of ethnic groups and religions. In some cases a village consisting of one ethnic group or religion could be adjacent to another village whose population consisted of a different ethnic group or religion. In other cases, single villages and small towns contained a number of ethnic and religious groups. Thus it was impossible to manage these very diverse peoples on the basis of territoriality.

The *millet* system was, in effect, an extension of Ottoman general administrative practice. It devolved to the *millet* community government of its internal affairs. These were directed and managed by the community's leadership. Except for taxation and security, the Ottoman government adopted a laissez-faire attitude to the internal affairs of these minority communities. In practical terms, the *millet* system meant that the minority communities were permitted to

> establish and maintain their houses of worship, often with the help of tax-exempt religious endowments. The minorities also operated their own educational institutions. The curriculum and language of these schools were determined by the community. Each community could also set up its own welfare institutions which depended on its own financial resources. To support their institutions, the communities were permitted to collect their own internal taxes. (A. Levy 2002: 2)

These communities also had considerable judicial autonomy. They had their own courts to adjudicate on a wide range of family and civil matters, such as marriage, divorce, inheritance, and financial transactions. Members of these minority *millet*s could also bring their cases before Islamic courts, which they often did, perhaps recognizing the greater executive authority needed for certain kinds of legal disputes. Life under such a system was one of relative segregation whereby language, customs, and culture were promoted in separate schools. But there was also significant acculturation and borrowing through the regular professional and commercial interactions between communities and in the service of the Ottoman elite (physicians, bankers, merchants, and craftsmen were especially well-represented professions among the minority communities). Inter-community relations gave rise to multilingualism, especially among the professional and commercial classes (G. Levy 2002).

This system of governance, however, was inherently biased. There was a fundamental inequality between Muslims and non-Muslims. Christians and Jews paid higher taxes than their Muslim neighbours. Non-Muslims were kept back from holding the higher government positions, though they often made up for such injustices by developing close professional links with the ruling elite. There was also always some sentiment of rivalry, distrust, and even hostility within one *millet* towards another. Christians were looked down upon as second-class citizens both by the Muslim public and by the government. 'Their dress was distinctive, and if Christian or Jew wore the *fez* (felt cap distinctive of a Muslim subject) he was required to sew on it a strip of black ribbon or cloth, not to be concealed by the tassel' so as not to dissimulate his non-Muslim affiliation (Davison 1954: 862). Yet these negative atti-

23

tudes rarely erupted into intercommunal violence. Even in the seventeenth and eighteenth centuries, when the Ottoman Empire became more marginal, economically, to Europe and life became more difficult, there were no incidents of wide-scale intercommunal violence.

Ottoman Identities and Social Transformations in the Nineteenth Century

In the Ottoman Empire of the early nineteenth century, religion provided a man with a label—in his own eyes as well as those of his neighbours and those who governed his life. He was a Muslim, Greek Orthodox, Gregorian Armenian, Jew, Catholic, or Protestant, before he was a Turk, Arab, Greek, or Bulgar, and also before he saw himself as an Ottoman citizen. The empire itself was governed by Muslims on laws based on Islam. The numerous Christian and Jewish communities had their partial autonomy, with the *millets*' ecclesiastical hierarchy supervising the religious, educational, and charitable affairs of the community. In practice this meant that Christians and Muslims lived side by side in the same state under the same sovereign, but were subject to different laws and different officials. Law was personal rather than territorial.

With the growing influence of Europe among the Ottoman Christian minorities came the transformative and revolutionary ideas of equality and liberty (connected to nationalism). From America came the proclamation that 'all men are created equal' and from France the 'Declaration of the Rights of Man and the Citizen'. By the early nineteenth century there was growing acceptance of these ideas among the Christian *millets* in particular, through their close contact with France and the French mission schools. This was coupled with the rapid spread of separatist movements in the Balkans, supported by both the Habsburg and Russian Empires. As a result, between 1839 and 1876 the Ottoman governing elite introduced sweeping reforms (the *Tanzimat*) to modernize all aspects of the administration of the empire. A building programme to modernize the infrastructure of the major cities was set up, and great strides were made in turning the Ottoman Empire into a modern rival to its European contemporaries. By the end of the nineteenth century, for example, Damascus had been restructured, with its major roads widened and extended; a tramline connected the old city with its outlying suburbs and telegraph and railway connected it to a string of other cities, making it as modern as many European cities of similar size at the time. More important for us here was the emphasis the Ottoman government placed on reassuring its minorities that their future lay within the Ottoman Empire rather than with a small, separated, national successor state.

The Ottoman leadership elite began to issue a series of decrees to reshape the nature of belonging and Ottoman sovereignty. Whereas the traditional concept of the state was essentially Muslim, with unequal membership by non-Muslims, now an attempt was made to add on two further elements. Pluralism and equality before the law were grafted onto the traditional concept of a solely Muslim state. In 1830, for example, Sultan Mahmud II declared: 'I distinguish among my subjects, Muslims in the mosque, Christians in the church and Jews in the synagogue, but there is no difference among them in any other way. My affection and sense of justice for all of them is strong and they are indeed my children' (Karal 1982: 388). The idea was to blur the traditional perception of Ottoman society as divided between a ruling Muslim people and non-Muslim subjects, even though by the time of these pronouncements the basic tenet of Ottomanism—Muslim superiority—no longer held in practice. By this point in their history, many of the Ottoman Christian and Jewish subjects held powerful positions in the government and in commerce, and formed a growing and thriving middle class in some ways more privileged than their Muslim counterparts (McCarthy 2001). As these Christian groups increasingly took up the Western ideas of liberty and nationality, and as education and literacy increased among them (thanks to the Catholic and also largely American Protestant missions), they began to complain frequently and loudly about their lack of equality. They also found ready supporters among the Western powers (France and Russia) who traditionally acted as protectors of Christians in the Middle East.

The early nineteenth century saw the Ottoman leadership make the decision to press for changes to try to stop the empire's territorial disintegration. They embarked on a programme to reorganize it along Western lines, which inevitably brought them up against the same problems of equality that had faced the Western states. Though not a major issue facing the Ottoman reformers, the question of the equality of Christian, Muslim, and Jew ran like a thread through many phases of the overall conceptualization and implementation of Ottoman reform and modernization (Davison 1954: 863). What is perhaps most significant in early nineteenth-century Ottoman history is that the doctrine of equality did, in fact, become official policy. In 1829 Sultan Mahmud II (r. 1808–39) issued a clothing law which attempted to do away with the sartorial order based on class, religion, and occupational membership. Such clothing laws had for centuries been used to maintain class, status, ethnic, religious, and occupational distinctions between men and women, not only in the Ottoman Empire, but also in Western Europe and in China (Quataert 2000: 65). The 1829 law set out to eliminate the visual difference among males by requiring all male subjects to wear identical headgear, the fez. Thus all government employees looked the same: the different turbans and robes of honour were gone. The only exceptions that were made were for religious clerics, Muslim and non-Muslim alike. The sultan's presumption was that equality of dress would lead to a wider equality among all men.

It was, however, a little later in the nineteenth century—in the era of the *Tanzimat* reforms (1839–76)—that the doctrine of equality between Christian and Muslim was most categorically put into place. This era of reform was initiated in 1839 with the *Hatt-i Sherif* or Imperial Decree, which included a commitment to equal justice for all Ottoman subjects, regardless of religion. The stated purpose of the decree was to promote each individual Ottoman's loyalty to the state (*devlet*), the religious community (*millet*) and the country (*vatan*). Bringing the *millet* into the equation was a significant step towards promoting the loyalty of all Ottoman subjects to their state and country. By 1840 the Ottoman state had introduced legal reforms modelled on European codes of law to implement the principle of equality of all before the law. By mid-century minority groups were represented in municipal, provincial, and state councils. This trend culminated in 1876 with the promulgation of the first written constitution in Ottoman history, establishing a limited monarchy, all of whose subjects were considered 'Osmanli whatever religion or creed they hold'. The constitution, furthermore, affirmed that 'all Osmanli are equal before the law … without distinction as to religion'. These statements relate to Articles 8 and 17 of the Ottoman constitution (See Davison 1954:

864). The representatives at the first Ottoman parliament of 1876–7 came from a range of religious backgrounds. Out of 125 deputies there were 77 Muslims, 44 Christians, and 4 Jews—a diversity perhaps unique in the history of multi-ethnic empires.[2]

In 1856 there was another decree, more extensive than that of 1839, which promised equal treatment for followers of all creeds in the empire. This was the *Hatt-i Humayun*, and it made specific mention of equal educational opportunities, appointments to government posts, and the administration of justice, as well as taxation and military service. Throughout the period of the *Tanzimat*, these decrees and edicts as well as their application in law did raise the status of Christians in the empire. Christians were accorded better access to education, to government, and to military service, but the advance was slow and piecemeal, and was not always accompanied by a change in people's attitudes. Many would argue that equality between Christians and Muslims was never actually attained in the nineteenth century despite the goodwill and intention of the Ottoman statesmen and lawmakers.

*Millet*s, Nationalism, and the *Tanzimat* Reconsidered

Many European writers of the time, as well as contemporary historians, have examined the *Tanzimat* period and the question of equality that ran through it to try to understand why it ultimately failed. Some have looked at it as part of a European effort to deal with the Eastern Question (the Ottoman Empire). They regarded the era from the perspective of the European statesmen and diplomats who were constantly reminding and prodding a less-than-committed Ottoman government to live up to its promised reforms regarding equality and citizenship. These European statesmen were expecting to see results achieved as they would have been in Europe. Others looked at this period as a phase in the ongoing internal decay of the Ottoman Empire, all efforts to restore health to the 'sick man of Europe' having failed. Some have gone as far as to judge the promises of equality as largely hypocritical, with no real effort made to overcome the oppressive rule over 'downtrodden Christians'.

Whether the Muslim Ottomans would have accepted a fusion in which Christians were their equals remains an unanswered and unanswerable question. For many, there was the inherited religious tradition of tolerance for 'people of the book', those who like Christians and Jews possessed a book of divine revelation and paid tribute to the Muslim government. There was also the remarkable degree of religious syncretism across Greater Syria, Anatolia, and also in the Balkans (along with mysticism and the many heterodox notions of Sufism), which could have provided a climate sympathetic to Christianity and Christians. Despite the widespread religious tolerance and syncretism, there remained among many Muslims an intense feeling of the superiority of Islam over Christianity, which it considered to be only a partial revelation. In their eyes Christians were not equal to Muslims. Along with this religious dogma came the slow, but nevertheless shocking, recognition that the *Tanzimat* reforms implied that somehow the traditional Ottoman way of life did not compare favourably with the way some things were done in Christian Europe.

This dawning revelation among Muslims coincided with an era of pronounced Christian sectarian friction within the Ottoman Empire; squabbles arose over privileges in the holy places, over whether the Greek hierarchy should include the Bulgars, over the shifting of individuals from one *millet* to another in order to gain some small political advantage or greater foreign protection. Furthermore, the Christian rebellions along the European borders of the Ottoman Empire (which will be summarized later) generally antagonized Muslim sentiment. During this period of reform and search for federated governance, many largely Christian regions were in general revolt. In 1867 Crete rebelled, forcing the sultan to remove many Muslim Cretans from the island and offer them safe haven on the Syrian coast as well as in the Muhajiriin quarter of Damascus. The uprisings in Bosnia, Herzegovina, and Bulgaria in 1875–6 and the open war against the Ottomans in Serbia and Montenegro resulted in mounting anger amongst Ottoman Muslims against both the Christian rebels and what seemed to be the weakness of the Ottoman government in dealing with such rebellion.

It was, however, the continuous interference of the European powers in Ottoman affairs that most angered the Muslims. The European states were fundamentally influenced by the domestic sympathies of their constituents for the Christian minorities in the Ottoman Empire. Such public opinion led to European military intervention in the creation of an independent Greece, Serbia, and Bulgaria, all the while maintaining diplomatic support for the territorial integrity of the Ottoman Empire. But more striking, and certainly a stance which would be repeated in the twentieth and twenty-first centuries, was the callous disregard by the European powers and the growing media of the reports of murder and forced migration of the millions of Muslims caused by the creation of those very states (McCarthy 2001: 21).

Furthermore, European imperialism constantly undermined the Ottoman reforms. No matter how much the European powers criticized the Ottomans and called for reforms, none of them wanted to see the Ottomans succeed. Nor did they want to see the empire's total collapse, at least not in the nineteenth century. Great Britain, France, Germany, and Austria sold more to the Ottomans than they bought. Ottoman purchases of textiles and other finished goods helped to keep the mills of Europe working, so a reformed Ottoman Empire with a revived manufacturing base was not in the interests of European powers.

Russian Meddling and Ottoman Decline

It was the Russian imperial agenda that caused the most damage to the Ottoman Empire. The Russians wanted Ottoman lands. Unable to expand further into Europe, or for that matter into Asia, they saw the Ottoman Empire as their natural route to expansion. Specifically they wanted Constantinople, the Dardanelles and Bosporus Straits, in order to gain access to the Mediterranean. More generally, they aimed to dismember the empire, dividing it between themselves, the Habsburgs, and a renascent Byzantium. The Western powers tended to oppose Russian expansion (as in the Crimean War), preferring an equilibrium between Russia and the Ottomans, but were sympathetic to the argument that Christians within the empire were oppressed. The Russians repeatedly invaded the Ottoman Empire, capturing lands both in Europe and in Asia. They forced the creation of an independent Bulgaria, Serbia, and Romania, by defeating the Ottomans in wars they themselves initiated. Then the Russians would demand reparations for their wartime losses. These demands were often mediated by the European powers to soften the blow to the 'sick man of Europe'. The Russians, as detailed by Justin McCarthy, dispossessed and ejected the native populations of Circassia and Abkhazia in the Caucasus, forcing the Ottomans to take in more than 800,000 Caucasian peoples at great human and civil costs. A further 900,000 Turks were also forced out of these border lands into the Ottoman Empire, which then had to find food and shelter for them when the existing population was already poor (McCarthy 2001: 21). Much of the economic and military disaster that constantly threatened the Ottomans in the nineteenth century was due to the intrigue of the Russian tsars.

Greek Independence

On 25 March 1821 the Orthodox bishop Germanos of Patras proclaimed a national uprising, with simultaneous uprisings planned across Greece, Crete, and Cyprus. Attacks were launched against tax collectors and all things Muslim. In southern Greece nearly 25,000 Muslims were killed in Morea. The Ottoman authority retaliated with mass deportations and a massacre on the island of Chios. Although the British and French suspected that the uprising was a Russian plot to seize Greece and possibly Constantinople from the Ottomans, the news of this massacre and other atrocities resulted in sympathy and support for the Greeks in Western Europe. The Europeans did not see the realities of the rebellion as being as much about hatred of tax-collectors and murderous acts against Muslims as concern with nationalistic ideals (Hobsbawm 1997). The elite intellectuals and politicians of Europe read the Greek struggle as a war between Christianity and Islam, and came down on the side of Christianity. After years of inconclusive fighting between Greek separatist militias and the Ottoman military, in October 1827 the British, French, and Russians intervened without a declaration of war, attacking and destroying the combined Egyptian and Ottoman fleet at the battle of Navarino. The following year the French landed troops in the Peloponnese to protect the Greeks and help them to regroup and form a government of their own. In the same year Russia invaded Ottoman Europe, defeating the Ottomans in the war of 1828–9. The Ottomans were thus forced to recognize an independent Greek kingdom. In March 1829, in London, a conference was held by the European powers to define the independent Greek state and delimit its northern border and island holdings.

But it was not until the Convention of 11 May 1832 that Greece was recognized as a sovereign state. However, due to the constant bickering of the Greek national leadership, the European powers again imposed their will. They decided that Greece would be a monarchy and the Bavarian Prince Otto, rather than someone of Greek origin, was chosen as its first king (Hobsbawm 1962: 181–5).

Romanian Semi-Independence

In the mid-nineteenth century another war erupted which was a harbinger of things to come. This was the Crimean War (1854–6). Its direct root cause could be traced back to the 1851 *coup d'état* in France. Napoleon III had his ambassador at the Ottoman court insist on the recognition of France as the 'sovereign authority' in the Holy Land. Despite two treaties nearly a century earlier (1757 and 1774) granting Russia sovereign authority over the same lands, the Ottoman sultan, Abdul Majid I, agreed. Russia quickly protested at this change of authority. After much prevaricating, as well as a show of force by the French navy in the Black Sea, the Ottoman sultan transferred control over the various Christian holy places—as well as the keys to the Church of the Nativity—from the Greek Orthodox Church to the Catholic Church.

The Russian tsar, Nicholas I, regarded this as an act of injustice towards the Greek Church. He decided to remedy the situation by taking over Moldavia and Wallachia (the Danubian principalities), and followed this by destroying the Ottoman fleet at the battle of Sinope in 1853. The heavy Ottoman casualties alarmed Great Britain and France, and, after issuing an ultimatum to Russia to withdraw from the Danubian principalities, both countries entered the war on the side of the Ottoman Empire. At the conclusion of the Crimean War in 1856, the Treaty of Paris agreed the return of the Danubian principalities to the Ottomans under a shared tutelage with its allies, Great Britain, France, and Austria. Moreover, the European powers pledged to respect the independence and territorial integrity of the Ottoman Empire. The Treaty of Paris stood for nearly a decade, but, one by one, each of its commitments unravelled. In 1859 the principalities of Moldavia and Wallachia merged to become the precursor of modern-day Romania.[3] Moldavia and Wallachia began to distance themselves ever more assuredly from their former Ottoman masters. The Ottoman Empire continued to shrink territorially as one after another its European provinces, with European interest and support, rebelled and seceded. In 1850 approximately 50 per cent of all Ottoman subjects lived in the Balkans, yet by 1906 the remaining Balkan provinces only made up 20 per cent of the Ottoman population (Quataert 2000).

Serbian Independence

Serbia's separation from the Ottoman Empire was a long struggle compared to that of Greece. Serbs in the north-west corner of the Ottoman Empire rebelled in 1804. Initially, as with earlier uprisings in previous centuries, it was not so much a secessionist movement as an appeal to the sultan to correct what they regarded as abuses at the hands of the local Ottoman administration and the Janissaries (the Ottoman elite corps), who were behaving more like an occupying army of plunderers than an efficient military force. Serbian Muslims, Jews, and Christians alike shared this hatred of them. Not getting a satisfactory response from the Ottoman sultan, the Serbs appealed to Russia for aid. There followed a complex struggle between Russia and the Ottoman state with the Serbs in the middle. In 1815 there was a second uprising. By 1817 both Russia and the Ottoman Porte had agreed to the establishment of hereditary rule by a Serbian prince. From that point on Serbia became a semi-autonomous principality. From direct rule, it was now under a form of vassalage. Its full independence would eventually come about at the conclusion of the later Russo-Ottoman war of 1877–8, discussed below.

Bosnian Rebellion (1875–6)

In 1875 rebellion erupted in Ottoman Bosnia. It, too, began as a protest against local landlords and the high rate of taxation. Most of the rebels were Bosnian Serbs, but they had sympathy from other communities in Bosnia who had little love for tax collectors. The nature of this rebellion soon changed character, and guns, money, and men began to arrive from Serbia and Montenegro, supported by Russia, which was

pursuing a 'pan-Slavic' ideology. Instead of attacking government officials (tax collectors), these nationalists began to attack Muslim villages.
In other words, instead of fighting against their perceived oppressors,
the government representatives, the Serbian nationalists turned against
those who they perceived might possibly become agitators for another
'nation' in their midst. The Muslim villagers, who had little, if any,
nationalist sentiment, responded with equally vicious revenge attacks
on Serbian villages. Bosnia was now caught up in its own civil war.

By the end of 1875 the European powers had entered the fray,
demanding that the Ottomans make concessions to the Bosnian rebels.
Russia, Austria, and Germany required the Ottomans to end the system of tax collection known as tax-farming, lower taxes in general, and
make other reforms. The Ottomans agreed to these conditions, thus
meeting the initial demands of the rebels; but the movement had by
then become a nationalist revolt that went far beyond any straightforward economic reforms. The Bosnian Serb rebels wanted Bosnia to be
joined to the Kingdom of Serbia, and so continued their revolt. The
Ottoman army responded by putting the rebellion down by force.
Serbia then declared war on the Ottomans in July 1876, and was
defeated two months later. At this point Russia intervened and threatened to invade the Ottoman Empire if it continued its attack on Serbia.
The Ottomans withdrew.

The Bulgarian Uprising of 1876

Meanwhile, in Bulgaria, another group of nationalist rebels attempted
to revolt—taking advantage of Ottoman military involvement elsewhere, in Bosnia. Guerrilla bands in Serbia and Romania crossed into
Bulgaria and attacked Ottoman posts in an effort to create a nationalist
revolt among the Bulgarian peasants. These efforts all failed due to lack
of popular support in the countryside and also the renewed strength of
the Ottoman military—recently reformed during the *Tanzimat* era. In
May 1876 fighting occurred in three towns in Bulgaria. These initial
actions led to ever increasing levels of violence, and eventually Russia
intervened. At first the rebels killed about a thousand Muslim villagers
in the surrounding region. The Ottomans, with most of their regular
troops tied up in Bosnia, called upon local Muslims, and also resettled
Circassians, to put down the revolt.[4] This they did with ferocity, killing

not only the rebels but many innocent Bulgarians as well. From an initial massacre of a thousand Muslims, there were now reported to be between 3,000 and 12,000 Bulgarians dead (McCarthy 2001: 46). Eventually the regular Ottoman army was moved out of Serbia and Bosnia and into Bulgaria to put an end to the unrest.

The Ottomans were successful in putting down rebellions in Bosnia and in Bulgaria. They also defeated the Serbian Kingdom. These internal rebellions and civil uprisings were within the ability of the Ottoman military machine to manage. However, European public opinion was not on the side of the Ottomans. Britain, for example, had long been a diplomatic ally of the Ottomans (taking their side in the Crimean War along with France a few decades earlier). But media reports of events in Bulgaria and Bosnia made support for the Ottomans difficult to justify to the public. British newspapers reported the deaths of Bulgarians as the 'Bulgarian Horrors'. Muslim deaths went unmentioned. The same was true for Serbian attacks against Muslim Bosnians. William Gladstone, at the time opposition leader in the British House of Commons, who held strong evangelical Christian convictions, organized a mass campaign against the Ottomans, helping to turn British public opinion against them. Benjamin Disraeli, the prime minister at the time, who sided with the Ottomans against the Russians, was held back from taking any action by this growing negative public opinion.

The Russo-Ottoman War of 1877–8

In April 1877 Russia crossed the Danube and invaded the European Ottoman region. By July Russia held all of northern Bulgaria, then Thrace, and by January 1878 she took Edirne, leaving Constantinople now virtually undefended. In the east, Russia took Kars and encircled the Ottoman garrison in Erzurum. Surrounded on two flanks, the Ottomans were forced to capitulate and signed an armistice in January 1879. In the first round of negotiations, two months later, Russia forced the Ottomans to sign the Treaty of San Stefano. Under its terms a Greater Bulgaria was created, stretching from the Black Sea to Albania and south to the Aegean. This would, in effect, vastly increase the Russian area of domination and influence and destroy the European balance of power. British public opinion now changed and turned against Russia, which was seen as threatening British interests in the

Middle East. Austria also was upset by this creation of a new Balkan rival. The German chancellor, Otto von Bismarck, proclaimed himself an honest broker and offered his 'good offices' as a mediator. This resulted in the Congress of Berlin. The negotiated Treaty of Berlin then took away most of the Russian gains in Balkan territory. Russia was forced to accept a much smaller Bulgaria and to settle for only the land in north-east Anatolia and southern Bessarabia, from which all Muslims were dispossessed and expelled to Muslim lands.

These wars in the Balkans led to massive dispossession and forced migration of peoples—it was to become the characteristic mark of nationalism. Unknown numbers of Bulgarians left Macedonia for Bulgaria when Macedonia was returned to the Ottomans. But it was the Muslims of the Balkans who suffered by far the most from the Russian conquest: 17 per cent of the Muslims of Bulgaria—262,000 people—died during and immediately after the 1877–8 war. Some 515,000 Muslims, almost all Turkish speaking (generally now called Turks) were driven out of Bulgaria into Asia Minor and Greater Syria (the Levant). They were the victims of a kind of state-sponsored programme of rape, plunder, and massacre by Bulgarian revolutionaries, Russian soldiers (especially Cossacks), and Bulgarian peasants. In the end, 55 per cent of the Muslims of Bulgaria were either killed or evicted. In Bosnia, which had been formally handed over to Austria, the mortality during the 1875–6 civil war resulted in a decline in the Muslim population from 694,000 to 449,000, a loss of 35 per cent (McCarthy 2001: 48).

The Russo-Ottoman war of 1876–7 and the ensuing treaties of San Stefano and Berlin of 1878–9 resulted in the loss of most of the European areas of the Ottoman Empire—the territories south and south-east of the Danube and the Caucasus. The decades that followed saw the Ottoman Empire lose additional European territory and the forced migration of many more hundreds of thousands of Muslim Turks into Thrace, Anatolia, and Syria.

Armenian Nationalism

There was general agreement that Armenians only made up between 5 and 6 per cent of the total population of about 21 million people in the

Ottoman Empire. They were spread out far and wide, and thus did not make up a majority—or even a significant minority—in any place. The only exceptions were perhaps Van (where they formed 25 per cent of the population at the beginning of the twentieth century) and Bitlis (perhaps 30 per cent of the total population at this time). Armenians had lived in south-east Anatolia for millennia. This tight ethno-religious community was recognized by the state and had its own Patriarchate and *millet* within the Ottoman Empire. By 1850 Armenians also had Protestant and Catholic *millet*s, as American and European missionaries converted some of their dissident members.

Armenians were found in all the major cities of the Middle East. They had always played an important role in Ottoman trade and industry, specializing in money changing, goldsmithing, jewellery, foreign trade, and medicine. After Ottoman Orthodox Christians left Anatolia to become part of the newly created Kingdom of Greece in 1832, Armenians filled many of the administrative positions left open by their departure. Because of their knowledge of foreign languages, Armenians rose high in particular ministries such as Finance, the Interior, Foreign Affairs, Education, Justice, and Public Works.

In 1855 and 1877 Ottoman Armenians are known to have assisted the Russians in their invasions of Ottoman Anatolia. These numbered tens of thousands of Armenians (Shaw and Shaw 1977). In the 1860s and 1870s Armenian revolutionary groups began to appear in Constantinople and further east. These groups made attempts to gain Russian support for their communities, especially in Van and Zeytoun. Between the 1880s and the First World War, Armenian nationalist groups set about organizing an Armenian revolution in order to attract the European powers to help them create an Armenian state (Rogan 2015: 167–72). During this period Armenians found increasing support in the international media through reports from European missionaries. The events in Bulgaria, where a small group of revolutionaries had killed large numbers of Muslims, causing massive retaliation and subsequent intervention by Russia, was a model which some of the Armenian revolutionaries believed would work in Anatolia. The problem, however, was that 'there was not a single large area in the Ottoman Empire where the Armenians were in a clear majority' and where a claim to statehood could be entertained (Shaw and Shaw 1977: 202).

Ottoman Response to Mass Influx

The nineteenth century, labelled the 'century of refuge', also saw the first organized response to a mass influx of forced migrants. Contrary to much popular thinking, this kind of response was not a twentieth-century invention, having actually emerged much earlier. After each Russo-Ottoman war in the first half of the nineteenth century, forced migrants had little time to prepare for exile, and often travelled with little more than the clothes on their backs and whatever they could pile onto their ox-carts. Their survival on the road depended on the kindness of local people and municipal authorities as they made their way south. Many died on the road from starvation or disease. In time these expulsions were accompanied by the development of localized and decentralized Ottoman organizations to assist and resettle the migrants. Local towns and cities opened up their mosques and churches to shelter and feed these exiles. Various local authorities levied additional municipal taxes per head to help in their feeding and clothing. As the sheer scale of the mass influx became clear, so did the need for a centralized organization.

In 1857, in response to the massive numbers of forced migrant Muslim Tatars from the Crimea, the Ottoman Sublime Porte promulgated a Refugee Code (also translated from Ottoman Turkish into English in some texts as the Immigration Law). Responding to the grave need to provide shelter and food for its subjects, expelled initially from the Crimea but also from other border-land regions with Russia, the Ottoman government set out to swiftly disperse and integrate its forced migrants. It aimed to provide 'immigrant' families and groups with only a minimum amount of capital, with plots of state land to start life anew in agricultural activity. Families who applied for land in Rumeli (the European side of the Ottoman Empire) were granted exemptions from taxation and conscription obligations for a period of six years. If, however, they chose to continue their migration into Anatolia and Greater Syria then their exemptions extended for twelve years. In both cases the new immigrants had to agree to cultivate the land and not to sell or leave it for twenty years. Ottoman reformers were eager to see the largely depopulated Syrian provinces revived by these new migrants after several centuries of misadministration, war, famine, and several pandemics of the plague (Shaw and Shaw 1977: 115). The twenty-year clause also meant that these newcomers were released from the pressure of nineteenth-century property developers, as there was a kind of lien on the property, prohibiting its onward sale for twenty years.

These forced migrants were also promised freedom of religion, and were permitted to construct their own houses of worship. News of this decree spread widely along the frontier zones and in Europe as the Ottomans advertised—also in European newspapers—for immigrant families wishing to settle as farmers in the Levant. As requests for plots of state land from forced migrants and potential immigrants rose, in 1860 the Ottoman authorities set up a refugee commission (the Ottoman Commission for the General Administration of Immigration) under the Ministry of Trade. The following year it became a separate public authority (Shaw and Shaw 1977: 115). The commission was charged with integrating not only the Tatars and Circassians fleeing from lands conquered by the Russians north and west of the Black Sea, but also the thousands of non-Muslim immigrant farmers and political leaders from Hungary, Bohemia, and Poland, Cossacks from Russia, and Bulgarians from the Balkans (Shaw and Shaw 1977: 116).

Throughout the 1870s and 1880s the commission also oversaw the management of the growing international aid—much of it missionary—coming into the empire. Before all else, the commission saw its principal role as to coordinate in-country aid and the feeding, clothing, and sheltering of forced migrants as they progressed through or near cities, towns, and villages to take up new lives as farmers on state land deeded to them.

The End of the Ottoman Empire

Much of the—largely involuntary—movement of people in the eastern Mediterranean in the nineteenth century was supported by a system of government which encouraged and tolerated variations among people, drawing out differences between neighbours and encouraging the formation of unique identities based on culture, language, or religion. In the heartland of the Ottoman Empire, belonging was not based on a physical birthplace alone, but specifically included the social

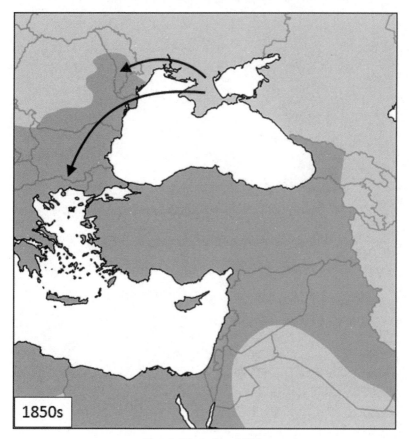

1850s

Map 2: Time slice 1850s

community of origin (Humphreys 1999; Kedourie 1984). It was rooted in the connections and links between and among a specific group of people as much as, if not more than, in a territory. The empire upon which such identities were based—the Ottoman Empire—came to an end with the First World War.

Amid the rubble of the war was a startling range of movements of communities. Among them were social groups in the Russian–Ottoman border lands such as the Armenians, the Circassians, and other northern Caucasus peoples (Barkey and von Hagen 1997; Brubaker 1995). Other dispossessions had their origins in the lines drawn on maps by the Western Great Powers to create new nation-states (Bocco et al. 1993;

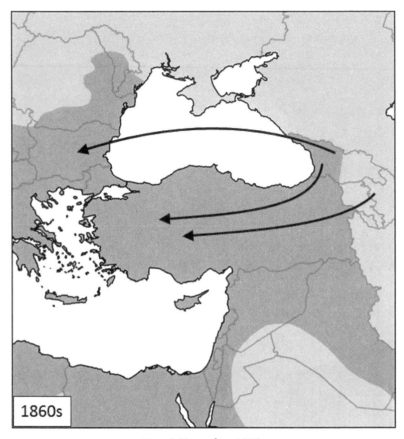

1860s

Map 2: Time slice 1860s

Gelvin 1998; Helms 1981; Morris 1987; Wilkinson 1983). These included the Palestinians, the Kurds, the pastoral Bedouin, and a variety of 'stateless peoples'. And in some cases, such as those of the Yazidis, the Assyrians, and some Armenian groups, migration was closely linked to the regional efforts at creating a pan-Arab, socialist, or Islamic society (Al-Rasheed 1994; Khalidi 1997; Lerner et al. 1958). Given such competing forces, many social communities with single identities were forced to move, and to seek protection elsewhere in the region or abroad. Many of these refugees and 'exchangees' found new homes and built or created new communities in Greater Syria (*Bilad al-Sham*) and, more specifically, in the territorially smaller modern state of Syria. They

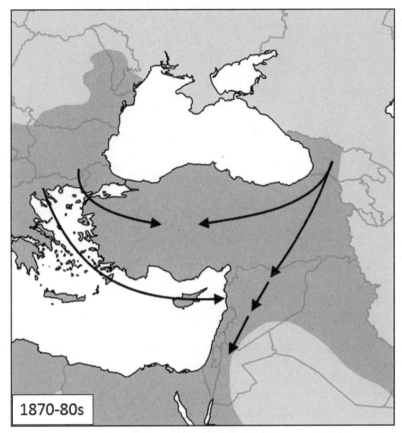

1870-80s

Map 2: Time slice 1870–80s

established themselves in new soil, but managed their memories so as not to put down new roots, but rather to keep the past alive in such a manner as to strengthen the commonality and trust in their immediate social network. They were creating moral communities with social capital that oiled internal social cohesion; there were processes of integration in their new state of Syria, but they remained separate and non-assimilated in important aspects (Chatty 2010b).

In the Middle East, where dispossession and forced migration have indelibly marked the landscape, the mass movements of people into the region over the past 150 years makes the attempt to regard the area as a set of homelands or cultural regions bewildering to say the least. The

41

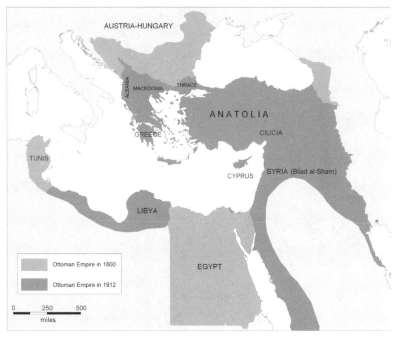

Map 3: The Ottoman Empire in 1912

Assyrians, once largely found in pre- and post-colonial Iraq, have reappeared in London and Chicago, just as the Iranians who fled the 1979 revolution have arisen phoenix-like in Los Angeles. The Circassians have their diasporic headquarters in New Jersey, and Iraqi refugees and exiles have found new community nodes in London and other major Western cities. The 'here' and the 'there' have become blurred in such trans-local or diasporic situations and the cultural certainty of the 'centre' becomes as unclear and as uneasy as that of the periphery. Thus the experience of displacement is not restricted to those who have moved to the periphery, but also affects those in the core (cf. Bhabha 1989).

In many states in the region, including Syria, the sense of national unity in the modern 'nation-state' understanding was created through the struggle for independence following the First World War (Brandell and Rabo 2003). Beginning in 1920 with the awarding of the League of Nations Mandate to the French administration, Greater Syria was divided into a number of states: Lebanon, Syria, Iraq, Transjordan, and

Palestine. Through common cause and hostility to the foreign power the populations of the territorially reduced modern Syria rebelled against the Mandate and continued to fight against the French policy of 'dividing and ruling' the truncated state even further as six separate statelets. However, it was not until 1936 that the new Syrian state's 'National Block' was able to persuade the French government to reunite the territory of Syria administratively into a single state. The exceptions were the areas that had been attached to Mount Lebanon to create the new state of Greater Lebanon, and the Sanjak of Alexandretta, which was promised to the Republic of Turkey in 1938. With independence in 1946, the Arab Republic of Syria had to build a

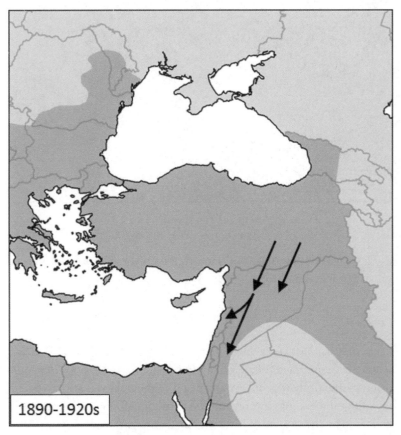

1890-1920s

Map 4: Time slice 1890s–1920s

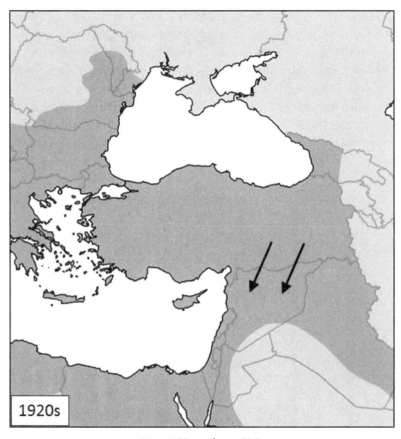

Map 4: Time slice 1920s

modern functioning state and integrate its diverse peoples within its greatly reduced territory.

Conclusion

Over the past 150 years the modern state of Syria, and the Levant as a whole, have provided refuge and asylum to numerous groups of people dispossessed of their property as a result of the upheaval leading to and including the end of empire, and the ensuing neo-colonial enterprises endorsed by the League of Nations. For Circassians, Kurds, Armenians, Assyrians, Palestinians, and Iraqis Syria has provided comfort and relief

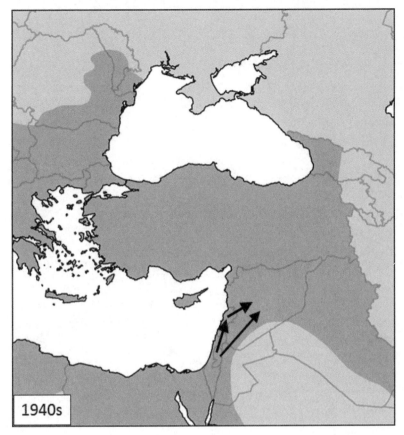

Map 4: Time slice 1940s

both on an individual basis and also for social groups. Perhaps as a residual trait of the tolerance which the Ottoman Empire had enshrined in its *millet* system towards multi-ethnic and plural society, the states to emerge from the Arab Ottoman provinces all tolerated, if not actively supported, the development of these minority cultures.

Those early Muslim refugees of the nineteenth and early twentieth century knew they could not look back. They had to create their homelands on new spaces. None of the populations exchanged after the 1923 Treaty of Lausanne had any ambiguity about their condition. They had to create a new community, both imagined and moral, in which new ties or kinship and trade could emerge. The Kurds, perhaps, more

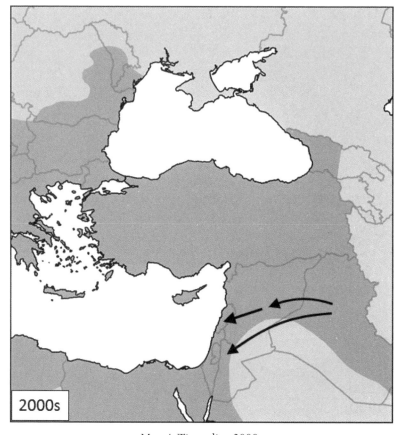

Map 4: Time slice 2000s

than any other group, held out for a return and alternated between a realistic hope and a nostalgic dream.

Today, many Palestinian refugees live within a hundred miles of their original villages and urban neighbourhoods. Some can even see the lights of their home towns and settlements at night. Some Armenians have travelled back to visit the homeland—both in Turkey and in the Republic of Armenia. So, too, have the Circassians and other Caucasians. A few Kurds among the twentieth-century forced migrants to Syria have managed to smuggle themselves across the border, sometimes on the backs of Peshmerga fighters, to visit their mountainous places of birth. Few have remained for more than a brief period of time. Some have recognized that the locations they visit are the spaces where their imagined homelands once existed. But they are not the same; they no longer contain the social ties and networks that made the space a homeland or a 'neighbourhood', and so they return to their contemporary homes with new memories of their 'imagined' home-land. The effort to reverse the misfortune of displacement and dispos-session and to 'emplace' then becomes a strategy for survival, and its success is a measure of the resilience of the forced migrant as seen in the new communities established by Circassians, Armenians, Palestinians, and Kurds in Syria and the Levant.

How successful forced migrants are in re-creating and re-placing themselves depends on the nature of the displacement and dispossession itself. The way people experience movement to a new place and the extent to which this is a shocking and disruptive experience is determined by the conditions under which they move and whether they can extend their notions of territorial attachment to new areas not necessarily adjacent to each other. Thus the Cretan Muslims were able to re-create their identity in several new locations outside Crete, on the northern coast of Lebanon and Syria as well as in Turkey.

For most forced migrants, however, the move is generally conducted in more traumatic conditions. The task of re-creating a place, a home or neighbourhood, of 'producing a locality', is dominated by the effort to re-establish some continuity with the past places of origin. This work of maintaining continuity and managing memory is clearly articulated in the writings of Hirschon (2001), Malkki (1995), Loizos (1999), and Chatty (2010b). The nature of post-Ottoman Arab society—as separate from its politics—has been such that it has tolerated and acknowledged multiple layers of belonging in the struggle to make new places in the world. Although not physically displaced, the peoples of the Arab prov-inces of the former Ottoman Empire have spent most of the twentieth century creating new identities, and *em-placing* themselves in a new social order. Those dispossessed and entering the region during the late nineteenth and twentieth centuries, a time of widespread regional upheaval and destruction, found social environments conducive to the task of re-building, re-placing, and re-creating homes, neighbourhoods, and attachments to place. The following chapters will both describe and analyse how the Circassians, Armenians, Kurds, Palestinians, and

Iraqis managed to re-build and re-create homes and neighbourhoods in the modern Syrian state. The final chapter then sets out the irony of the displacement of people from Syria into the neighbouring states, carrying with them the memory of earlier forced migrations, dispossessions, and local efforts at accommodating the stranger.

The ethnic minority communities in the modern state of Syria, and the Levant generally, found a way to integrate themselves physically and socially in their new surroundings, but at the same time resisted the natural phenomenon of assimilation over the long term. Although discrimination in one form or another existed, the pull to remain different, to maintain their otherness, was more powerful. Patronage and real as well as fictive kinship networks were powerful positive forces; so too were the religious and charitable associations that these groups set up to help those less fortunate in their communities.

These are the very people who are now being asked to host the latest wave of refugees in the region. Whether the current wave of dispossessed, from Iraq into Syria and from Syria to Lebanon, Jordan, and Turkey, can weather the storms of dislocation as successfully as their forerunners did is an open question. Whether lessons from the late Ottoman reforms with regard to integrating refugees and other forced migrants can still be learned remains to be seen.

2

THE CIRCASSIANS, CHECHNYANS, AND OTHER CAUCASIAN FORCED MIGRANTS REIMAGINING A HOMELAND

My grandfather moved his family from Dagestan when my father was only two years old; he was just a baby. The move was decided as an outcome of the last of the Ottoman Russian wars when much of Dagestan fell to the Russian Orthodox armies. They didn't want to live under a Christian Orthodox force. First the family settled in Georgia and then they moved to Turkey, to a town called Amasya, looking for a new place to call home. My grandfather died there. My father and his two other brothers grew up there and did their compulsory Ottoman military service in Diyarbakir. As he was about to leave the service, he was encouraged by the tribal chiefs to join the gendarmerie [police service] which he did and he was sent to Damascus. In Damascus he was commissioned as an officer and he was sent to Karak [in present-day Jordan]; at that time Amman was a small Circassian village. On my mother's side, her grandmother was by now over 100 years old. She was very religious and she insisted that she be moved to the holy land, Sham al-Sharif [Syria]. So my grandfather agreed and he moved from Amasya in Turkey to Damascus.

(Adnan, Damascus, 2006)

In my interviews with Circassians in Syria, Sham al-Sharif was often cited as the place where the columns of Caucasian forced migrants, moving southwards on ox-drawn carts, decided to stop. Sham al-Sharif (Damascus the Noble, the Honourable) was the other name for Damascus, linking it religiously with Mecca, as the city that Muhammad, the Prophet of Islam, had refused to enter, considering it to be a paradise on earth. The title 'Sharif' generally was associated with Muhammad and his family and tribe among Sunni Muslims. Many of the Circassians I interviewed in Syria explained that their grandparents or great-grandparents decided to stop their migration once they reached Syria, based on their belief that they had reached a 'noble' place connected with the Prophet. One of my first interviews with a Circassian elder in Damascus confirmed this special association. Having arranged with an acquaintance in Damascus to interview her ninety-one-year-old grandfather, I had been warned that he hardly ever spoke about his family's journey to Damascus from the Caucasus mountains. Yet, no sooner had I entered the family's formal sitting room than I found myself facing not just my elderly informant but also his sons, daughters, and grandchildren, all gathered round to hear him tell the story—for the first time—of his journey to Syria. Fearing that this interview might be difficult with such a large audience, I carefully and methodically pulled out my two digital recorders. But before I could even push the start button, he began: 'My grandparents suffered great hardship in our journey from Abkhazia to Sham al-Sharif. We came on horseback and on ox-drawn carts. My father was a small boy and he was carried in the saddle bags of my grandfather's horse ...' (Abdul-Salam, Damascus, 2005). Though it was the first time his own children and grandchildren had heard him tell this tale, it was delivered with animation, intelligence, and poignant detail, the past coming into sharper focus for this nonagenarian than the present.

Who are the inhabitants of the Caucasus—that borderland between Europe and Asia bounded by the Black Sea to the west and the Caspian Sea to the east? Frequently referred to as 'Circassians' as a blanket term, they are a collection of largely tribal peoples associated with this mountainous terrain. The entire region is one of great linguistic and cultural diversity: among the peoples of the region are the Circassians proper, Abaza, Ossetians, Ingush, Chechnyans, Adjar, Azeri, Laz, Tatars, and Abkhaz. Circassians often refer to themselves as Adyghe (Men), a common self-appellation among peoples cut off from mainstream human circulation either by mountainous terrain, as here, or by extreme climates, as is the case among the San of the Kalahari desert. This chapter focuses on the massive expulsion, migration, and then integration into Syria of Circassians and others from the region bordered to the north by Tsarist Russia and to the south by the Persian Empire (Iran). Beginning at the end of the eighteenth century and continuing until the early 1920s, historical records reveal the mass expulsion of between 4 and 5 million Muslims from the Crimea and the Caucasus, largely forgotten in contemporary discourse. This massive forced movement of peoples may have been ignored in Western reportage because their movement was generally south into Anatolia and Greater Syria (the Levant) and not west into Europe.

Much of what the Circassian forced migrants experienced on the move and later in their efforts to integrate in the Levant can also be generalized to the other peoples of the Caucasus. The differences among the Circassian tribes were of minor importance. No Circassian tribal community excluded members of another in the new homelands they created in Syria. Marriage within and between tribal groups was common, and social and cultural continuity was very much focused on the larger group rather than the tribal affiliation. The hierarchical nature of Circassian society as recorded in the Caucasus did not translate well into the settler society in the new Ottoman lands, since Ottoman authorities actively sought to separate out the elite tribal leadership from the rest of that society. The tribal elite were instructed to settle in the cities of the Levant, while the rest were encouraged to create agricultural settlements on the border lands between agriculture and herding (the *Ma'moura*). In the early period of migration into Syria the Circassian slave trade and the agricultural servitude peculiar to Circassian society were a problem. Ottoman government estimates during the first large wave of Circassian forced migration in the 1860s were that 150,000 of these immigrants were of slave or serf status. Some scholars consider that these figures were probably too high, but that they do show that the number of slaves entering the Middle East with their masters was significant. The great majority of them were attached to their masters, commonly referred to as *emirs* or *beys*. In times of peace back in their Caucasian homelands they had cultivated the land of their masters and in war they had fought under their masters' command. In their new homelands in Greater Syria some slave families began to rebel against this system, and some of the poorer families who had sold children to slave dealers in order to continue their journeys into exile also began to protest. However, the traffic in young Circassian women for the harems of Constantinople and other cities, particularly Cairo, continued with little protest until the 1880s (Toledano 1982). Only then did this tradition of servitude or agricultural serfdom unravel due to Ottoman and Western European pressure, particularly the British anti-slavery movement.

Certainly from the middle of the nineteenth century the Caucasus was both a crossroads and a frontier between Asia and Europe, and between a Christian Russian empire and a Muslim Ottoman state. Many Circassians converted to Islam when Ottoman rule was established in the western part of Caucasia at the beginning of the sixteenth century. The remaining population seems to have converted in the eighteenth and early nineteenth centuries when the Islamic Sufi Muridite movement from Dagestan reached the upper regions of the Caucasus (Karpat 1979). Muridism grew out of local resistance to Russian military expansion into these lands. As a movement it preached a doctrine of social equality and liberty as well as resistance to foreign occupation. This was translated into Muslim Circassian solidarity against Russian occupation.

As a group, Circassians have long captured the historical imagination; the prowess and valour of their men, reinforced in the *mamluk* (warrior-slave) tradition of the Islamic caliphates, has been referred to often in historical tracts. The Ottoman government's successful use of informal Circassian militias in holding back or slowing down the advance of Russian imperialism and later Balkan nationalist aspirations reinforced the reputation of the region's menfolk as powerful fighters. The romanticized conceptualization of the physical beauty of Circassian women both within and outside the sultan's seraglio (household) was remarked on by many writers of the eighteenth and nineteenth centuries, and was captured in the paintings of the French Romantics.

During the European Enlightenment, Voltaire, for example, took it for granted that Circassians were a handsome people, a trait that he associated with their practice of inoculating babies with the smallpox virus. In his letter on the English Voltaire wrote:

> The Circassian women have, from time immemorial, communicated the small-pox to their children when not above six months old. ... The Circassians are poor, and their daughters are beautiful, and indeed, it is in them they chiefly trade. They furnish with beauties the seraglios of the

Turkish Sultan, of the Persian Sophy, and of all those who are wealthy enough to purchase and maintain such precious merchandise. (François Marie Arouet de Voltaire (1694–1778) *Letters on the English*, Letter XI, On Inoculation)

In the nineteenth century Johann Friedrich Blumenbach, the founder of physical anthropology, invented the concept of the 'Caucasian race' partly in reference to the widely understood beauty of Circassian women. He considered that the peoples of the Caucasus, particularly the Circassians and Georgians, represented something close to the ideal human form, having 'degenerated' less than others since the creation. Early anthropologists thus sought to elevate Europeans by linking them to the Circassians in a common racial category.

Circassian women were equally renowned as high-status slaves or concubines, particularly during the five centuries of Ottoman rule between the sixteenth and early twentieth centuries. Roxelana (1502–58), the wife of Sulayman the Magnificent, was the first former slave to be elevated from the status of concubine to legal wife. Furthermore, she made history in another sense by giving the sultan five sons. Prior to her rise in the seraglio, royal concubines were only permitted to give birth to one son in order to prevent sons fighting among themselves. Roxelana may not have been 'properly' Circassian, as historical evidence suggests that she was kidnapped from the Ukraine as a child and sold to the sultan's household in Constantinople while still a teenager. However, many Circassian slave girls and women did reach elevated standing in the imperial harem. Nor were Circassian wives and concubines limited to the imperial family. Sir Henry Elliot, the British ambassador to Constantinople in 1870, was reported to have realized that it was particularly indelicate to raise the subject of Circassian slavery since the grand vizier's Circassian wife had been a slave, and so had been—or were—the wives of many other important officials in the sultan's government (Lewis 2004; Toledano 1982: 170).

At the time of the Crimean War (1853–6), many Circassian militias fought with the Ottomans and with British soldiers against the Russian Empire. A kind of 'Circassophilia' in the English-speaking world seems to have emerged from that time. However, earlier travel accounts show that these romantic attitudes towards the Circassians had deeper roots. Admiration for the Adyghe people seemed to stem in part from the general respect accorded to independent mountain peoples who resisted Eastern empires, which in turn was linked to the disdain that most Westerners felt for Asian—and Russian—civilization.

Both the Circassian reputation for beauty and their heritage of achieving political power outside their homeland through their military prowess stemmed in part from the particular niche in the political economy of the Middle East that they had long occupied. For centuries even before Ottoman rule, the Circassians had specialized in providing fighting forces for various entities. They were the *mamluk*s, boys and men recruited or sold into bondage to be trained to serve as elite fighters for the ruling class. Circassians were not the only *mamluk* soldiers of the Muslim world—some came from Albania, Kosovo, and other Balkan territories—but they were the dominant group in Egypt over an extended period of time.

A Century of Dispossession and Forced Migration into the Balkans and the Levant

Beginning late in the eighteenth century and accelerating into the nineteenth, the Muslim inhabitants of the Caucasus and the adjacent Crimean peninsula experienced wholesale dispossession and deportation to the Balkans and to Ottoman Anatolia. This came about in several stages as Imperial Russia succeeded militarily in extending its rule and imposing its religion south and west into the diminishing domain of the religiously more tolerant Ottoman Empire. The first wave of expulsion from the Caucasus region took place at the end of the eighteenth century, following the Russo-Ottoman war of 1774. This was the first of a series of wars fought over the next century between these two empires which saw the Ottomans lose territory or effective control over their lands bordering on Russia. The Treaty of Küçük-Kaynarca (Kaynardzha, Bulgaria) signed on 21 July 1774 marked the defeat of the Ottomans in their struggle to keep control of the northern shore of the Black Sea, particularly the Crimea and the region we know today as southern Ukraine. As with most treaties during this modern era, a balance of power was negotiated so that no one side was totally vanquished. Russia returned some territory in exchange for extended rights and territory in other areas. Russia returned Wallachia and Moldavia to the

Ottoman Empire, but was given the right to intervene in case of Ottoman misrule. The Crimea was declared independent, but the sultan remained the religious leader of the Crimean Muslim Tatars. In 1783 the Crimea, though nominally independent, was formally annexed to the Russian Empire.

Unwilling to live under Russian Orthodox rule, some 500,000 Muslim Tatars were reported to have left the Crimea during this period (the 1780s) for Ottoman lands. As was to be a pattern later, they settled first in the nearest Ottoman province of the time, Bessarabia, and only later were moved on when that land, too, was lost to Russia. Of the original group of half a million, those who eventually reached Anatolia were reported to be 300,000. The loss of life on these journeys into exile was exceedingly high, in some cases reaching as much as 40 per cent. One can hardly imagine the hunger, thirst, and disease that must have accompanied these migrants. There were no religious charities or any national or international agencies to feed, shelter, or water the columns of forced migrants as they made their way south. The second mass expulsion of Muslim Tatars from Crimea, also nearly half a million, was in the nineteenth century after the Treaty of Edirne at the conclusion of another Russo-Ottoman war (1828–9). Many of them were first moved and settled in Rumeli, as the southern European Balkans of the Ottoman Empire was then known. But with the next Ottoman defeat in its war with Russia, the Tatars were expelled for a second time and forced to resettle in Anatolia and the southern Syrian provinces (Tekeli 1994: 209–10).

The next large-scale forced migration of Muslims came forty years later as an outcome of a major European conflict, the Crimean War of 1854–6, in which Great Britain and France (and Sardinia) allied themselves to the Ottomans in an effort to stop Russian expansion into the Ottoman Danube provinces of Moldavia and Wallachia (Romania today). Despite some inconclusive battles, including the Charge of the Light Brigade in the battle of Balaclava (made famous in Tennyson's poem), overall loss of life was huge, put by some historians at more than 750,000 lives. It was the first modern war fought in the trenches and, after an eleven-month siege of Sebastopol, Russia eventually gave in and pulled back. By the terms of the Treaty of Paris (1856) which concluded the war, Russia was meant to reduce its presence on the

Black Sea and remove its naval base, but this did not happen and Britain and France were not strong enough to insist upon it. It was estimated that 400,000 Muslim Tatars were forced to leave the Crimea at this time. Most sold their property and moved to the southern Balkans (Rumeli), as had the earlier group of Tatar forced migrants. Then, twenty years on, as tensions rose over Russia's lack of respect for the terms of the Treaty of Paris, the Ottomans went to war again without their British and French allies in the Russo-Ottoman war of 1877–8. The Crimean Tatars, who had settled in Rumeli just a few decades before, were moved on for a second time and resettled on the Anatolian plateau and in the Levant, with concentrations in and near Izmir, Ankara, and Konya (Karpat 1985: 66). The total number of Tatars forced to migrate deep into Ottoman lands between the end of the eighteenth century and the beginning of the twentieth is estimated to be about 1.5 million, of whom one in every four was reported to have died on the road. This level of fatalities in forced marches anticipated that experienced by the Armenians in their 'death marches' a century and half later.

Another wave of dispossessions was taking place in the Caucasus. These started largely after the 1860s as Russia continued its expansion into Ottoman lands throughout the 1870s, 1880s, and 1890s. There were Circassians and Abazas who had been unhappy with the outcome of the Treaty of Edirne at the close of the Russo-Ottoman war of 1828–9, which gave Russia the coastal strip of the Caucasus along the Black Sea, but who stayed on in their lands and resisted the continuing Russian campaigns to occupy their homelands. These groups were finally defeated in 1865, a few years after the Russians captured their leader, Shaykh Shamil, in 1859 (Tekeli 1994: 210). Shaykh Shamil or Imam Shamil (1797–1871) was a political and religious leader of the Muslim tribes of the northern Caucasus. He was the third imam of Dagestan and Chechnya (1834–59) and led the resistance to the Russians. During a thirty-year period of fighting Russian incursions (1830s–1860s), few Circassians left their homeland. Only in the 1860s did the emigration of Circassians turn into a mass displacement.

The methods that the Russians used to force the Circassians out were essentially the same as those they had used earlier to clear out the Muslims of the Crimea. Russian soldiers entered the villages, burned down the houses, stole the cattle and other belongings, and left the villagers with barely enough to live on. The British consul Gifford Palgrave, who rode through the Crimea to collect information for his reports, found that three-quarters of the Muslims he met were preparing to emigrate. McCarthy quotes Count Leo Tolstoy, who saw the carnage in the Caucasus first hand: 'It had been the custom to rush the aouls [villages] by night, when taken by surprise, the women and children had no time to escape, and the horrors that ensued under the cover of darkness when the Russians made their way by two and threes into the houses were such as no official narrator dared describe' (McCarthy 1995: 33).

At the Treaty of Paris at the conclusion of the Crimean War, Russia insisted that the Ottomans transfer peoples from these newly acquired lands (Pinson 1972: 74). Russia wanted to create a Christian majority in its newly conquered areas along the northern rim of the Black Sea and the Caucasus. Thus, treaty conditions determined that the Greek Orthodox from the eastern Black Sea region were to be sent to Russia and the Muslims in this frontier area were to be moved out and into the Ottoman heartlands. However, although as many as 520,000 Muslims had been forcibly moved out of their homelands now occupied by Russia and into the Ottoman Empire by 1865, only a few thousand Greek Orthodox subjects from the Ottoman Empire had agreed to migrate north into Russian-held territory. Of the few thousand Greeks forced to leave the empire for Russia, by 1869 many were reported to have returned to the eastern Black Sea region (Sinop, Trabzon, and Samsun), unhappy with conditions in the Russian state (Tekeli 1994).

During the Russo-Ottoman war of 1877–8 the Ottomans sent two Circassian units to help in the fight against the Russian invaders in the Caucasus. Inevitably the local Circassian population rose up against the Russians. In view of the Ottoman defeat and local Caucasian rising, Russia was able to insist in its treaty with the Ottomans at the close of the war that the Circassians on these newly acquired Russian lands now be moved out and resettled far away from the new Russian border. The Russians did not want to see these 'warlike' Circassian peoples settled in the relatively close areas of the Balkans. As a result, 2 million people were forced to leave the Caucasus for Anatolia in terrible conditions, travelling overland and by sea between 1878 and 1879. An estimated 500,000 died along the way from disease and starvation. It was perhaps the first ethnic cleansing or genocide in the modern era. These forced migrations of Muslim groups from the Caucasus regions carried on throughout the 1880s and 1890s (1881 through to 1914), and increasingly included Chechnyan and Dagestani refugees from new areas of Russian conquest in the Caucasus. This last wave of forced migrants was estimated at another 500,000 people (Karpat 1985: 67–70).

Table 2.1

Conflict	Expulsion	Population displaced
Russo-Ottoman war of 1774	Tatars	500,000 to Bessarabia and Rumeli
Russo-Ottoman war of 1828–9	Tatars	500,000 to Rumeli and Anatolia
Crimean War of 1854–6	Tatars	400,000 to Rumeli and Anatolia
'Shamil' campaign of 1859	Circassians	520,000 to Rumeli, Anatolia, and Syria
Russo-Ottoman war of 1877–8	Circassians	2,000,000 to Rumeli, Anatolia, and Syria
Balkan wars 1910s	Circassians	500,000 to Anatolia and Syria

Source: McCarthy 1995.

The transportation of these Circassians, Chechnyans, and Dagestanis was so large an operation that both governments had to co-operate to carry it out. Tens of thousands were evacuated by sea. The two governments had to employ warships—after their guns had been removed—as well as hiring numerous steam and sail vessels from other countries to effect this mass transfer. The majority of Circassians being sent to Anatolia were landed at Trabzon and Samsun on the Black Sea. One contemporary observer estimated that the mortality for the entire emigration was 50 per cent. Those refugees headed for Bulgaria were landed at Constanta or Varna. Conditions there were no better. One observer estimated that 80,000 Circassians landed at Varna, destitute, and suffering from fever, smallpox, and dysentery. Soon the beaches were covered with the dead. The Ottoman authorities had to bring in convicts to bury the dead or throw them into the sea (Pinson 1972: 74).

Muslim refugees who travelled by land were even less fortunate. In terms of loss of life and general suffering the Bulgarian Muslims' forced migration through Bulgaria was one of the most terrible in history. The vicious treatment of refugees by the Christian Russians and Bulgarians, and the fact that the migration was mainly undertaken in winter, were the main factors. But the inability of the Ottoman Empire to reach these refugees and provide them with aid on their journeys south into the shrinking Ottoman territory was another factor. Massacres by Russians and Bulgarians were the main impetus behind their flight. McCarthy (1995: 78–9) described how

> the refugees left quickly, taking only what they could carry. They walked, drove ox-carts and whenever possible clambered onto trains to escape south. At Hasskoy northwest of Edirne, more than 8,000 refugees gathered in January, waiting without shelter for trains to take them away. At Filibe station 15,000 waited. At Corlu 20,000. As the countryside became more unsafe and winter of 1877 deepened, refugees moved along the train tracks to the relative safety of stations guarded by Ottoman soldiers. Many froze to death along the tracks and observers grew used to seeing heaps of bodies along the lines.

McCarthy wrote that refugees had huddled together for warmth and froze together in death. This suffering and mortality of the Bulgarian Muslim refugees was chronicled in gruesome detail by European diplomatic consular briefs and reports. One stated that 'one little girl was found by a German railway official amongst a heap of 400 men, women and children who had frozen to death on the hills near Tatar Bazardjik and of whom she was the sole survivor'[1] (the consuls continually remarked on the number of naked bodies they saw, including women and children. It was clear to them that what clothing the refugees possessed was often seized by Russian troops and Bulgarians).

The Russo-Ottoman war of 1877–8 and the Treaty of Berlin that followed it saw several new nation-states—among them Romania and Bulgaria—being carved out of the European Ottoman Empire. Between 1 and 2 million people were driven from the Balkans to the Ottoman heartlands as a result of this peace treaty. About 500,000 people, or one in every four, were reported to have lost their lives in these forced marches. Those that survived were by and large resettled by the Ottoman authorities on agricultural lands in Anatolia and in

Levantine Syria. But that was not the end of the expulsions and forced migrations. Between 1893 and 1902 72,000 Muslims and Jews were expelled from Bulgaria. And then between 1912 and 1913, during the Balkan wars, which saw Serbia, Bulgaria, Montenegro, and Greece successfully defeat Ottoman forces with Serbian forces moving triumphantly through Kosovo and Albania to the Adriatic coast, a second large wave of Muslims and Jews fled the Balkans for Ottoman lands to the south. This specific involuntary emigration was estimated to be of 64,000 persons (Tekeli 1994: 210) and included Kosovars and Albanians, who largely emigrated to Syria, where many found work on the construction of the Hijaz railway linking Damascus with Medina in the Hijaz of what is now Saudi Arabia.

Table 2.2

Balkan conflicts	Expulsion	Population displaced
Bulgarian conflict 1893–1902	Muslims and Jews	72,000 to Greater Syria (the Levant)
Balkan wars (1912–13)	Muslims and Jews; Kosovars and Albanians	64,000 to Anatolia and Greater Syria

Source: Tekeli 1994: 210.

Surviving Expulsion and Finding Refuge in Syria

As the mass expulsions grew in scale, the need for a centralized organization to respond efficiently and fairly to these huge numbers of destitute and needy migrants became clear to the Sublime Porte. In 1857 the Ottoman government issued a Refugee Code offering land to immigrant families and groups, as described in chapter 1. Settlers were promised freedom of religion, whatever their faith, and were permitted to construct their own places of worship. News of this decree was published in European newspapers, but also spread rapidly by word of mouth, both along the frontier zone with Russia and in Europe. Requests from Circassians for land poured in; but also from potential immigrants in Poland, Switzerland, Bohemia, and Germany. Also taking advantage of this novel 'Immigration Code' of 1857 were thousands of Bulgarians, many of them 'emplaced' at the beginning of the nineteenth century in the Crimea where they had been had been forced to move by the Russians to replace the expelled Tatars (Shaw and Shaw 1977: 116).

In order to process the rising requests under this code, a refugee commission, the General Administration of Immigration, was set up in 1860, at first under the Ministry of Trade and then later as an independent agency in 1861 (Shaw and Shaw 1977: 115). This commission was the first modern response to a mass influx of refugees and exiles—especially the Tatars and Circassians fleeing from the lands conquered by the Russians north and west of the Black Sea. The commission also took responsibility for the thousands of non-Muslim immigrant farmers, political and intellectual leaders from Hungary, Bohemia, and Poland who arrived in Ottoman territory having responded to the advertisements in European papers. Over the following decades the commission additionally took over the management of the rapidly expanding—mainly missionary—international aid coming into the Ottoman Empire. More importantly, it tried to coordinate emergency in-country aid—the feeding, clothing, and sheltering of the migrants as they progressed through or near cities, towns, and villages—as well as the actual resettlement process. It took some time before the hosting provinces of the southern Ottoman Empire were able to meet the basic needs of these newcomers. In February 1878, for example, the governor of Damascus, where thousands of Circassians had arrived penniless and hungry, found that he had to levy a tax of 4 piastres (approximately $10 at today's purchasing power) per head on the registered male population of the governorate in order to feed and clothe these new immigrants in the initial phase of their resettlement (Lewis 1987: 99).

In eastern Anatolia and in the Syrian Levant the Ottoman authorities set out greater incentives to encourage refugees and immigrants to settle. In line with the Ottoman Refugee Code/Immigration Law of 1857, these forced-migrants-turned-settlers were given 70 donums (about 17 acres) to start farming. They were also provided with seeds, draft animals, and money to buy farm equipment. They were expected to build their own houses—often in the style of their original homelands—or get local people to build for them. In addition, and almost as though prescient of more contemporary resettlement concerns, they were prohibited from selling this land for twenty (though that was later dropped to ten) years so as to make sure these rural areas remained inhabited and to give time for the newcomers to adapt and acclimatize. These settler grants—both in materials and in land—were eventually cut back as more and more forced migrants appeared in the Ottoman heartlands and the Syrian Levant. However, their terms were generous, and they were based on realistic expectations regarding the effort and time needed to integrate and acclimatize. In modern times we have no similar 'resettlement' packages of such generosity. Up until 1878 these forced migrants were resettled primarily in rural areas. Only after 1878, when productive land and areas not associated with malarial disease became scarce, did the Ottomans permit and carry out the construction of immigrant social housing districts in the neighbour-hoods of towns and cities. The Muhajiriin district of Damascus is one such example, originally built for Muslim Cretans, but then later extended to Muslims from the Balkans and the Caucasus.

The Refugee Commission resettled these Muslim forced migrants, exiles, and immigrants following certain fundamental principles: create a border area or frontier zone; populate it with these new migrants, putting them between pre-existing rival or feuding social groups; resettle the incomers in an area as environmentally similar as possible to their homeland; and prevent any one group from becoming a major-ity in the region or province. Thus in Syria it encouraged the Circassians and Chechnyans to create frontier villages and towns between areas where Kurds and Bedouin herders were fighting over pasture lands in the Jazireh region between the Tigris and Euphrates. Further south, in the Jaulan of Syria, the Ottomans encouraged Circassians to build new settlements in areas between the fighting Druze and Bedouin villages. In promoting settlement in the Jaulan Heights, the Ottomans were specifically attempting to match the terrain and climate of the new territory, as closely as possible, with that of the newcomers' place of origin. Thus many Circassians felt 'at home' in their new settlement on the Jaulan Heights. The authorities also sought to create new popula-tion mixes so that no one group would become a majority and thus try to dominate the others. In the case of the Circassians, however, their warrior ethos and popularly acknowledged ferocity was such that the Ottomans took early steps to make sure they were widely dispersed.

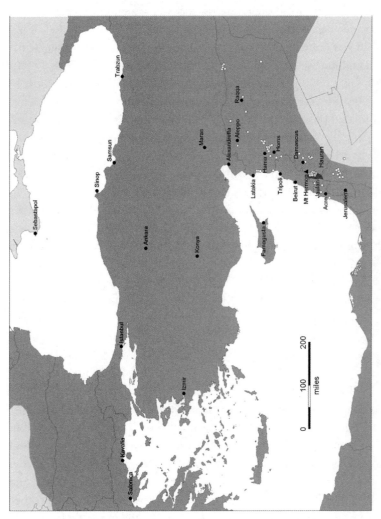

Map 5: Circassian and Chechnyan settlements

Between 1876 and 1895, official statistics compiled by the Refugee Commission showed that more than a million—largely Muslim—refugees had survived their perilous forced marches and sea voyages and entered the Asiatic Ottoman Empire. However, historians have estimated that, with the deprivations, disease, slaughter, massacres, and genocides that occurred between 1912 and 1922—the period of the Balkan wars, the First World War, and the Turkish national struggle for independence—the population of Ottoman Anatolia and the Levant fell by nearly 30 per cent (from 17.5 million to 12 million). Most of these deaths were due to dispossessions, expulsions, forced migrations, and related deprivation. The loss of life among Muslims was 2.5 million, among Armenians between 750,000 and 1,000,000, and among Greeks 310,000. By contrast, the total loss of life in Germany and France during the First World War was estimated at between 2 and 3 million, or 2–3 per cent of their populations (McCarthy 1983).

The Circassians, Chechnyans, Dagestani, Abkhazi, Abaza, and other smaller Caucasian groups were expelled from their homelands as a result of military defeats between 1860 and 1914. They made up the largest European or Eurasian forced migrant group to enter the Middle East in modern times. The first Circassian groups were removed to the European provinces of the Ottoman Empire on the other side of the Black Sea in about 1860, following Russia's defeat of Shaykh Shamil and his Chechnyan and Dagestani militias in the eastern Caucasus. Having routed this population, the Russian then eliminated Circassian resistance in the mountains above the Black Sea, pushing out more Circassians, Abkhazi, and Abaza. The Circassians were literally stuffed into boats at Russian-controlled ports. They were given neither assistance nor supplies, and at the first port of call, Trabzon, they died in great numbers of smallpox, typhus, and scurvy. In the winter of 1863 between twenty and fifty Circassians were dying each day in Trabzon. By the worst days of the following spring, 500 a day were dying; and 30,000 may have died at Trabzon alone. Those who landed at other ports, such as Samsun and Sinop, suffered a similar mortality rate. At the height of the immigration fifty refugees a day were dying at Samsun (McCarthy 1995: 36). Over the next few years, hundreds of thousands of Caucasian peoples were shipped to Ottoman territory or travelled overland. The figures are disputed, but it is generally accepted that as many as half of those who were forced from their homes in the Caucasus died on the journey into their first exile in the Ottoman territory of Rumeli.

The Refugee Commission had only been set up in 1860 to deal with these swelling numbers of other forced and voluntary migrants. Despite the early inadequacies of this newly created organization and the overwhelming numbers of refugees, those who survived the journey from the Trans-Caucasus region were given plots of land and permitted to build homes in Rumelia, Bulgaria, and Thrace as well as elsewhere in the European provinces of the empire (Karpat 1979; Toledano 1982: 152–68). Within fifteen years, however, nearly all of these Caucasian settlers were uprooted and driven out again. The Russians insisted that the Circassians should all be expelled from the European provinces of the Ottoman Empire, arguing that they were too dangerous and unreliable a community to have along a sensitive border. The other European representatives all agreed that 'the colonisation of Circassians in European Turkey shall be absolutely forbidden and those already established in Roumelia shall be sent back as far as practicable to the Musulman Asiatic provinces of the Ottoman Empire' (quoted in Lewis 1987: 96). Although the Ottoman authorities rejected this proposal, the Circassians were in fact expelled from Bulgaria and eastern Rumelia at the close of the Russo-Ottoman war in 1878 when Russia defeated the Ottomans and occupied much of the region. Many of these Circassians took refuge southward in Thrace or Macedonia that winter, but they were too many to be permitted to settle permanently. The Ottoman authorities reluctantly moved them on and undertook their transportation to Anatolia and Syria from the ports of Salonica, Constantinople, and Kavalla in February 1878. A few travelled overland on ox-carts (for Tatar migrations see Tekeli 1994: 213).

> *My parents came here when they were very young. There had been a war in their homeland. The Circassians helped the Turks in the war against Russia, but they lost. Then they had to leave these conquered places. My parents used to tell me about their first impression of Damascus in Marjeh.[2] It was a vast green meadow. The ox-carts all stopped there and formed circles. Inside the carts, fifteen to twenty families were squeezed in. Their journey had started back in Caucasia and from Abkhazia. They came by sea, some came overland. Most who came by sea drowned. Whole ships sank. Only a half million made it to Turkey. Some people chose to stay*

in Turkey. Some of our relatives stayed there. Others chose to come to Sham al-Sharif (Syria). Our ox-carts all passed through Aleppo, Homs, Damascus, and Jaulan and then dropped down into Jordan, a few families stopping here and there. The Turks dispersed us in different places to protect various locations. For the Turks we were a weapon. It was like having pistols in their pockets which they used whenever they needed to protect an area. My family settled in Jaulan. They were part of twelve Circassian villages which were built there. Most villages had 150 families, but ours was very small it had only fifty houses. Our village was the closest to Quneitra. All our Circassian houses had red tiles for roofs.

(Abdul-Salam, Damascus, 2005)

Over a period of six months between February and August 1878, 1,000 Circassians landed by ship at Beirut and were sent to Damascus to set up villages in the orchards (Ghouta) surrounding the city; another 2,000 landed at Tripoli and headed for Homs; 1,300 came from Salonica to Lataqiyya; and finally 13,000 arrived at Tripoli. Lewis recounts the fate of the Austrian Lloyd steamer *Sphinx* which set out from Kavalla for Lataqiyya on the Syrian coast with 3,000 Circassians but was forced by a storm to divert to Famagusta in Cyprus. Forty people were washed overboard and drowned, and a fire which broke out on board killed another 500. The numbers of refugees arriving by ship continued, with another 500 arriving in Tripoli and 1,200 in Acre in July, and 1,200 in Beirut in August (Lewis 1987: 97).[3] In the course of this one year, 25,000 Circassians arrived in Syria, and between 10,000 and 15,000 came into the province of Aleppo by ox-cart (Karpat 1979:19).

For the most part, Ottoman government officials in the provinces were unprepared for the mass arrival of so many refugees over such a short period of time. These refugees all needed food, accommodation, and ways of making a living. The authorities in the ports where many of them first arrived made what arrangements they could to provide temporary accommodation and food. Often small tax levies were raised in the towns and cities where their numbers were large in order to provide them with funds. But not all these new immigrants received help. Some were reported to have resorted to robbery, banditry, and even the sale of their children. Many also became ill; in March 1878, for example, smallpox was reported to have swept through the mosques and *madrasa*s of Damascus where many of these newly arrived forced migrants had taken shelter.

The problem was not one of antipathy to the refugees, but rather of logistics. The cities could not cope with these large influxes of forced migrants and needed to move them out and into the countryside as quickly as possible, where they could be settled as farmers and become self-sufficient. One example of this logistical nightmare for the provincial authorities was the planned settlement of about 10,000 Circassians in the district of Hama. Although the government did make some help available, the inhabitants of Hama donated 6,000 kilograms of wheat and 4,000 kilograms of barley for the first sowing by these new farmers. It seems that there was not enough assistance even with these private donations, and some 3,000 Circassians returned to the port of Tripoli, where they demanded passage back to Constantinople. Eventually the situation improved, logistics began to work more smoothly, and the newcomers were sent to settle in districts that were near or on the frontier of settlement where there was also plenty of uncultivated land.

Some scholars have argued that the Ottoman government was actually quite cautious in its Circassian resettlement plans, having learned some hard lessons from the Balkan experience. For the Ottomans, the Circassians were potentially dangerous, because of their deep commitment and loyalty to their tribal chiefs—even to the extent of disregarding the authority of the central government. Consequently the government decided to take care to disperse the larger Circassian tribes by settling them in different areas and placing their traditional leadership elsewhere. Many of the community and tribal leaders were given army positions, while wealthy and notable families were allowed to settle in cities, rather than becoming part of the new rural farming settlements. Thus divided, the Circassians were prevented from reorganizing themselves into armed bands and from attacking the indigenous populations, as they had occasionally done in the places of first resettlement in the Balkans and Anatolia (Karpat 1979: 18).

After centuries of neglect the southern provinces were being slowly reclaimed by the Ottomans and local governance was giving way to a more centralized approach to rule (Rogan 1999). This was reflected in the development of a modern infrastructure with the construction of roads, the establishment of telegraph lines from Damascus through the length of Jordan to the Hijaz, and the building of the Hijaz railway connecting all the southern provinces with Damascus and thereby

Anatolia, as well as cadastral land surveys and land registration establishing ownership of land and boundaries.[4] The sponsored settlements of the new immigrants along the centuries-old contested *Ma'moura* (cultivated land) and Badia (semi-desert grazing land) was part of the policy of taking back control of these regions. When central government was strong, the Ma'moura was pushed out into the Badia. When it was weak, the *Badia* was pushed into previously cultivated land by the strong nomadic pastoral tribes (Chatty 2013a [1986]). These new settler communities ran in a line from Aleppo to Amman and further south to Ma'an, and became the focus of contestation for control between the Bedouin pastoralists and the new farmers.

As Lewis points out, it was the fact that these settlers were located in these frontier districts rather than their actual numbers or the amount of land which they cultivated that made them historically significant (Lewis 1987: 100). For many of the migrants from the Caucasus, it was rarely a matter of simply adopting the hoe and getting on with farming. Many had to learn to become farmers, having come from pastoral traditions. But it was their capacity to protect themselves and their families from local elements as well as marauding Bedouin that drew attention to them. The Circassians were very well fitted for the role of frontier settlers. They were able and willing to take on the Bedouin and the local peasantry, who often held counter-claims to the land upon which the Circassians had just settled. There were numerous recorded disputes, in which the Circassians were generally the victors, partly because they were impressive fighters, but also because the Ottoman authorities generally took their side. Again according to Lewis, the authorities deliberately directed some of the Circassian settlers to areas that were particularly turbulent so that they could assist in subduing the prevailing feuds. The government settlements of Circassians on the Jaulan Heights in areas near the Druze settlements of Hauran and Mount Hermon are one such example. The Druze, a semi-autonomous ethno-religious community originally settled in southern Lebanon and the hill areas of Aleppo, had come into conflict with the Christian Maronites of Mount Lebanon in the 1860s. The latter, with backing from French and other European powers, established their hegemony over the mountain (formerly known as Jebel Druze). Many Druze left and established new settlements in the

Hauran as well as around Mount Hermon. The areas, however, were restive, and the Ottoman policy of settling Circassians in between two major Druze settlements was an effort to control the latter. Many of the Circassian men in these settler groups took up employment in the Ottoman army or in the mounted rural gendarmeries. Those who didn't were occasionally called up anyway for special service in the military to quell sporadic disturbances either with the Druze or local Bedouin tribes.

After this wave of forced migrants at the end of the 1870s, people from the Caucasus continued to arrive. For some it was as a matter of having found Russian rule unacceptable, or an unwillingness to let their young men serve as conscripts in the Russian army or to pay tax in lieu. They were also encouraged to come by the Ottoman government. The sultan, Abdul Hamid II, clearly saw these new immigrants as potential settlers and soldiers. He also took a personal interest in their affairs and, after 1887, was reported to have given instructions for provincial government officials to do whatever they could to expedite the settlement of these refugees and immigrants. For example, in 1887 he agreed to the creation of a special settlement of Caucasian forced migrants (Abaza) on his own lands, Marj al-Sultan, in the orchards and pastures for his horses surrounding Damascus. Part of this personal property was divided up between 150 of the forced migrant families. They were provided with tools, seeds, and labour to build their new village, in the style to which they had been accustomed back in their old homeland.

From a reading of British embassy dispatches and reports in 1905 and 1906, Lewis has summarized the numbers of Circassian families in the Syrian provinces as 1,949 families settled in Quneitra, on the Jaulan Heights, and 670 families near Homs (Lewis 1987: 101–2). In the *wilayat* of Beirut there were about 550 families, with a total for both Beirut and Damascus *wilayat*s estimated at 25,000 individuals. However, another embassy report puts these figures at over 30,500.[5] What is striking is that between the first great wave of deportees entering the region in and around the 1860s and the early 1900s, when these reports were made, there had been little change in population numbers of those resettled. This may have been due to a number of factors: a low fertility rate; a very high mortality rate in the first few decades after their arrival; or high departure rates. However, it is noticeable that most of the Circassian villages failed to grow significantly in size. This static population growth would account for why the Circassians, once established in their settlements, did not try to expand their areas of cultivation or occupancy after the First World War.

Caucasian and Chechnyan Forced Migrant Settlers in the Syrian Provinces

One of the first and largest groups of Caucasian exiles to reach the Syrian provinces in the 1860s was a group of 5,000 Chechnyans who settled at Ra's al-'Ayn on the Khabur river. These settlers arrived in one large group following the defeat and capture of Shaykh Shamil by the Russians in 1859. It is reported by Lewis that this group was aware of the Ottoman Refugee Code and interpreted it to mean that that they could take what land they wanted. Without any instructions from Ottoman authorities (or perhaps because no documentation has been discovered), this group chose to settle on an area with abundant springs next to the Khabur river. It was not an empty or abandoned area, and the local farmers and sheep herders were not happy with this invasion of outsiders into their midst. The nomadic pastoral sheep-raising Bedouin tribes in the area were also not consulted, resulting in numerous disputes and violent raids and counter-raids between the Chechnyan settlers and the Bedouin. The Chechnyans were very aggressive and often took the offensive, defeating even the noble camel-raising Shammar Bedouin in raid after raid. Inevitably they were feared by both the local peasantry and the Bedouin, and came to constitute a settlement whose right to remain was not to be challenged.

As a community, however, the Chechnyans initially failed to thrive in their new settlements. Their population numbers did not appear to rise over the ensuing decades. It is most likely that, although they had chosen very fertile sites on the Khabur river to build their new villages, these sites were also highly malarial, resulting in significant infant and adult mortality. Smallpox, cholera, and other diseases also reduced their numbers. What saved these settlements from collapse was that other Chechnyans, forced out of their homelands, arrived at Ra's al-'Ayn in the 1870s and 1880s, helping to replenish population numbers (Lewis 1987).

Forty years after the Chechnyans settled at Ra's al-'Ayn, a Circassian group arrived at Raqqa on the Euphrates. These were forty-seven Kabarday families, part of a larger group who had arrived by ship in Alexandretta in 1905. The Kabarday had left Russia largely of their own accord, fleeing not so much violence and armed conflict like the Chechnyans, but rather the prospect of being forced to renounce their Muslim faith and convert to Russian Orthodox Christianity. Their resettlement was planned and organized by the Ottoman provincial authorities. It was originally determined to settle the Kabarday in Raqqa, Khanasir, and Manbiju along the middle Euphrates on the Aleppo–Baghdad trade route, and thus create a string of Circassian villages in the area around Raqqa from which a gendarmerie could be recruited. Consular observations from Aleppo also reported that this group's leader, Talustan Anzor, came to be highly respected as a mediator and conciliator in the Raqqa district.

Damascus District Settlements

With the large influx of Circassian refugees passing through Damascus from the port of Beirut, a number of Circassian settlements are known have been established both to the north around Homs and nearby in the vicinity of Damascus. Marj al-Sultan, in the fertile orchards ringing Damascus, was a well-organized and carefully planned settlement which quickly took root and thrived. In later years, as the flow of migrants slowed down and dwindled to more manageable size, and as the Ottomans began to allow settlement in the cities, a number of Circassian immigrants settled in the Muhajiriin and Diwaniyya districts of the city.[6]

> In 1878, twenty-five Circassian families who were forced to emigrate arrived in Marj al-Sultan. They had come from Turkey and before that they had been in Bulgaria, in the Balkans. Actually we have gone through five forced migrations. In 1864 it was to the Balkans [from the Caucasus]. Then after the Berlin Agreement of 1878 it was to Turkey from the Balkans. Some came by land and others through Greece, Salonika and Cyprus, you know the story of the Sphinx ship, to the Syrian coast. The twenty-five families who settled in Marj al-Sultan came to Damascus by land—through Aleppo, Homs, and so on. They were mainly Shabzugh and Abazah tribes. At the time, Madhat Basha was the Governor of Damascus. His wife was a Circassian and he liked the Circassians. He met with those who were on their way

to al-Marj al-Sultan and the Jaulan and suggested that they stay closer to Damascus in a place called Mezzeh. At that time Mezzeh was an unpopulated land devoted to cactus fields. The Circassians refused as they were afraid that they would become assimilated if they lived so close to the city. Some went on to the Jaulan where the geographic nature of the place was very close to that of their homeland: heavy rain, snow, woods and mountains. Others came here to al-Marj. It was spring-time. In spring this area used to be extremely beautiful with plenty of water, trees, and grass. It was the private property of the sultan himself. In the spring and fall, Sultan Abdul Hamid had his 3,000 (mainly military) horses grazing in this area.

The Ottoman government gave each family two cows, two oxen, poultry, food sup-plies, and tents. Originally they chose to establish their town along the south eastern area. But when they started digging, they discovered that this place was an old Roman cemetery and so they had to move west. They started to build their small homes, using unburned bricks [adobe] and pressed wet soil. The roofs were made of poplar trees which were plentiful in the area. There was a very clear style. No house was to be built directly on the side of the street. They were all set back. After building the houses they set out to build the mosque in the next year, in 1879, in the Shabzugh quarter. All the houses were of one storey. Only three houses were two storeys. The second storey in these houses had only one room and that was used by the head of the tribe as a guest area. The reason that all the houses were built as one storey was so as to provide privacy for the women of the house.

(Adel, Marj al-Sultan, 7 April 2006)

As with so many of these planned Circassian settlements, they were located on fault lines or frontiers of conflict. The villages in the Ghouta, the important agricultural artery for the city, had long been harassed by Bedouin, particularly the powerful Aneza tribes who sought to extract *khuwa* (tribute) from the local farmers. Long a thorn in the side of Ottoman tax collectors, *khuwa* payment diminished what could then be collected by the government in taxes. The Circassian settlers in the Ghouta quickly established their strength and unwillingness to pay tribute to the Bedouin. They did not need Bedouin protection as they were quite able to protect themselves. In due course they entered into agreements with the Bedouin leadership to work together for the mutual benefit of both communities. Sometimes, however, these agree-ments broke down.

The last big clash of the Circassians in Marj al-Sultan with the Bedouin was in 1954. There were about 2,000 Bedouins. The village had only 350 people includ-ing men, women, and children. What made up for the difference in number was that most of the people in the village were well trained in using arms. Previously, the village was attacked during the Syrian revolution.

(Adel, Marj al-Sultan, 7 April 2006)

Marj al-Sultan thrived as a village, and rapidly became a focal point for Circassians on their way to settlements in the south in the Jaulan and Transjordan or later for those passing through for trade and other business in Damascus, Homs, or Aleppo. For the next generation seeking higher education in Damascus was important, but the pull to remain in Marj al-Sultan was strong. Although the second generation replaced Turkish with Arabic as the language with which to address officialdom, the Circassian language, Cherkasi, remained the language spoken at home.

Other immigrants from the Balkans and from Anatolia continued to arrive in Syria throughout the early decades of the twentieth century. One small community of Balkan refugees slowly grew on the outskirts of Damascus, settling in the orchards on the edges of the city. Here they were initially fed by the local community and then informally allowed to farm small patches of land in these orchards to grow vegetables and fruit. They had no title to the land, but over time their settlement was not challenged by the state and thus attracted other Balkan migrants. These immigrants were mainly Kosovar and Albanian refugees. They were fleeing the unrest during and following the Balkan wars of 1912–13 as well as what they perceived to be a threat to their freedom to worship as Muslims in the new nation-states being created in the Balkans. As one elderly resident of this 'Arnaouti' community in the Diwaniyya district of Damascus recalled:

My father was born in Kosovo in 1894. He came to Damascus in 1914. He knew no Arabic, only Turkish, but he was able to get a job on the Hijaz railway. He started as a labourer, then a locomotive driver, and ended as an inspector of boilers. He died in 1996, without mastering Arabic. He was 102 years old when he died. My father got married only to settle down. He married without being able to speak Arabic. He married a woman from Damascus, the daughter of a pious sheikh. His wife was an Arab woman who could not speak Albanian. He built the house we are sitting in by his own hands, room by room. First one room then another then another. When we children were born we learned to speak Arabic and Albanian to both our parents. When I finished my five years of schooling I too joined the Railway and have worked there all my life. I am a Syrian, but not an Arab. I prefer to be known as Syrian

'Arnaouti'. ... The problem for me is that I was born here and grew up here and have memories here. I love Damascus.When you ask about my homeland, I cannot abandon Syria as a homeland. But there was also another homeland, that of my father. It is not the same for the Palestinians or Armenians. Our fathers came here to have the freedom to practise their religion [Islam]. But they lost what they had had before [their homeland].We fight to live here in dignity.

(Barakat, Diwaniyya, Damascus, 18 October 2005)

Jaulan Heights Settlements

It appears that Quneitra had been an abandoned settlement for much of the eighteenth and nineteenth centuries. In that void, much of the area around it had been claimed as important pasture land. The Fadl, the Na'im, and numerous Turkmen nomadic pastoral tribes claimed the area as belonging to their 'traditional tribal territory'. Rough and rocky, it was prime grazing land for sheep, though also potentially suitable and previously used for agriculture.

The first Circassian settlers arrived there in 1873, most probably from Sivas in Anatolia. They came with their ox-carts and animals, and seem to have held back from pursing any cultivation for about five years. Then, in 1878, another 2,000 Circassians arrived from Bulgaria and the community started trying to cultivate the land. These newcomers, as well as the original settlers, were now given title to between 70 and 130 donums of land, depending upon the size of their families. By this time Quneitra was a village of 100 houses, and there were about seven other villages nearby (Oliphant 1880: 44). Ten years later on, Quneitra had grown to a town of 260 buildings with a population of approximately 1,300 Circassians and a few Arab government offices and soldiers. One visitor to the Jaulan in 1885, Gottlieb Schumacher, described the Circassians he came across:

> As a consequence of the Russo-Turkish War, they wandered out of Bulgaria, and in the spring, 1878, in a starving and pitiful condition reached 'Akka. ... By indomitable industry and solid perseverance they soon attained a certain degree of prosperity, built villages, cultivated fields, bred cattle, dried grass for the winter and drove the Bedawin out of their neighbourhood.

(Schumacher 1888: 57)

He continued to describe these new settlements:

It does one's eyes good, after having seen so many devastated places, to arrive at a flourishing, evenly-constructed, clean village, whose inhabitants, with their Kaimakam (magistrate), an energetic, industrious old Turk, immigrated from the neighbourhood of the chief Turkish town, have more feeling for European systems than the citizens of many towns in this country. ... Looking too at the towering hay-cocks, the swift rattling Circassian carts, the preparation of dried bricks from the fine earth of the neighbourhood, and above all the cleanliness of the streets, one asks involuntarily, 'Am I in the Jaulan?'

(Schumacher 1888: 208)

Relations with the surrounding pastoral tribes were uneasy at first, particularly with the highly respected Al Fadl Bedouin, who stood to lose some of their pasture lands to the Circassian farmers. This tribe, with deep historical roots in Syria, had about 320 tents as well as winter villages in the area at the time of Schumacher's visit. He reported that the Fadl deeply resented the Circassians. Both the Fadl and the Circassians had bloodied each other, with the amir, Shaykh Shedadi al-Fadl, having died in one battle with Circassians (Schumacher 1888: 87). Eventually the early skirmishes and jockeying for control gave way to a *modus vivendi*, and reports in the late 1870s by Oliphant and other travellers indicated that a *majlis* (in this sense, a consultative council) run by the *kaimakam* (governor) of Quneitra also included representatives of the Fadl, the Na'im, the Turkmen, and the Druze to discuss matters related to the smooth functioning of the villages, as well as the use of the land for agriculture and for pasture.[7]

The Circassians on the Jaulan were drawn into much more serious and sustained conflict with the Druze than they had experienced with the Fadl. Some historians claim that the Ottoman authorities selected the Jaulan as a settlement site for the Circassian immigrants because they need to place a militarily strong potential force in a strategic position between the Druze of the villages around Mount Hermon and the Jebel Druze. Jaulan was in just the right place. British embassy reports also suggest that in 1883 the *wali* of Damascus wanted to settle some Circassians in the southern Bekaa Valley (of contemporary Lebanon) in order to place a wedge between the Druze of Lebanon coming to the aid of those in Mount Hermon and the Jebel Druze in Syria. Although this planned settlement did not come about, Circassian cavalry was used by the Ottomans against the Druze, causing resentment and distress for years to come.[8]

My mother was born in Turkey in 1870 at the time of the war against the Russians. She was carried here [to Syria] in the saddlebags of our grandfather's horse. They came to Jaulan and settled in one of the twelve Circassian villages. Ours was the closest to Quneitra. Our house was the best, our villages were the best. Even the French who were familiar with the whole area admitted that ours were the best villages. All the houses had red tiles for roofs. We lived with my parents and grandparents. We had oil lamps and we used wood for heating. We had forests and we used to bring the wood from there to burn for heating. Until 1947 we had no electricity. We had an Arab school and a Circassian school, but that was closed down in 1936. Some families, mainly who supported the Circassian school, wanted to return to Circassia but others wanted to remain. We learned Arabic in school and spoke Circassian at home. When I finished school, I worked on the land for four years and then I joined the army. It was the time of the French Mandate.

(Abdul-Salam, Damascus, 25 October 2005)

For the next fifty years these Circassian villages thrived. The Circassians prospered as army officers and civil servants, as well as farmers. The second and third generation had become well-educated—in both Arabic and their local Circassian language—loyal citizens of Syria. For many it was their third homeland, having been removed from the Caucasus, then sent to the Balkans, before arriving in the Jaulan and setting down new roots. Then, during the Six Day War in June 1967, the Circassians were again violently dispossessed of their lands, most fleeing and taking refuge in Marj al-Sultan, but some also in Damascus itself, accepting any shelter they could find.

Then just when we started to feel at home [in the Jaulan], we were driven out. I came [to Damascus] with my wife and children except for one who went missing in the fighting [the June 1967 War]. Three of my sons were already in Damascus. Two in the armed forces and one was studying. As I was a civil servant I was not eligible for any assistance. We stayed in an apartment of three rooms—three families in three rooms. One son who was a student in the Faculty of Mechanical Engineering, Mounir, is now a retired general and Talaat is in America. The three of them were living in one room and the families of friends of our sons in the other two rooms. So instead of living comfortably in my fine house with a garden full of flowers in Quneitra, here we were three families in a cellar. I became very frustrated and at a complete loss. I became absent-minded and started to wander about. Finally we were allowed to stay in an empty apartment of a Circassian going to America for two years. This was the chance we needed to regroup and set about becoming self-suffi-cient once again.

(Abdul-Salam, Damascus, 2005)

Settling in and Becoming Integrated

The early period of the Circassian and Chechnyan migrations and set-tlement in the Syrian provinces was met with some apprehension, especially by the non-Muslim (Christian) inhabitants of the region. There was a fear that these newcomers, uprooted from their native homes by Christian governments (Russia, Bulgaria, and Greece) might become violent to local Christians. They were said to have been unruly while living in the Balkans, attacking Bulgarian Christians and abduct-ing women as well as resorting to robbery (Karpat 1979: 23). In a report by the British ambassador in Constantinople to the Marquis of Salisbury, the British foreign secretary, in 1878, an explanation was given for the variety of lawless actions perpetrated by the Circassians, which went back to the enormous hardships their eviction had inflicted as they were forced to travel from one part of the Ottoman Empire to another in conditions of dire poverty and ill-health. In a sympathetic and frank description, he explained that the breakdown of the Circassian social order was as a result of these migrations, which brought many to the brink of starvation. In order to survive, the ambassador argued, some were forced to steal, while others had to settle in rural areas where they were viewed as interlopers supported by the state. Surrounded by unfriendly neighbours such as the Bedouin, Kurds, and Turkmen, who all resented the Circassian usurpation of their own grazing lands, they had to establish their prowess and gain respect by force of personality and physical strength (Karpat 1979).[9]

Thirty years later (1906) British consular reports suggested that the Circassians had acclimatized and gained the respect of their neighbours by sheer force of will and hard work, refusing to be browbeaten into paying *khuwa* to the Bedouin. The reports of these consular officials regarded the Circassian immigrants now largely as peasants

> employed in agricultural work on *miri* or Crown [state] land. ... In other parts of Syria there are large and flourishing [Circassian] communities, a few being scattered a considerable way south along the line of the Hedjaz

77

Railway. In many of these districts the Circassians have transformed barren tracts into well-cultivated and prosperous lands.[10]

By the early decades of the twentieth century the Circassian and Chechnyan communities were well established in the Syrian provinces of the Ottoman Empire. They were clustered in villages along the Euphrates and along a frontier line between the desert and the sown near Homs, Damascus, and Jaulan. With the defeat of the Axis powers, these settlers found themselves no longer Ottoman subjects. They threw their weight behind the newly created state of Syria. In the following years their image changed from that of pioneer settlers, both feared and admired for their energy and vigour, to respected civil servants, army officers, and government office workers. The Six Day War turned the Circassians who had been settled in the Jaulan into 'refugees' again, internally displacing them. Nearly 25,000 Circassians were driven out when the Israelis occupied the Jaulan. Most fled to Damascus where they were given assistance by the Syrian Circassian welfare societies as well as government and international agencies. Some received assistance from the Tolstoy Society and from relatives who had previously emigrated to the United States, particularly Paterson, New Jersey. Most of them settled in Damascus, however, and after some initial difficulty started to rebuild their lives.

For many Circassians, the safety net and focus of social and cultural life of the community revolved around the Circassian charitable associations which were formally organized in Damascus in 1948. Much of Circassian social life centred around these organizations: promotion of education, Circassian language teaching, newspapers and magazines, public libraries, sports clubs, and even the setting out of guidelines for the appropriate *mahr* (bride price) to be contracted on marriage. For these proud people, the associations were set up and designed to ensure that no Circassian or Chechnyan ever had to ask the state for welfare or a handout, if they fell on hard times. In recent years these associations have become an important focus for the transmission of Circassian language through the numerous courses they offer. They have also become an organizational point for the numerous visits to Caucasia that have taken place with increasing regularity since the fall of the Soviet Union.

Not only is language acquisition promoted, but general higher education is also widely supported by the Circassian charitable societies.

Circassian youth are encouraged to enter university and pursue professional degrees. Although military careers still represent important options for the Circassians in Syria, a wide range of professions is also taken up by Syrians of Circassian origin. As in many refugee and settler societies, higher education is highly valued and the Syrian Circassian Society, with support from the Circassian republics in the Caucasus, provides ten to fifteen scholarships each year to students willing to pursue higher education abroad.

With the fall of the Soviet Union, the imagined Circassian homeland has become a real space. Large numbers of Circassians, from Turkey, Syria, and Jordan as well as the United States, have begun to make trips, especially in the summer, to find long-lost relatives and make real their pictured villages. Often these visits to the homeland community generate a shock of non-recognition of the 'self' in others. The self, which is often conceptualized abstractly in terms of cultural belonging, is also perceived as having particular physical characteristics. As Shami relates of these encounters, the Circassians visiting from Turkey, Syria, and Jordan were surprised to find that their countrymen and women in the homeland left behind in the nineteenth century were generally shorter and darker than they had imagined. In the Middle East, Circassians were proud of the general perception of them locally that, as a people, they were fair, and tall in stature. This disjunction was explained by some as being because it was the nobility (hence the taller and more fair) who had fled whereas the poor and the slaves had largely remained in Caucasia. Although there is no historical evidence to support such a version of the emigration, it has now been repeated enough to have acquired a finish of historical respectability (Shami 1995: 89).

Conclusions

The European Caucasian Muslims, mainly Circassians, Chechnyans, Dagestani, Ossetians, and Abkhazi as well as Albanians and Kosovars, arrived in the Middle East towards the end of the nineteenth century as forced migrants and refugees, sometimes displaced twice over in the space of a few decades. Although their dispossession and migration was, in the main, anticipated by the Ottoman state—as an outcome of treaties of peace with its arch-enemy, Russia—their actual arrival in the Syrian provinces generally overwhelmed the awaiting officialdom. The early years of these settler migrants were highly insecure, as Lewis, McCarthy, and Karpat have so carefully documented (Karpat 1974; Lewis 1987; McCarthy 2001). Many of the original settlements in Syria, Jordan, and Palestine failed to thrive. Some died out entirely or were abandoned before replenishment arrived with the next wave of dispossession and forced migration at the end of the nineteenth and early twentieth centuries.

For many of these forced migrants there was a physical environment to adapt to as well as a transformation in livelihood. Most of the original settlers came from mountainous terrain and were expected to carve out livelihoods on the largely flat open ground on the frontiers of the semi-arid steppe. They were expected to farm the land, eventually providing revenue for the state once their period of 'exemption' from tax-farming had lapsed. They were also expected to pacify the region of their settlement, establishing their superiority over quarrelling neighbours and repulsing the Bedouin efforts to coerce them into paying a form of protection money. These settlers could and did protect themselves from marauding tribes as well as the hostility of their immediate neighbours. Going one step further, they often entered into alliances with Bedouin tribes such as the Fadl in Jaulan and the Beni Sakr near Amman, and thus brought stability to a wide area of agriculture.

Within the Circassian community, concepts of family, group solidarity, and leadership were shaped by the cultural ideals of the old homeland and influenced the new social order which the Circassians set out to create.[11] Most Circassian settlements were organized with neighbourhood leaders, each with a guest house where men of the community would gather to discuss settlement matters, mediate disputes, or plan defences. They were also places where the elders could reminisce about the Caucasus, while the younger generation might actively consider visiting or returning to it one day. In many of these settlements the distinctive two-wheeled carts of the Circassians could be seen taking their own produce to market towns, occasionally also carrying barley cultivated by Bedouin (Hacker 1960). The other Circassian settlements in Quneitra as well as places like Marj al-Sultan were by the mid-twentieth century 'small, self-contained, largely self-sufficient communities of a few thousand inhabitants each—middlemen, trading agricultural products for simple manufactured articles, for cloth, tea, sugar, kerosene and household utensils brought from Damascus and Jerusalem' (Hacker 1960: 20).

The Circassians in general were determined to succeed in their new homelands, and many of those I interviewed in 2005 and 2006 talked about the decades of hard work, making their communities successful, whether in Marj al-Sultan, Jaulan, or Amman. Although belonging to different tribes and elaborating slight differences in custom and some-times 'invented' traditions, these Muslim Europeans were decidedly progressive in the emphasis they placed on educating their youth, and determined to maintain their languages and keep a social distance from non-Caucasian communities. Marriage, with its elaborate ritual of elopement, was kept very much to Circassian and other Caucasian peoples, although close-cousin marriage, as preferred by the Arabs, was not acceptable.

Towards the end of the British and French Mandates, and as the Great Depression loosened its grip on the Middle East, these Circassian settlements began to thrive. They were no longer implanted immigrant groups in an Arab landscape, but a community integrated into the local, sometimes heterogeneous, population as well as the wider government. The focus of social life for many Circassians continued to be their charitable associations and sports clubs. Their newspapers and libraries were well known—and unique, considering that the Circassian rural farming communities continued to be relatively small. In time, more of the young migrated to the cities and entered into government service, education, and other professions. Their numerous charitable societies were, and still remain, active associations looking after the elderly, the infirm, and the young.

For all the strength of Circassian social customs and traditions, the unity of these communities remains very much at an ideational level, with an emphasis on the importance of community solidarity, good citizenship, and political awareness. Political leadership, however, is limited to the community level. Even the remembered and partially imagined homeland is not a source of political capital. Many Circassians today do return to visit their places of origin. Some have entertained notions of remaining, and others have seen their children marry and put down new roots in Caucasia itself. But for the most part, the

Circassians, as refugee and settler groups, have been absorbed into the states they found themselves in after decades of turmoil and dispossession. Today Circassians form sizeable communities in Turkey, Syria, Jordan, and Palestine. The figures are impressionistic, as few national census statistics separate out the Circassians as an ethnicity. Shami (1995) gives the following figures: 1 million in Turkey; 50,000 in Syria; 30,000 for Jordan and 2000 in Palestine.[12] In the Russian Federation there are three republics (previously autonomous regions of Kabardino-Balkaria, Cherkessk-Karachay, and Adygei) with significant Circassian populations. The estimated Circassian population in the Caucasus is about 500,000 (Shami 1995).

After the Six Day War some Circassian families from the Jaulan set out to recover their lost homelands, and travelled to the Soviet Union in search of relatives and roots. Some remained there. Others found it not so easy to either stay or return, and entered into cycles of movement between the old and the new homelands. The relative freedom of movement—depending on economic capacity—made the homeland both more real and more imagined at the same time. Those I was able to interview in 2005 and 2006 had visited once if not more often. Some had bought land and built houses with the idea of remaining, only to find after a few months that, as beautiful as the Caucasian landscape was, they remained deracinated. Their social ties and networks were rooted in their Circassian communities in the Middle East and no longer in the Caucasus region.

I went to visit the Caucasus twice. I met with about forty relatives all from the Kaghados. They offered me land and help to settle there with my children. But the idea did not appeal to me so much. Life there was different from our life here. A person who was born in Syria has become used to a certain style of life and would find it difficult to take such a step. Nothing can compare to [the] Caucasus. It is more beautiful than Switzerland. It has magnificent mountains, woods and valleys. The soil is so fertile. If a branch fell to the ground, it would grow into a tree. I am not exaggerating. They would have easily given me a house and helped us settle, but my wife would not consider the idea. Even our children, when they were little, they felt like going back, but my wife refused. Her family and friends are here [in Damascus]. However, she likes to go for visits to Circassia. We make the utmost use of the improved relations [in the post-Soviet era] and regularly communicate now with the Kabardai Republic. There are a number of good package tours and some of the Circassians who came here married Circassian girls from Syria. In addition a

*number of Syrian Circassian students who went on scholarship got married to girls
from there. Some stayed there and others brought their wives back here.*

(Qahtan, Duma, 2006)

I asked Abdul-Salam, who was born in the Jaulan in 1916 and whose
grandparents had travelled to Syria from Abkhazia via Anatolia,
whether he would return to the Jaulan or to his forefathers' homelands
in Abkhazia had he the opportunity. His children and grandchildren,
listening to his interview with me, all replied, 'Abkhazia, of course.'
Abdul-Salam hesitated before answering:

*I would not mind going back to Abkhazia if it were to become independent. But no
one recognises the Abkhaz Republic. If the Jaulan were returned to Syria, I would go
back. I would, for sure, go back leaving everything behind. If I could go back to
either, I think I wouldn't have as many people who know me in Abkhazia as in
Jaulan. (One son interrupts: 'If you go back to Abkhazia, it would be better for
you!'). I am old now. It is no good for me anymore. If I were young, I would go on
foot [to Abkhazia].What would I do there now at 90 years of age?*

(Abdul-Salam, October 2005)

For Abdul-Salam, his remembered Circassian homeland in the Jaulan
beckons more attractively than his imagined homeland in the Caucasus.
Of course, age is a factor in his preference. But the enthusiasm of
youth, as expressed in the response of his children and grandchildren
to my question about return and making the journey of discovery of
kin and imagined ancestors, is offset by the wisdom of age which rec-
ognizes the need for real kinship ties and social networks. For Abdul-
Salam, his 'homeland' is where his family and friends are rather than in
the virtual place in spaces left long ago.

Self-identification of individual Circassians remains firmly based on
ethnic qualities, language, culture, and customs. For many, these markers sat comfortably with those of national identity. Being Circassian and
being Syrian were not considered contradictory. The homeland was a
place that no longer existed in space. And the recent opportunity to
return to the space of the original homeland, though enthusiastically
visited, was not, for the majority, a reality that sat easily with their
imagined pasts. Integrating but not assimilating was one of a number
of solutions to the complex responses of being the 'Other' in a larger
heterogeneous society also made up of numerous others such as Syria
had become.

SYRIA

The Circassians and Chechnyans of Syria, and the Levant in general, are a distinct ethnic group although they belong to the 'majority' Sunni Muslim population of the country. Their displacement from their homelands in the Caucasus between the 1860s and 1920s was, at times, forced by expulsion orders and at other times 'voluntary' when choices had to be made regarding possible pressure to convert to Christianity. Some of the Circassian groups were forced to move several times before reaching the Levant. In all cases, these Circassian migrants made decisions to make the successor states to the collapsing Ottoman Empire their homes. In Syria, over several decades, they became model citizens, successful farmers, civil servants, and members of the armed forces and security services. One might say the peoples of the Caucasus lay down the warp on a loom. The forced migrant groups that followed over the next century then completed the multi-ethno-religious weft that made up the peoples of modern Syria.

3

THE ARMENIANS AND OTHER CHRISTIANS SEEK
REFUGE IN GREATER SYRIA

My father was born and educated in Zeytoun. He then attended and graduated from the Sultaniyye High School [in Aleppo] in 1912. He was fourteen at the time. Ah, being graduated from that school this was really something at that time. You were taken immediately into the administration [Ottoman government]: railways, banking system, things like that. You see, there was little discrimination at that time; these people graduated from this school. They had a special dress, somehow military, like St Cyr in France. It was a uniform, a special dress. Then my father was also taken into the railway administration. So he escaped from the deportation or massacres, because he was working, because he was working in the Ottoman administration.

(Vahan, Damascus, 2005)

I had met Vahan several times at the French Institute for Near Eastern Studies (IFPO) in Damascus before realizing that he was Armenian. All of my encounters with him had been in the office of the Syrian director of research at the Institute, and our language of discussion had floated between French and English. The director of research had encouraged me to interview him, as she told me he had a most unusual story to tell. And indeed he did. Vahan had been born in Beirut, to Armenian parents who had not experienced the Armenian deportation or genocide. Instead, his father had worked for the Ottoman rail authority and had been stationed at Rayak Station, a small outpost in the Bekaa Valley in Lebanon, for most of the First World War. After the war Vahan's father had been encouraged by a Jesuit priest in Beirut to

85

enrol in the University of St Joseph and take an engineering degree. By the time he graduated he was on hand to assist in the second deportation of Armenians from Cilicia in 1921 after the abrupt departure of the French forces. Later in the early 1940s Vahan's father began to build two Armenian villages in Anjar and near Tyre in Lebanon to house the third wave of Armenian deportations from the Hatay province of Syria when it was given up to Turkey by the French Mandate authorities. Vahan visited these settlements, and was aware of the extent to which refuge was being provided by the local communities of Christian and Muslim Arabs. His father had insisted that he attend the Lycée Française de la Mission Laïque in Beirut. There was an Armenian school in Beirut at the time, but his father wanted him to learn French and English as he himself had done.

> *Forty years ago, when I was thinking about this situation, I wondered how to assist Armenia and at the same time be a good Syrian citizen. Armenians were being massacred and the Syrians saved us. How can you forget? So I thought that I could do something useful by enriching the libraries of Armenia with books about the Arab East. I was a student and I began in 1947 to send books to the Armenian Academy of Science. I sent some 25,000 books, Orientalist, academic, encyclopaedias. I wanted Armenians in Armenia to have Arabist perspectives. Our future is with these people. … In the past when there were book fairs here in Damascus or Beirut, I used to invite people from the Armenian Academy of Science here to buy books. I have in the past invited them and then the Institute [IFPO] was kind enough to sign a convention so every year one or two people come from Armenia to use the library. So I am a very Syrian patriot but I am also an Armenian-Arab nationalist.*

> (Vahan, Damascus, 2005)

Vahan's mother had a similar story. She was the daughter of a well-to-do family in Marash. In order to escape the unrest that was brewing in eastern Anatolia, the heartland of Ottoman Armenia, she was sent to Constantinople to a very famous finishing school where students could study residentially. So between 1914 and 1916 she lived in Constantinople and then afterwards came to join her family, by this time based in Beirut. I was intrigued by the story of these well-educated, professional Armenians who had avoided being caught up in the deportations and death marches and had found their way independently to Syria and Lebanon. Nearly all that I had read before was focused on survivors of the death marches. How was it that some

Armenians survived, perhaps even thrived, in areas outside eastern Anatolia where the Armenian genocide was focused? And how did the experience of their 'kith and kin' shape the way in which they integrated into Syria (and Lebanon) in particular?

Of all the formally recognized minority communities of the late Ottoman Empire, the Armenians, after the Greek Orthodox, held perhaps the most prestigious place in its multi-layered and plural urban society. As the empire began to fail and the Greek Orthodox community largely withdrew to its newly created nation-state of Greece (1829), some Armenians became caught up in the nationalist fervour that was sweeping Europe and impacting on the fringe European provinces of the empire. With growing success, ethnic majorities were laying claim to state spaces in the European regions of the Ottoman Empire, and one after another the Bulgarians, the Serbs, and the Romanians were recognized as nations and states: nation-states. The Armenians, perhaps as a result of centuries of successful trading and business throughout the empire, were widely dispersed. Nevertheless, at the end of the nineteenth century and the early decades of the twentieth, they made a concerted effort to garner international support for a state of their own. Their bid for secession largely collapsed because their heartland was an integral part of the Anatolian plateau and, perhaps, because European encouragement and support did not match the earlier commitment to nation-building in the Balkans.

I don't justify what the Turks have done, but Europe wanted to destabilize the Ottoman Empire for various reasons; for colonialism, or for the colonial extension. So Europe encouraged our young people to use the same slogans that they are now using to destabilize the Arab world. You see 'Freedom, This and This', 'Social Justice', 'Dictatorship'. It is very interesting to find these slogans being repeated now nearly 100 years later to encourage opposition forces. Europeans encouraged those Armenians who studied in France and Britain. They would come back with these ideas of the French revolution. It was very well manipulated. It was all then exactly what they are doing now. By killing tens of thousands of people [in Iraq] they [the West] think they can extend Democracy. Back then, when the counter Ottoman massacres came, they didn't help. The French, the British, when they saw what was happening, they didn't do anything. The US made no declaration of war at that time. So they saw and they didn't do anything or launch a war against Turkey. So ethnic cleansing began in Turkey, I don't justify it, but it was encouraged by the West.

(Vahan, Damascus, 2005)

Massacres, Death Marches, and the Armenian Genocide

There are many theories related to the tragic conclusion of the 'Armenian question' in Eastern Anatolia. They tend to fall on two sides of a seemingly impermeable divide: an Armenian position and an Ottoman/Turkish position. Historians and other scholars generally fall into one camp or the other.[1] However, the facts are fairly robust. In an era when people were being dispossessed and expelled from their homelands in their millions (see chapter 1), the Armenians, too, were dispossessed, massacred, and forced out of their lands on death marches (Karpat 1985). Here again opinion is divided as to what provoked or explained the ethnic cleansing of the Armenians of eastern Anatolia in the period between the outbreak of the First World War and the founding of the Turkish Republic in 1923.

Between 1914 and 1923 more than 'a million Armenians were killed in mass shootings, massacres, deportations and induced starvation' (Melson 1996: 142). This mass destruction was called the first domestic genocide of the twentieth century, and has been the subject of immense scrutiny. A number of theories abound to explain why it happened. One theory traces the origins of the genocide to the provocative behaviour of the Armenians themselves—or at least to their nationalist and revolutionary parties. As Rogan so carefully reveals, Armenian activists in Constantinople and eastern Anatolia did little to hide their celebration in the face of imminent delivery from Turkish rule once the British and French fleet approached the Dardanelles. For the Turks this was a moment of existential threat. In eastern Anatolia, Armenian armed bands attacked or ambushed Ottoman gendarmes; other groups of Armenians fled to Tiflis (modern Tbilisi in Georgia) to seek Russian arms and support. The Armenian uprising and eventual defeat in Van then sealed the fate of Armenians in eastern Anatolia. They were clearly regarded as a 'Fifth Column', and the deportation of Armenians was conducted openly by government orders; secret orders for the mass murder of Armenian deportees followed soon thereafter (Rogan 2015: 172).

Another theory puts the primary cause of the genocide at the door of the perpetrators. It advances the position that in the revolutionary situation of the Ottoman Empire after the overthrow of Sultan Abdul

Hamid in 1908, the Young Turks—with their secular pan-Turkish, rather than Ottoman or pan-Islamist, ideology—came to power. And although they were to be recognized for having contributed significantly to the creation of the modern Turkish state, they were also responsible for the Armenian deportations, which became genocide by any definition of the term.[2] Whether as an outcome of their failed revolutionary aspirations, or as a result of their population concentrations in what was increasingly becoming the heartland of the empire, the Armenians paid dearly for their late expression of nationalism and their reliance on unstable European alliances.

The concern of this chapter is with those Armenians who survived and went on to find new homes and communities for themselves in *Bilad al-Sham* (Greater Syria). Yet to build a picture of those who escaped death we need to have a general sense of numbers. Any extensive massacre or genocide will lead to controversy over the number of victims; the Armenian massacres are no exception. Here it may be useful to briefly look at the figures that Arnold Toynbee used to gauge the extent of the destruction of Armenian lives. Toynbee estimated a pre-deportation figure of 1.6 million (an average of the Armenian Patriarchate figures and those of the Ottoman census). He estimated that some 600,000 Armenians escaped the deportations. Among these were 182,000 who fled as refugees into the Russian Caucasus, and 4,200 who managed to get to Egypt. He also pointed out that the Armenian populations of Smyrna and Constantinople were not deported; nor were Armenian Catholics, Protestants, and converts to Islam. Of the million who were deported he estimated that 500,000 (later revised upward to 600,000) Armenians died.[3]

The Armenians who survived were dispersed throughout the southern provinces of the empire. Many of the parentless children were taken in and brought up in Armenian Church-sponsored orphanages, or adopted through the offices of various humanitarian agencies such as Near Eastern Relief and given new lives in Europe and the United States. The widespread and extensive Armenian trade and commercial links provided respite and succour to these refugees in their darkest hours. In the intervening decades the Armenians have emerged as successful communities in the diaspora as well as throughout the Middle East. In the Levant, particularly Lebanon and Syria, they are today successful minorities well integrated into the political (especially in Lebanon) and social life of the nation-states which were once the Arab provinces of the Ottoman Empire.

Historical Background

From the beginning of the eleventh century until the First World War the Orthodox and Apostolic (Gregorian) Christian population of Anatolia was gradually replaced with Muslims. In the final century of Ottoman rule, the nineteenth century, a large in-pouring of Muslim refugees into eastern Anatolia from Transcaucasia and the Russian border zones took place. By the beginning of the twentieth century Anatolia was a mix of Muslim and non-Muslim communities. The Greek Orthodox of Anatolia were found in the coastal provinces of the north and west. The Jews lived in western Anatolian cities. Armenians had a long history in eastern Anatolia, and, in addition, had spread into central and western Anatolia. In the east, smaller Christian splinter groups, especially Syrians (Catholics and Orthodox), Chaldaeans, and Nestorians of the Assyrian Church of the East, remained in largely agrarian village pockets in their traditional homelands in Anatolia and the Euphrates valley as well as Persia (Baum and Winkler 2003).

For most of the nineteenth century the Ottoman Empire was embroiled in a series of wars with Imperial Russia. It had lost all but the Crimean War. With each loss more territory was taken from it, largely in the Balkans and in southern Transcaucasia. The latter remained a contested area for a further fifty years, and left the Armenian population straddling the Russian and Ottoman Empires. Its menfolk served in both the Russian and Ottoman armies. On one side the Armenian heartland was receiving millions of Muslims that Russia either expelled or drove into the Ottoman Empire, while on the other hundreds of thousands of Armenian Christians were fleeing into the Russian-held Armenian lands (McCarthy 2001).

Between 1880 and 1910 Ottoman Anatolia experienced what was perhaps the most prosperous period of its history. The population in Anatolia was said to have grown by 50 per cent during this period (McCarthy 1983). Although the empire was renowned for the census figures it kept of its subjects, those related to the Armenians were heavily contested. Solutions to the 'Armenian question' raised at the Berlin

Congress of 1878 needed figures to support the various points of view. Both Russia and England expressed interest in eastern Anatolia. British statisticians began to study Ottoman census figures as well as those of the Armenian Patriarchate and make estimates of their own. Perhaps the most important and detailed figures of Armenian numbers were presented by the Armenian Patriarchate immediately after the First World War, at the Versailles Peace Conference. They were intended to convince the delegates and world opinion that before the First World War there had been more Armenians than Turks in the Armenian areas of eastern Anatolia and that in 1919 a large enough population of Armenians remained to create a viable and stable Armenian state (McCarthy 1983).

A Protected Minority

During the late Ottoman period the Armenians had been granted considerable autonomy within their own *millet*, and lived in relative harmony with other groups in the empire. As explained earlier, in the nineteenth century empire religion 'provided a man's label' (Davison 1954). Although the empire was governed by Muslims and was based on the religious laws of Islam, the various Christian communities and the Jewish community enjoyed partial autonomy. Christian groups in the empire, however, maintained and exploited their close and often intimate association with European state representatives. After 1800 these Christian minorities were gradually absorbing Western ideas of liberty and nationality. They began to complain frequently and loudly about their lack of equality. The first response of Sultan Mahmud II (r. 1808–39) was crucial, in that he made it clear that in his view all his subjects, of whatever creed, were equal (Temperley 1936). The significant era of reform came in the *Tanzimat* period of 1838 to 1876, when serious efforts at Westernization were made and the doctrine of equality of Christian and Muslims was proclaimed in several imperial edicts. In the mid-nineteenth century the empire had a total population of 35 million, of whom about 14 million were non-Muslims. The overwhelming majority of non-Muslims were Christians, with perhaps only 150,000 being Jews. The Greek Orthodox population was the largest Christian minority, followed closely by the Gregorian Armenian.

The Armenian ethno-religious minority of the Ottoman Empire was tightly managed and controlled by its Gregorian Church, and had its own Patriarchate and *millet*. When the Kingdom of Greece was created in 1832, many Orthodox Christians left the empire to join the new nation-state. They left behind many important government posts, which the Armenians took up, in ministries such as the Interior, Justice, Finance, and Foreign Affairs. Hence, from the second quarter of the nineteenth century the Armenian *millet* acquired greater importance and influence, politically and economically. The Armenians were then considered the most reliable element in the empire and were called *millet-i-sakika* (the loyal *millet*: Barsoumian 1997). By 1850 Armenian influence was such that they were granted a Protestant and Catholic *millet* in addition to their Gregorian or Apostolic Church *millet*.[4]

Several years before, another Christian minority sharing much the same area and homeland as the Armenians, and previously administered by the Ottomans as a subsection of the Armenian *millet*, was granted its own separate *millet*. This was the Assyrian *millet*. The Assyrians largely inhabited the Hakkari mountains between Lake Van in Anatolia and Lake Urmia in Persia. This area, which was home to many Armenians and Kurds as well, was also known as Kurdistan. In their rugged mountain villages these Christians followed the Assyrian Church of the East, also called the Nestorian Church.[5] The Assyrians spoke a dialect related to Syriac: Aramaic. Like their closest Christian neighbours, the Armenians, they were also persecuted, and became victims of massacres at the outbreak of the First World War.

By the 1870s the reform movement of the earlier decades and its push for Westernization had come to an end. The *millet* system, which had been so beneficial to the economic and political growth of non-Muslim communities, was dramatically reformed. When Abdul Hamid II ascended to the caliphate in 1876 he suspended the constitution as well as the parliament. The liberal spirit of the *Tanzimat* reform era ended. While nationalist movements in the European parts of the empire were gaining ground, Abdul Hamid heavily repressed similar political movements in Anatolia, which he believed were threatening separatism; foremost among these were the Armenian nationalist and, later, separatist movements.

Armenian nationalism was slow to start. Perhaps this was due to the Armenians' close attachment to their church and the Patriarch's constitutional position as head of the Armenian Gregorian *millet*, which gave him a place in the Ottoman system of government. Nevertheless, local Armenian support for Imperial Russian expansion into Transcaucasia and the eastern frontier of the Ottoman Empire eventually did shape much of the Armenian nationalist movement. Between 1800 and 1877 Russia expanded into Transcaucasia. It annexed Georgia (1800), took over areas that are today the Republics of Azerbaijan and Armenia (1829), and twice attacked Anatolia (1855 and 1877). In each of these invasions, Armenian militias aided the Russians, perhaps in the hope that Christian Russia would help them create their own independent Armenian homeland. Yet the peace conferences at the end of these campaigns compelled the Russians to retreat from some of their gains in Anatolia. In these withdrawals, tens of thousands of Armenians who had fought with them also fled (McCarthy 2001). During this period the forced displacement of peoples—largely Circassian and Abkhazian Muslims—was taking place into areas which held substantial Armenian minorities, creating tensions, hatreds, and fears (McCarthy 2001).

Armenian nationalist groups began to appear in Constantinople in the 1860s and 1870s, and also further east. These Armenian revolutionaries made numerous attempts to gain Russian support for their nationalist struggle. But the outcome of the Treaties of Berlin and San Stefano at the end of the Russo-Ottoman war of 1877–8 did not accommodate their aims. Thereafter, and up until the First World War, Armenian nationalist groups, both in the Ottoman Empire and abroad, set about creating a revolution which would engage the attention of the European powers and help them to create a state for the Armenian nation. With offices in London, Paris, and other European capitals, Armenians began to garner support in the international media. Three Armenian political parties were founded: the Armenakan Party, founded by young Armenians in Van; the Hunchakian Revolutionary Party (Hunchaks), founded by Russian students and Armenian émigrés in Europe; and the Dashnaktsuthian Party (Dashnaks), founded by Armenian students in Russia.[6] Emboldened by the way in which Bulgaria had been created as a nation-state in 1878, these students and revolutionaries aspired to do the same for Armenia.

Having recognized the weakness of their position vis-à-vis Europe and Russia, the Armenian nationalists set out to put their struggle on the European political map. This was to be a campaign of 'terror' which would result in greater repression and then an outpouring of European sympathy, as had been the case in the 'Bulgarian Terrors' a decade earlier. In that case Russia had intervened, caused mass expulsion and death among Bulgarian Muslims, and created a new Bulgarian state. But it is rare that history repeats itself exactly; while Bulgarians were a majority in Bulgaria, Armenians were never an absolute majority in eastern Anatolia, making the drive to put their plight on the European mental map difficult. According to McCarthy, the initial attacks took place in the Sasun region against Kurdish traditional leaders who had coerced Armenian villagers to pay tribute to them. As in the southern Syrian provinces, the people of this rural and remote area had the double burden of having to pay off the pastoral tribes with tribute as well as paying the Ottoman tax collector. In the summer of 1893 numerous Armenian villages took up arms and resisted both the Kurdish chiefs and the Ottoman tax officials, who then complained to the regional governor. He responded by sending a military unit to the area to assist both groups of collectors. After a month's resistance, the Armenians agreed to lay down their arms in return for an amnesty. However, once disarmed, they were subjected to looting and burning, torture, murder, and rape. As many as 3,000 Sasunites died in that massacre (Walker 1980).[7]

Word of the Sasun massacre quickly spread. The British consuls in Armenian Anatolia relayed the details to the British ambassador in Constantinople. Missionaries and correspondents broadcast the details of the massacre to Europe; a general outcry was registered, and British, French, and Russian ambassadors proposed a joint commission of inquiry. This was rejected by the Ottoman state, but a compromise allowed the European observers to accompany a governmental commission of inquiry which was held in early 1895. The outcome was predictable. The Ottoman commission found that the Armenians had engaged in 'seditious' action which required pacification by armed force. The Europeans disagreed and noted instead that the 'absolute ruin of the district can never be regarded a measure proportionate to the punishment even of a revolt' (Great Britain 1896).

After lengthy diplomatic exchanges the British, French, and Russian ambassadors sent a memorandum to Sultan Abdul Hamid reminding him of his obligations to the Armenians under Article 61 of the Treaty of Berlin, including that he consolidate the Armenian provinces of the empire, nominate governors for these provinces, grant Armenian political prisoners amnesty, allow émigrés to return, provide reparations to the victims of Sasun and other affected districts, and appoint a high commissioner to execute these reform provisions (Great Britain 1896). Inevitably the Sublime Porte tried to seriously dilute these recommendations, which the sultan most likely regarded as a dangerous precedent for the empire's sovereignty.

By the end of the nineteenth century the Armenian nationalist revolutionary plan had achieved a partial success. The educated, elite Armenians were a sizeable minority in Constantinople, and actively engaged in debates regarding constitutional rights. The rural Muslim population in eastern Anatolia, however, was inflamed by the activities of the Armenian revolutionaries in their midst. The Ottoman army was subduing the Armenian rebels and civilians in an inexcusable manner, but, unlike in Bulgaria, there was no European intervention. The British and Russian representatives in Constantinople had both protested at the Armenian massacres. The British considered a plan to sail into the Dardanelles and depose the sultan, and to accede to Armenian demands for a state of their own. But Russia did not wish to see the Ottomans replaced with British, French, Austrian, or international control. In the end, none of the European powers were ready to go to war with the Ottoman Empire or with each other over Armenia in the 1890s. Although public opinion in Europe was concerned about the Armenians, European governments were far more interested in the balance of power between Russia, Great Britain, France, Austria, and Germany (McCarthy 2001).

Armenians had lived in Cilicia for millennia, but the region was an ethnic and confessional mixture. Armenians had played a major role in commerce, in crafts, and in the new developing industry, and were taking advantage of the educational opportunities provided by American and European mission schools in Adana, Tarsus, Aintab, Marash, and elsewhere. After the 1908 Young Turk revolution many Armenians felt that the time had come for them to insist on their rights as Ottoman citizens and to enjoy freedom of speech. Instead, there was a massacre at Adana the following year. There are many versions of its origins, but most accounts lay some blame on the Armenian prelate of Adana, who took to promulgating nationalist rhetoric and proclaiming that the centuries of servitude had passed and now was the time for Armenians to defend themselves, their families, and their communities. For Muslims, this new era of constitutionality appeared threatening to their traditional relationship with Armenians. At the same time, a counter-coup was taking place in Constantinople to restore Abdul Hamid to the throne. Traditionalists and conservatives attacked the Armenians of Adana. The violence soon spread to the outlying villages. When Ottoman authorities finally intervened, two days later, more than 2,000 Armenians were dead. After an uneasy ten-day truce, violence broke out again, this time spreading throughout Cilicia all the way to Marash in the north-east and Kassab in the south.

An Ottoman parliamentary commission of investigation reported that there had been 21,000 victims, of whom 19,479 were Armenian, 850 Syrian, 422 Chaldean, and 250 Greek (as quoted in Hovannisian 1997a; Papikian 1919). This was perhaps the first massacre of the Young Turk era, and several Ottoman officials as well as Armenians were hanged in Adana for provoking the violence. Once the Young Turks regained control of Constantinople, they claimed that the massacres were the work of reactionaries and conducted a public memorial service for both Turkish and Armenian citizens of the empire. Over the next four years, between 1908 and 1912, the Armenian Dashnak Party remained loyal to the constitutional regime. It was, however, actively criticized by other Armenian political groups for its continuing collaboration with the Young Turks. Nevertheless, despite this growing unease among some Armenian nationalists, when in 1912 the combined armies of Greece, Bulgaria, Serbia, and Montenegro invaded Macedonia and Thrace, the last remaining Ottoman possessions in Europe, the Armenian nationalists generally exhorted their followers to fight to defend the Ottoman state.

Wars in the East and the Armenian Massacres

On 30 October 1914 the Ottoman government entered the First World War on the side of Germany. In essence two wars were to be fought, one along its northern and western frontiers against Europe,

and the other to the south and east against Russian armies encompass-
ing an intercommunal war between the Armenians and Muslims of
eastern Anatolia and the southern Caucasus (McCarthy 1995). Many
Armenians enlisted in the Ottoman army. An Ottoman unit of 8,000
Armenian soldiers fought against Russia at Sarikamish in Caucasia.
However, Armenian volunteer partisan units began to operate with
Russian forces against the Ottomans along the eastern front (Walker
1997). Between 1914 and 1920 the wars on the eastern front of the
empire were perhaps among the worst in human history (quoted in
McCarthy 1995; Singer and Small 1972). Cities such as Van, Bitlis,
Bayazit, and Erzincan were left in rubble and thousands of villages were
destroyed (McCarthy 1995; Niles and Sutherland 1919). Millions of
Armenians and Muslims died. The Armenians came out of these struggles with a rump Soviet Armenian republic and the Young Turks were
left with a country in ruins.

The defeat of the Ottoman army in the Caucasus in January 1915
marked a turning point for Armenians in the empire. Although Enver
Pasha publicly thanked the Armenians for their conduct during the
Sarikamish campaign in a letter to the Armenian bishop of Konya
(Lepsius 1897), the end of that month saw violent measures initiated
against them. Many of those who had enlisted in the army were forced
to give up their arms and were consigned to manual labour.[8] Between
April and August 1915 Armenians from most of the major centres of
the empire were ordered to leave their homes and were forced to
march—to almost certain death—towards the Syrian desert and then
Mosul. Very few ever reached Mosul itself.

The operations began in Zeytoun on 8 April, and in Van two weeks
later. They spread to Cilicia and other major cities of Ottoman Anatolia.
According to Walker (1997), the pattern was the same: first the fit
Armenian men from a town or village would be summoned to the
government building. They would be held in jail for a few days, and
then marched out of town, where they were generally shot. Shortly
afterwards, women, children, and old men would be summoned in the
same way, but were told that they had to leave for new homes. They
were then driven out by gendarmes along designated routes. Many
collapsed and died along the way. Muslim villagers were instructed not
to harbour any Armenians on pain of death. Those who could not con-

tinue the journey were shot. They were largely driven south-westward in the direction of Aleppo. This city became the main staging post for the deportees; from there they were sent east along the Euphrates to Dayr al-Zor. Occasionally, eyewitness accounts as well as records kept by the British army towards the end of the war indicated that local residents took pity on these desperate people and arranged marriages for the young Armenian women as well as 'fostering' arrangements for young men and children.[9]

By the end of August 1915 a large proportion of the Armenian population of Anatolia had been driven out of their lands, pillaged, raped, starved, and murdered. The Armenian leadership in Constantinople had been destroyed, Cilicia was in ruins, and the mainly Armenian cities of Van, Bitlis, Mush, and Sasun largely emptied of Armenians and replaced with the 750,000 or more Muslim refugees fleeing the fighting in Transcaucasia. Some Ottomans had opposed these violent policies of the Young Turks, both at the official and the popular level. In several localities decrees had been issued making it illegal for Muslims (Turks or Kurds) to harbour or shelter Armenians. However, many local families violated these orders, and after the war ended thousands of Armenian children re-emerged, having been kept alive in Muslim households during the conflict (Lepsius 1897).

Like the Armenians, the Assyrian Christians of the empire were also accused of supporting Russian imperial ambitions in the Trans-Caucasus and Ottoman Armenia. They were caught up in and suffered from the same periodic massacres as the Armenians, including the events of 1894–6 and the 1909 Adana massacres. Some 25,000 Assyrians were massacred at Diyarbakir when anti-Armenian rampages turned generally anti-Christian. Once the Ottomans had entered the First World War the Assyrians were accused of being collaborators with the enemy, and were targeted by the Young Turks for extermination. An estimated 250,000 Assyrian Christians out of a pre-war population of about 600,000 were killed during the course of the war (Bloxham 2007; Gaunt 2009).

On 30 October 1918 the Ottoman government signed the Armistice of Mudros with the Allied powers. It was agreed that the Ottomans would be disarmed and the Allies would make only minimal changes to the Ottoman state and unoccupied lands until a final decision had been agreed by treaty. In the following two years, before the Treaty of Sèvres was signed on 10 August 1920, much changed. The Bolshevik Revolution saw Imperial Russia give way to a Soviet state with a determined ambition to hold on to all the territory that had been part of the Russian Empire. The Russian army in eastern Anatolia had melted away in the previous year, leaving behind only the Armenian troops. For a short period these troops belonged to the Transcaucasian Federation of Georgia, Armenia, and Azerbaijan. Georgia and Azerbaijan were rapidly absorbed into the new Soviet state, leaving only Armenia as an independent republic. In Anatolia itself, the defeated Ottoman troops, at first reluctantly and then with greater enthusiasm, repelled the provocative Greek, French, and also Italian land grab and thus, under the leadership of Kemal Atatürk (Mustafa Kemal), carved out a rump Anatolian state (Hovannisian 1987; McCarthy 2001).

During these two years Armenians made significant efforts to build a viable, democratic state in the Transcaucasian territory under their control. Three Armenian delegations from the new republic attended the January 1919 Paris Peace Conference (Hovannisian 1987). Their public relations success can be found in one of the first acts of the conference, which declared that 'because of the historical misgovernment of the Turks of subject peoples and the terrible massacres of Armenians and others in recent years, the Allied and Associated Powers are agreed that Armenia, Syria, Mesopotamia, Palestine and Arabia must be completely severed from the Turkish Empire' and provisionally recognized as independent nations subject to the 'administrative assistance' of a Mandatory power. Palestine and Mesopotamia were awarded to Great Britain, and Syria to France. But no nation among the Allies or associated powers was prepared to accept the Mandate for Armenia. The Allies tried to persuade the United States to do so, but as it had never formally declared war on the Ottoman Empire, it resisted taking any part in this Mandatory exercise or any other.[10]

By the end of 1919 Atatürk had won over much of the remaining Ottoman army and created a new government seat in Ankara. By 1920 it was obvious that the Allied powers had to redefine their obligations towards Armenians in the light of the growing successes of the nationalist Turkish struggle (Walker 1997). By May 1920 the Armenians based in the Republic of Armenia were increasingly faced with the

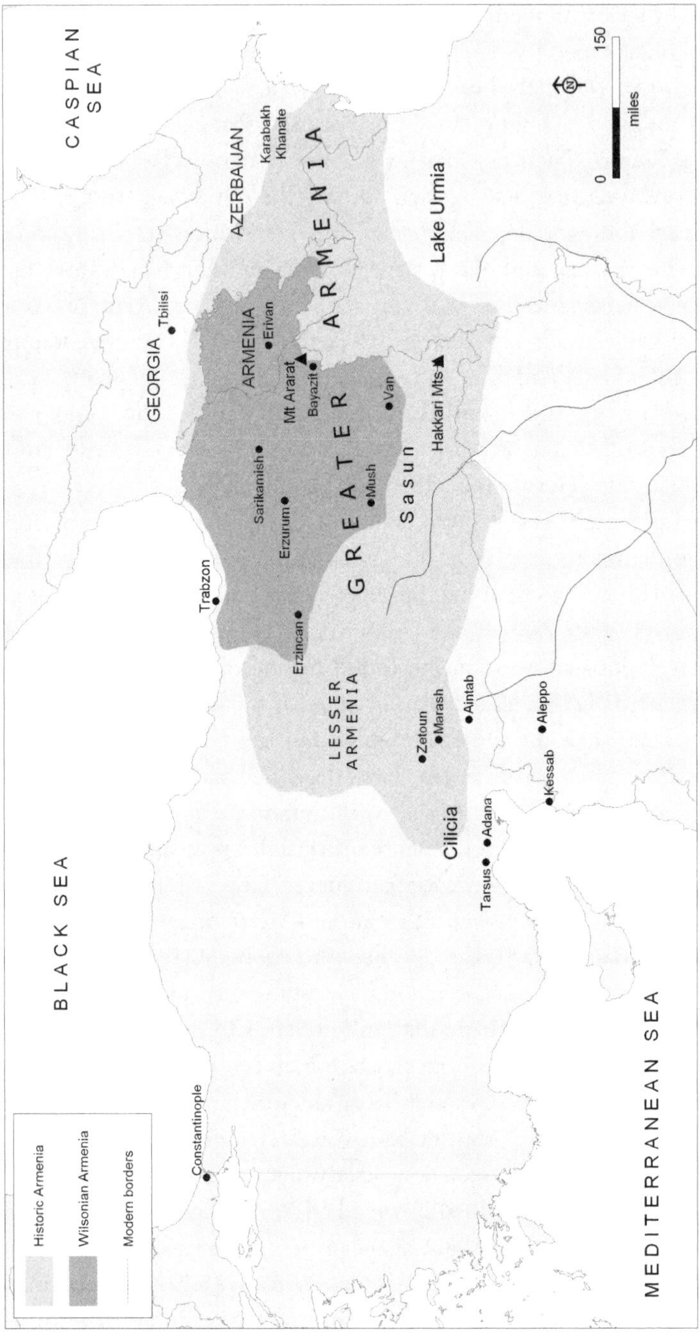
CASPIAN SEA
AZERBAIJAN
Karabakh Khanate
GREATER ARMENIA
GEORGIA
Tbilisi
ARMENIA
Erivan
Mt Ararat
Bayazit
Van
Lake Urmia
Hakkari Mts
Sasun
Mush
Sarikamish
Erzurum
Trabzon
Erzincan
LESSER ARMENIA
Zetoun
Marash
Aintab
Aleppo
Kessab
Cilicia
Adana
Tarsus
BLACK SEA
MEDITERRANEAN SEA
Constantinople
Historic Armenia
Wilsonian Armenia
Modern borders
0
150
miles

Map 6: Greater and Lesser Armenia

choice of standing up to a new Turkish invasion or succumbing to Soviet pressure and joining Soviet Russia.

In October 1920 the Turkish National Assembly in Ankara allowed one of the important veterans of the First World War, Kazim Karabekir, to take his forces and attack Armenia (McCarthy 2001).[11] This was swiftly accomplished. The Armenian Republic sued for peace, and in December 1920 the Treaty of Alexandropol was signed. The Armenians acquiesced to the new borders and gave up their claims to eastern Anatolia. The crippled Armenian government then had no choice but to save what little territory remained to it by opting for Soviet rule and seeking the protection of the new Soviet state and its Red Army (Hovannisian 1983).

Surviving the Deportations, Massacres, and the Death Marches

The humanitarian relief for the Armenians was largely an American effort growing out of the American Protestant missionary presence in the empire dating back to the 1830s. These early Protestant missions had quickly discovered that conversion from Islam was going to be unlikely, and so they turned their attention to Armenian Christians, who were capable of conversion to more evangelical denominations (Grabill 1971). They had great success, and by the time of the Armenian massacres of 1915 there were more than 551 Protestant elementary and high schools, eight colleges, and countless dispensaries serving Armenians and some Greeks in Anatolia (Richter 1910).

The first relief efforts reached the Armenians through private agencies, but in 1915 an influential group of missionaries, philanthropists, industrialists, and educators founded the Armenian Relief Committee. In 1918, with the Armistice of Mudros, the American public was able to renew and intensify its relief operations. The Armenian Relief Committee became known as the American Committee for Relief in the Near East (ACRNE), and raised $20 million in private donations in 1919. Early in that year a field mission to Anatolia and the Caucasus returned to the USA with reports of appalling conditions. By March 1919 the first ACRNE medical teams reached Armenia and took charge of eleven hospitals and ninety orphanages with 13,000 children. Another 30,000 orphans were eventually taken in by ACRNE.

By the summer of 1919 ACRNE had been incorporated as the Near East Relief, and had sent more than 30,000 metric tons of food and clothing to be distributed to the destitute in Constantinople and the western provinces of Anatolia.[12] In the same year (February 1919), the American Congress had created the American Relief Administration to administer a $100 million appropriation to assist non-enemy countries as well as 'Armenians, Syrians, Greeks and other Christian and Jewish populations of Asia Minor, now or formerly subjects of Turkey'. Herbert Hoover, a future president of the United States, was appointed the head of the American Relief Administration (Hovannisian 1997b). Many orphans or separated children survived solely because of the efforts of Near East Relief and the Armenian Church.

Near Eastern Relief and many other humanitarian agencies as well as the Armenian Church worked tirelessly to find and support these refugees. Because of the nature of the deportations and forced marches, very few of the elderly had survived, and so humanitarian aid was directed at the youth. Orphanages for Armenian children were opened throughout the region—in Aleppo, Beirut, Damascus, Cairo, and Alexandria. Most of these were sponsored by the Armenian Apostolic and the Protestant and Catholic Armenian Churches. Interviews in 2005 and 2006 in Beirut, Damascus, and Aleppo revealed the importance of both recovering contact with kin and coming under the wing of the Armenian Church for immediate survival, and later the support of the coalescing and greatly expanded community.

In Lebanon and Syria, where pre-existing and well-established Armenian minority communities were widespread, the new immigrants and survivors were quickly taken in and helped back on their feet. In nearly all these cases it was the Armenian Church that provided the first line of relief. These refugees may have spoken Armenian at home, but now had to learn Arabic in order to survive. Their social integration within the Armenian community was quick to come; wider economic integration through the established trades was slower, and required new language acquisition. Politics within the Armenian community was also widespread: the nationalist agendas of the main Armenian political parties continued to operate among the Armenians in relation to the new homeland, which was partially imagined and did not sit in the physical space that many preferred. But political involvement at a national level was one of studied neutrality, as in Lebanon, Syria, and Egypt, or full support for whichever party was in power.

The Armenian community in Greater Syria (Palestine, Lebanon, and Syria) was of long standing. The Armenian Patriarchate in Jerusalem was the focal point for Armenians in Egypt and Palestine, while in Lebanon and Syria (as well as Cyprus, Greece, and Iran) it was the Patriarchate (Catholicosate) of Cilicia, based in Antelias in Lebanon. The Armenians surviving or fleeing the forced marches managed in numerous ways to find family and to seek out and access Church support. In either case, the strength of the kin ties and the Church allegiance was striking. Many refugees moved between Syria and Lebanon—both part of the French Mandate between 1920 and 1943. In Lebanon, where the French were creating a new nation by adding tracts of 'historical' Syria—Tripoli and the Bekaa Valley—to Mount Lebanon, 'Armenianness' in a nation structured along sectarian lines became an important feature of the political landscape. In Syria, by contrast, pan-Arabism continued to remain an important feature of the new social order, perhaps reflecting the remnants of the old Ottoman multi-ethnic cosmology. There, multiculturalism and ethnic pluralism was an accepted part of the social landscape but not an integral part of the political scene.

When the French left the Sanjak [of Alexandretta] in 1939, there were many Armenians who did not want to remain and be ruled by the Turks so they left for Aleppo and for Lebanon. Many were very poor so the French built two villages for them. One was at Anjar and the other was near Sur in Lebanon. My father was the engineer responsible for these constructions. He was also responsible for many irrigation projects, in Aleppo, in Syria, in Lebanon. He used to travel a lot. I used to hear my grandparents cursing the British and the French for what was happening in Aleppo and Cilicia and Iskenderun. But we were told we had to learn French and English in school. We always spoke Armenian at home but we went to French school.

I studied civil engineering at the same school as my father in Beirut. But I had problems with the school. They approached me for school elections, but I was not a Lebanese Armenian, I was Syrian. It was a problem. So I left and went to Aleppo and studied engineering there. Then I travelled around Europe. I lived in Austria, in Sweden, in Finland, and France. Now I am here in Damascus. I am a newcomer to Damascus. We are maybe 6,000 Armenians in Damascus. We were once much bigger, but in the 1960s, during the economic reforms, many large businesses were affected. Armenians are special merchants; many left, but still we have a large presence. The

Church is very strong. We have a very coherent community. We have the Apostolic and Catholic Church. We have two choirs, we have social clubs and dance troupes. We have three schools, one connected with the Armenian Church, one with the Armenian General Benevolent Union and one with the Dashnak Party. We have a very coherent community here.

I am convinced that Armenia is an Oriental country. All these attempts to integrate Armenia into the West are silly. So I consider that Armenian–Arab relations are extremely important. We were being massacred and the Syrians saved us. How can you forget?

(Vahan, Damascus, 2005)

The Armenians of Syria, numbering perhaps 90,000 today, are a Christian and non-Arab population in an Arab-majority country. They speak a non-Semitic language and have their own alphabet. They run a number of communal institutions including schools, cultural clubs, welfare associations, and social and recreational organizations, as well as their own newspapers and journals. They are linked with the Armenian diaspora worldwide and with the Republic of Armenia. They are integrated without being assimilated. They have, as Migliorino states, found a way of expressing their 'cultural diversity within contemporary Syrian society, one that has seemingly found and cultivated a "diverse" way of being Syrian' (Migliorino 2006: 99).

Making a Home in Syria

By the end of the First World War the largest number of Armenian survivors in the Middle East found themselves in Syria; by the mid-1920s they were spread widely throughout the country: in the north in the region of Aleppo, the Euphrates region, and the Jazireh, in the major cities of Homs, Hama, and Damascus as well as Der'a in the south (Hovannisian 1967). The existing Armenian Church formed the central pivot around which the refugees constructed their lives. A system of institutions revolving around the Church grew rapidly, and included schools, charities, and cultural associations, all of which catered to the material and spiritual needs of the community (Migliorino 2006). A cultural identity which drew heavily from the past, but which also integrated the trauma of the recent genocide, developed and was encouraged both by the Armenian Apostolic Church and the nationalist political party leadership. The French administration of Syria also encouraged and created opportunities for the Armenians to develop their social and communal strategies with some autonomy. The religious authority of the Armenian Church was not undermined by the French; it was purposely respected as a continuation of certain aspects of the Ottoman *millet* administration (Thompson 2000).

Migliorino makes the important point in his book *(Re)constructing Armenia in Lebanon and Syria* (2007) that the French administration of the two states between 1920 and 1943 encouraged the Armenian community to develop and create a space for itself in both the social and political universe of each state. In Lebanon the Armenian community was drafted into the sectarian political structure, providing it with a formal role in government. In Syria, however, other than a lone representative of the community in parliament, it was encouraged to restrict its politics to its own internal affairs and those of the Armenian diaspora. Despite serious restrictions in the 1950s and 1960s, Armenian cultural identity and expression has flourished in Syria, leading Migliorino to use the term 'Kulna Suriyyin' [We are all Syrians] to describe the accommodation of Armenian ethnicity with citizenship in the state (2006).

Many of the Armenian refugees who arrived in Syria after the 1915 deportations had family to help them. However, many others did not, and had to turn solely to the Armenian Church for support. With the backing and encouragement of the French administration, the Church was able to draw on its traditional relations with its flock in Ottoman times and construct new ways of reaching out and looking after the welfare of this large new group of needy refugees. An internal system of housing provision, of food distribution and welfare, of education and job creation grew up around the Church. Just being Armenian was enough to get a start. The religious policy of the French Mandate in both Syria and Lebanon, which maintained a system of legally established freedoms in the area of religious affairs, together with the political support that was accorded to the Armenians, was crucial in the tremendous expansion of the Armenian churches in Syria (Migliorino 2006).

I was born in Damascus in 1934, in a very poor place, in a small house in the area near Bab Sharqi, near the Church of Anais. We were very privileged to have this space as there were others in much worse conditions than us. Before me, they had been living in Lebanon. We were five girls and three boys. My father came from Turkey, from Cilicia. There had been problems there for more than sixty years. My mother and father came to Damascus in the second Armenian migration, not the first one in 1915, but rather in the one of 1921. They came in February 1921. They were thrown out of Cilicia and then went to Aleppo for a little while. At that time all the family members were alive. None of our family members died on the road from Cilicia to Syria. My father was educated but he had no profession. But he was lucky. He was born in Marash in 1908. He was twelve or thirteen when he came here. At first he worked in the church as doorman, carrying goods, cleaning, simple things. But he liked learning. He taught himself Spanish, Italian, and French. Then he worked with the Franciscans. When he was about twenty he wanted to migrate to Argentina. But his parents wouldn't let him go. The grandparents wanted the family to stay together. They were afraid of war. So they didn't let him go. And they made him marry early. I was the firstborn, just a year or two after the marriage.

My grandfather had been a soldier in the Turkish army. The family used to live in the military sector of Marash. They were exempted from deportation. They were privileged—very few Armenians were—but they were. At that time all of Syria and Palestine were under the Ottomans. My grandfather had been stationed in Baalbek (Lebanon) and had fought against the French. When my grandfather decided to leave Marash in 1921, there had been about 4,000 Armenians who were killed. He took the family to Aleppo and then on to Rayak [the end of the train line from Aleppo to Lebanon]. From Rayak, they came to Damascus. They came here with nothing. The men could find no work. But there were some charitable associations here to help the Armenians. There were also Armenians from a long time ago who had settled centuries ago but who didn't speak Armenian, they only spoke Arabic, but they helped. The good thing was that many Syrians knew some Turkish, so they had a language they could communicate with. But for the most part there was no language in common.

In the beginning it was very hard. For us, our family was ten people: my grandfather and grandmother, my mother and father, and uncles and aunts. All of them were given a space under a tree and a blanket to make a tent. Then some help came from the Armenian Church here in Bab Sharqi. My grandfather was privileged. He was given some space at the cemetery of the Armenians near a mausoleum where they covered themselves in the cold of February and slept. In the daytime, the landowners of the Ghouta used to come to find day labourers for their fields. He wanted work and he would go round and round to try to be picked for the agricultural work. Eventually some relatives came from Aleppo with more resources and they worked together and established a 'camp'. This became the Armenian 'camp' near Bab Musalla. After a time, my grandfather moved us to a very small house with two rooms. We had a small space were we worked and made small goods for selling in the souq near the Umayyad Mosque. My grandmother used to cook in a big pot for the whole family. She used to cook one dish and give it out to everyone. We didn't even have a table, just a cloth on the ground. It was very primitive at the beginning. It is hard to imagine how we managed then. But I always tell my children that if we had to return to that time, I could live like that; but they couldn't [he laughs]. We had terrible times, but we have come out of it. And we are going to remain an Armenian community. If we had stayed in Turkey, maybe we would never have had what we now have.

(Sarkis, Damascus, 2005)

Some Armenian survivors of the death marches were orphans who moved from one location to another in Syria, looking for ways to survive. Often the experience left a strong desire to find others like themselves and to work tirelessly to (re)create a new community based on language and religious belief. But even in that endeavour, the relationship with other religious groups was never undermined.

My father was born in Adana [Turkey]. Even though just a child, he survived the massacres and made his way alone to Syria. First to Aleppo, then he went to Hauran and finally to Damascus. At first he found shelter in tents near Bab Tuma [organized by the Red Cross]. Then he became an apprentice to a shoemaker in the Armenian Quarter near Bab Sharqi. The Red Cross helped those who were very poor and those who couldn't afford to go to school. But as soon as he could he began to give out any money he had to various Armenian charities. There were many such associations in Damascus. Many of them set up schools. Eventually after he married an Armenian who also escaped the massacres in Adana, he decided to start his own business. He began first by just making parts of the shoe for other shoemakers. But then he started to make a limited number for customers on order especially those who had foot problems and needed especially tailor-made shoes. My sisters apprenticed with an Armenian dressmaker in the Quarter and then eventually when that lady left, my sisters set up on their own and started to have customers in their room in the house. They became very well-known dressmakers in the Quarter.

(Bedros, Damascus, 2009)

Conviviality and Integration

Armenians have been widely dispersed throughout the Middle East for centuries, serving as merchants and traders in the Ottoman Empire, in the British and French Mandated states in the inter-war years, and in the contemporary independent states of the region, particularly Syria and Lebanon. Surviving the waves of expulsion, massacres, and forced deportations at the end of the nineteenth and beginning of the twentieth centuries and reconstructing their society in new places meant reliance on the Armenian Church and the Protestant missionary relief agencies, as well as concerted efforts to integrate into the social and political contexts of their newly adopted nation-states.

In the process of locally integrating, language emerged as an extremely important marker of minority identity. Where once French and Turkish was a mark of higher status among Armenians in the Ottoman Empire, and use of Armenian suggested a more working-class background, the deportations became a leveller and Armenian became the language of the survivors in their new homeland and community. The first generation had to work to learn Armenian, even though French and then English became the language of the elite outside their homes. The second and third generations have also made great efforts to promote Armenian as the language of the home. Many of the survivors, confronted with inter-ethnic marriages among their children and grandchildren, insist on Armenian as the language spoken to the youngest generation. With other markers of separation among ethnic groups disappearing, language increased as an indication of identity among Armenians throughout Syria and Lebanon, and the rest of the Arab Middle East. The Armenian Church and the associated social clubs provide classes for the youngest generation and so perpetuate significant elements of the differentiation that allows the Armenians to integrate in their new homelands without assimilating.

The Armenian communities in Syria and Lebanon reorganized around the Church, from which social clubs, sports groups, schools, benevolent societies, nursing homes, and language and dance classes were run. They maintained strong cultural centres, elementary and secondary schools, athletics programmes, as well as literary and historical publications and newspapers. Armenians throughout Syria and Lebanon (and elsewhere) put significant effort into locating relatives and creating close ties with other Armenians. In nearly all of my interviews, it is striking the lengths that individuals went to in order to locate their families or create new fictive ties. Once together, they worked extraordinarily closely to support each other to gain a foothold on the economic ladder and to re-establish their social world made up of numerous proto-*millet*s or ethno-religious social groups. Living together among others from different religious and cultural backgrounds was often described by them as the uniqueness of their new home in Syria and Lebanon as well as a continuity with their past.

CHRISTIANS SEEK REFUGE IN GREATER SYRIA

I was born in Bab Tuma [Damascus] in 1939. When I was twenty we moved to Sha'laan quarter of Damascus. The neighbourhood was religiously mixed, Muslims and Christians. We got on well so we never felt any differences. We were six. My parents, my two sisters, and my brother. When I got married, I brought my bride to the house. The same for my brother. Many Armenians moved to this neighbourhood, Sha'laan and Salahiyya, from Bab Tuma when they could afford it. Here many people knew each other well; they were good neighbours. There was the Shanawani mosque and the Franciscan church, there was also a Latin church on the other side of the road and further up the street there was a church for the white Russian exiles in Damascus.

When we moved here to Sha'laan from Bab Tuma my mother was very lonely. She was quite shy and spoke poor Arabic, but her Turkish was good. As we always tried to speak Armenian at home she had little chance to improve her Arabic. When we had Armenian visitors she spoke Turkish. I have learned Turkish from them. So at home we speak Turkish and Armenian, but our Arabic is now also good. Four years ago we moved to Qasour. I was asked if I liked it better in Qasour as it was a Christian area. I did not hesitate to say that I liked it better living with Muslims in Sha'laan.

(Bedros, Damascus, 2009)

Armenian identity hinged on religious affiliation, language, and the 'myth' of origin and ties to the homeland. The fact that the physical place of the Armenian state had moved to a new locality, from 'Cilicia' to the south Caucasian territory of the former Soviet Armenia, was insignificant for most. The majority of Armenians interviewed had visited this new Armenian Republic. Few had chosen to stay for more than a few months. Among the wealthy there had been some exploratory effort to gauge business ventures, but few had decided to invest in Armenia. Yet, by and large, Armenians expressed dual identities: nationals of their adopted country in Syria and Lebanon as well as their Armenianness and ties back to the 'homeland' which has taken shape in the south Caucasus. The place, the homeland, was the same, but the space it had taken up had shifted. As a minority in Syria, Armenians carved out a special place for themselves among several other Christian minorities, including the Aramaic-speaking Assyrians, who had also fled from their homelands in south-eastern Anatolia escaping discrimination and massacres throughout the early decades of the 1900s. The Armenian emphasis on language and education resulted in the establishment of an education system in Syria operating in parallel to state-run schools. Moreover, Armenian schooling was hugely respected and placement in these schools was highly sought. The outcome of such education opportunities gave the Armenian community a special place in broader Syrian society.

The Armenians who survived the death marches, massacres, and genocide in eastern Anatolia during the First World War found sanctuary in Greater Syria among their co-religionists who had been long established in the Levant. In Syria, however, Armenians had a greater, more generalized impact on the social make-up of the state as a whole. Unlike in Lebanon, where Armenians were a recognized and distinct politico-religious minority, in Syria they were more widely integrated into the fabric of its cities, and often lived side by side with other Christian communities. Their quarters were distinguished by their churches and their educational establishments, the latter being highly regarded by both Christian and Muslim Syrians. The Armenians, along with the Assyrians, who were also displaced from Anatolia during the First World War and from Iraq in the 1920s, made up the second significant wave of refugees to find sanctuary and safety in modern Syria.

4

THE KURDS SEEKING FREEDOM
OF ETHNIC IDENTITY EXPRESSION

We fled after the revolution led by Shaykh Said in 1920 [1925]. The Kurds revolted against the Turks. They demanded a self-governed Kurdish state in Turkey. When Shaykh Said was hanged by the Turks, many Kurds fled Turkey and came to Syria. I remember we all travelled in big groups, seven or eight families and all of their sheep and cattle which they sold on the way at Ra's al-'Ayn. We all walked to Dayr al-Zor and then to al-Sham [Damascus]. We had relatives here who received us and helped us to settle. This quarter had only Kurds who spoke Kurdish. ... When we had been in Syria for six or five years we were granted citizenship [by the French Mandate authority]. Citizenship was granted to anyone who resided in the country for five years.

(Mohammed, Harat al-Akrad, Damascus, April 2006)

I first met Masood in 2007 at the opening of an art exhibition in central Damascus near the Sham Palace Hotel, a major meeting point for foreign journalists, security apparatchiks, and aspiring Syrian artists. He had several of his oil paintings on display at this trendy art gallery. I approached him and asked him what he would be doing next. He told me he really didn't know. He had just received a scholarship to study art in Germany, but he had no way of getting permission to exit Syria or to enter Germany. He had no passport, neither did his father. They had been confiscated, or recalled by the Syrian state, in 1962. His uncle had not had his citizenship rescinded, neither had any of the women in the family. Rumour had it that when Jamal Abdel Nasser had visited the Jazireh in 1958 during the period of the union between Syria, Egypt, and Yemen (the United Arab Republic) he had warned the minister of the interior that there were too many Kurds in the region, and that he should keep an eye out for any who entered the country illegally. As a result, about 100,000 Kurdish citizens of Syria, mainly members of the Kurdish group who had sought refuge in Syria in the 1920s, were stripped of their citizenship. For Masood this had become a personal tragedy. He could not take up his scholarship in Germany without travelling illegally, without permission to leave the country, and without a visa to enter Germany. He knew that as an illegal he would be denied entry and deprived of this scholarship. He had no choice but to remain in Syria as a stateless person, unable even to check into a hotel for the night when he travelled within Syria because he had no ID. Trying to make light of this last restriction, he told me, 'I have friends everywhere in Syria, I can always find someone to give me a bed for the night.'

There are today somewhere in the region of 25 million Kurds living in the Middle East. About 13 million live in modern-day Turkey and make up about 20 per cent of the population;[1] 4 million live in Iraq and make up about 23 per cent of the population of that country; in Iran Kurds number about 5.7 million and represent about 10 per cent of the population; and in Syria they are between 2 and 2.5 million, mainly living along the northern border with Turkey and Syria.

Many of the Kurds in Syria have been there for centuries; but in the 1920s a wave of Kurdish refugees arrived, escaping Turkish repression after their failed bid for independence during the Shaykh Said rebellion. Although the Kurds in Syria represent the smallest portion of this largely mountain-dwelling, tribal people, the forced migrations into Syria in the twentieth century most clearly illustrate the struggle of the Kurds for recognition as a nation. Turkey, Iraq, and Iran have similar mixes of indigenous and refugee Kurdish populations as a result of numerous intra-tribal power struggles and conflicts followed by group expulsions, as well as abortive efforts to establish a Kurdish state.[2] Similar power struggles among the Kurdish tribal leadership, as well as periodic nationalist uprisings, have left the border regions with Kurdish exiles, refugees, and forced migrants living among long-settled and variously resident kin. Their failed bids for recognition as a nation-state,

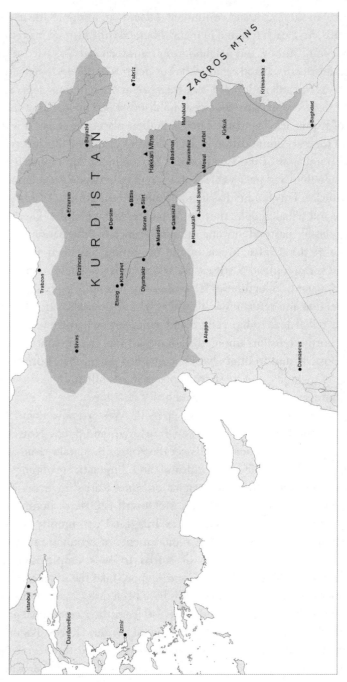

Map 7: Kurdistan

beginning in the 1920s and continuing, off and on, in the 1930, 1940s, and 1960s, have each resulted in many thousands of Kurds taking refuge in Syria, Iran, Turkey, and neighbouring Caucasian states as part of the general international and regional power politics of the day. Seen alternatively as valiant nationalist struggles or as treacherous separatist revolts, these events have displaced and dispossessed hundreds of thousands of Kurds, leaving many stateless in their places of refuge. It is the story of their accommodation in Syria that this chapter will address.

The homeland of the Kurds is the Zagros mountain range. It has served as a fluid and permeable frontier region between great empires for centuries. This fluidity has been of value to the Kurds. As a largely pastoral and tribal people, they could take advantage of the open border regions for pastoral movement, unrestrained by international frontiers, until the 1920s. Much of the migration has been seasonal, between spring upland pastures and winter villages. These migrations were important opportunities for trade—for example, carrying salt in one direction and returning with wheat. The regions also afforded the Kurdish tribal leadership refuge and sanctuary when they tried to exploit border tensions among the competing empires. In more recent times, borders and frontiers have become less permeable. Wire-mesh fencing, minefields, and air surveillance make it difficult for people to cross frontiers other than at official border crossings.

The international borders drawn up by the Western powers in 1919 define the modern states of Turkey, Iran, Iraq, and Syria. However, these 'created' formal borders dissect the Zagros mountain chain, cutting across the major socio-cultural and linguistic groupings of Kurdistan. In each of these modern nation-states Kurds are increasingly drawn into the national fabric. As McDowall (2004: 8) points out, there is now a tension between the 'imagined community' of the Kurdish nation and the practical requirements of economic survival, which pushed large numbers of Kurds to seek employment in Constantinople, Tehran, Baghdad, and Aleppo. Like the other pastoral tribes in the Middle East, many Kurds have been dislocated and dispossessed not only from their homes but also from their communal grazing lands by the creation of modern national borders. Kurds, Bedouin, and Turkmen, for example, had previously managed the permeable borders between empires to their advantage, and together provided most of the livestock or meat requirements of the region. The Kurds, like the Bedouin, have largely given up their international migrations and succumbed to pressure to become more settled. Even then, many continue to keep livestock, making herding along with language and cultural traditions (but not necessarily religion) important markers of identity.[3] In each country in which they seek safety or asylum, the Kurds slip into a remote, 'paperless' existence. Their official documentation does not give them permission to be in the country, and generally there are no mechanisms to become correctly documented. Some Kurds, such as those who took shelter in Syria in the 1920s, were granted citizenship by the French Mandate authority. But that status was withdrawn during the Syrian union with Egypt and Yemen in 1962. Many male Kurds who received citizenship during the Mandate period were stripped of their status, and then selectively granted official documentation by the local government officials (*mukhtars*). Many Kurds from this 1920s wave of immigrants live without documentation, or hold government papers which declare them stateless or *bidoon*.[4]

Background (Geography and History)

The region generally referred to as Kurdistan is centred on the Zagros mountain range which runs in ridges north-west to south-east along Iran, Iraq, and Turkey's common frontiers. To the west the mountains give way to rolling hills and the Mesopotamian plain (Iraq and Syria). To the north-west they merge into the Anatolian plateau (Turkey), and to the east they level out onto agricultural lands (Iran). The region is important for agriculture and animal husbandry. Until the early twentieth century animal husbandry was the most important economy activity in Kurdistan, providing much of the meat for Anatolia, Mesopotamia, and Syria. Large flocks were driven annually to Constantinople, Baghdad, Aleppo, and Damascus (McDowall 2004).

The term 'Kurdistan' was first used in the twelfth century by the Seljuks to describe the mountainous area and its people lying along the geopolitical fault line of three empires: Ottoman, Qajar (Persian), and Russian. Until the late nineteenth century none of these empires deemed it necessary to define the boundaries of Kurdistan. Only when the European powers became concerned about Russian intentions in the

East did sensitivity emerge in Europe as to how many Muslims (largely Kurds) lived in the region compared with Christians (largely Armenians and Assyrians). As long as the Muslim population was the majority, the European powers hoped that Russia would not use religion as a pretext to seize these eastern lands, which would give it access to the Mesopotamian plain as a natural extension of Christian Russia, or in order to protect the Armenian Christians of the Ottoman Empire. Apart from this issue, the Great Powers seemed to have little interest in how generously terms such as Kurdistan or Armenia were drawn across a map. That changed in the twentieth century, as each of the empires crumbled and was replaced by states anxious to impose their notion of homogenous identity on all the people in their territories.[5]

The Kurds speak an Indo-European language which, like Dari in Afghanistan and Farsi in Iran, is part of the Iranian group of languages. Two major dialects or languages exist today in Kurdistan: Kurmanji, spoken by most northern Kurds, and Surani, spoken by most southern Kurds. These differ from each other as German from Dutch or Spanish from Italian. There are several distinct dialects spoken by sizeable Kurdish minorities. In some enclaves in southern Kurdistan, Gurani is spoken, and in small pockets in north-western Kurdistan, Zaza is used by both Sunni and Alevi Kurds. Zaza and Gurani belong to the north-western group of Iranian languages, whereas Kurmanji and Surani belonging to the south-western group. It is likely that Zaza and Gurani speakers were already in the Zagros region when Kurmanji and Surani speakers entered. During this population movement, it is thought that Zaza speakers may have been pushed westwards into Anatolia while the Gurani speakers were enveloped and surrounded, becoming a distinct sub-group with their own dialect (McDowall 2004).

Most Kurds are Sunni Muslim. But there is some religious differentiation (following linguistic lines) which may also indicate some differences in origin. Many Zaza speakers are also Alevi Muslims, a heterodox Muslim Shi'ite sect with strong pre-Islamic elements of Zoroastrianism and Turkmen shamanism. In southern Kurdistan, many Gurani speakers are also Ahl al-Haqq believers. This religious offshoot is similar to Alevi Islam but without the veneration of the Imam Ali. In the Jabal Sanjar and around Shaykan and Mosul, among the Kurmanji speakers, are the Yazidis. This ethno-religious group follows a religion which is a synthesis of old pagan elements, Zoroastrian dualism and Manichaean gnosis with Jewish, Christian, and Muslim elements. About 15 per cent of Kurds, like most Iranians, follow Shi'ite Islam (Ithna 'Ashari Shi'ites or Twelvers), and live in the Kirmansha province of Iran. Kurdish religious distinctiveness has also been expressed in the strength of its religious mysticism. Sufi brotherhoods (*tariqa*s) are common among the Kurds and important markers of social organization, although the Turkish state has tried to control their membership over the past century.

Other religious communities existed in Kurdistan. Small Jewish groups, mainly in the urban centres and towns, date back at least 2,000 years. They have tended to be traders and artisans. Although there was an exodus to Israel between 1948 and 1952, still some remain and probably affiliate themselves to certain tribes. There was a sizeable community of Christians of various sects in Kurdistan: the Gregorian Christian Armenians of eastern Anatolia, the Nestorian Christians or Assyrians (sometimes referred to as the Assyro-Chaldaeans), as well as the Suryani or Syrian Orthodox.

The majority of the Kurds are probably descended from Indo-European tribes moving across Iran in the middle of the second millennium BCE. In the second century BCE there are references to the Kurds as 'Cyrtii', Seleucid or Parthian mercenaries dwelling in the Zagros mountains. Semitic tribes may also have inhabited the region at this time. By the eighth century CE, at the time of the Islamic conquests, the term 'Kurd' was used to refer to the nomads on the western edge of the Iranian plateau, and probably included Arab and Turkmen tribes. Within several hundred years the latter came to be recognized as Kurdish, although their Arab or Turkmen roots were generally acknowledged. Likewise, numerous Kurds who left Kurdistan to become professional soldiers with Muslim armies or in groups as herders or farmers or merchants lost some of the more obvious cultural attributes of Kurdishness—such as language—over time.

From about the twelfth century, the term 'Kurd', like 'Bedouin' in Arabia, came to mean a nomad or pastoral herder. Over the centuries both Bedouin and Kurdish tribes consolidated their presence in agricultural areas adjacent to their seasonal herding migrations and commonly held grazing lands. A pejorative sense of 'outlaw' or 'bandit' also came to be attached to the term, and gained widespread usage in the late seventeenth, eighteenth, and early nineteenth centuries. This was a time of particularly weak Ottoman rule and control over the Anatolian and Arab provinces. Kurdish tribal raiding of agricultural settlements and demands for tribute (protection payment) from peasants and villagers—in exchange for warding off the depredations of other tribes—were widespread.

By the nineteenth century the term 'Kurd' had taken on the meaning of tribespeople who spoke the Kurdish language. The dominant ideology of Kurdish society at the time was kin based and rooted in a myth of common ancestry. Most Kurdish tribal groups had their own real or imagined ancestor going back either to the time of Muhammad in the eighth century or to a hero in early Islam such as Khalid ibn al-Walid or in the later period to Salah al-Din al-Ayyubi (Saladin to the Europeans). The Kurds, like the Bedouin, had a range of terms to describe descending orders of social organization of the tribe. Many of these were the same in Kurdish and in Arabic. The highest order was the confederation of tribes, descending down to the tented encampment of related kinsmen and women. Each tribe had a strong sense of common origin as well as a sense of territorial identity—but not necessarily ownership. This applied not only to common lands held by the tribe for pasturing their livestock, but also to the villages and towns within their territorial domain and from which they could extract tribute. Regarding the latter there was a sense of responsibility to maintain order and control, but also an assumed right to extract payment for the management of security and political organization. This territorial universe was never entirely bounded or frozen, and could accommodate other tribes. For example, in the northern Jazireh of Syria the Arab Shammar Bedouin and the Kurdish Milli tribe—supposed enemies—shared certain pastoral grazing areas; the latter in winter and the former in summer (McDowall 2004: 15).

Among the Kurds, as with the Bedouin, leadership was instilled in particular individuals at all levels of tribal organization: the confederation, the tribe, sub-tribe, lineage, and the extended family. These chiefs (*aghawat*: sing. *agha*) were expected to act as arbitrators of disputes, allocators of resources, benefits, and duties. The chief of the tribe or confederation was also expected to act as a mediator with other tribes or with the state. Leadership was often dynastic, and passed down from father to son. The flexibility and latitude accorded the tribal leaders to negotiate access, to mediate conflict, and to represent interests was particularly suited to the confrontations with the rigid and inflexible mechanisms of Ottoman state control.[6]

Again as with the Bedouin of Arabia, the Kurds maintain an oppositional dichotomy which extends back to their imagined origins. Whereas the Bedouin consider their origins to go back to two mythical brothers, Qais and Yemen, who are the founders of their two confederations of tribes, the Aneza and the Shammar, the Kurds regard Zilan and Milan as the equivalent. This oppositional dichotomy is expressed today in the opposition of the Talebani and the Barzani tribal confederations and it extends to the two political allegiances of the Kurds between the Patriotic Union of Kurdistan (PUK) and the Kurdish Democratic Party (KDP/PPK).

Kurdish social organization had a fully developed hierarchy based on acquired and achieved status both among settled and pastoral folk. At the highest level was the chief or *agha*, who generally held both economic and political power. In agrarian areas the local landowner held enormous power over the peasantry, often controlling land, water, livestock, equipment, seeds, and labour itself. The *agha* was leader of a community and the title was generally granted by the Ottoman state. An example of how the title of *agha* was awarded can be found in eighteenth-century Damascus. This was a period of general decline and pronounced in-migration of peasants, Bedouin and Kurds, from areas in eastern Anatolia and the northern Syrian semi-arid steppe where insecurity and famine was pronounced. Local Damascene religious scholars frequently mentioned their disdain for the *aghawat* who were moving in on the periphery of the city and setting up their own systems of management and governance. Khoury describes this growing independent power base in the city, which threatened the old guard:

> In a section of the sparsely settled suburb of al-Salahiyya, to the northwest of Damascus ... Kurdish immigrants unable to penetrate the old city set up home there. Their chiefs created paramilitary forces composed of their tribesmen and the state awarded them the title of *agha* for policing the countryside. (Khoury 1983: 22)

Some of these newcomers became part of the Damascene ruling class. The Kurdish Yusuf family and the Shamdins, for example, came to prominence in the second half of the nineteenth century when they were competitors for the same Kurdish clientele in al-Salahiyya. A marriage alliance between the families produced a son who became one of the richest men in Damascus and held one of the most prestigious posts in the Ottoman Empire, the Commander of the Pilgrimage (*Amir al-Hajj*), in the late 1890s.

The Ottoman state's relationship with Kurdish tribal leaders has its origins in the early sixteenth century. At that time, Kurdistan, with all its tribal principalities and fiefdoms, was threatened by the rulers of Persia who sought to annex the region. In 1514, during a major battle in the north of Kurdistan, Kurdish tribal leaders fought alongside the Ottoman sultan, Selim, and contributed significantly to his victory. As a result, Sultan Selim concluded a pact with the main Kurdish leaders. This Kurdish–Ottoman pact formally recognized sixteen independent Kurdish principalities in Kurdistan (Kendal [Nezan] 1980: 22). The tribal leaders of these principalities were given significant independent status: they could strike coinage, and have their names recited at the Friday public prayer; they did not have to pay tribute nor were they accountable to the sultan. However, they were not permitted to change the frontiers of their principalities or fiefdoms. These tribal chiefs (termed *beys* and sometimes *pasha*s by the Ottomans) in effect became vassals of the sultan. They were free to manage their fiefdoms as they pleased, their power was generally absolute and hereditary, but they were expected to fight for the sultan in the empire's campaigns, particularly against the Persians. These sixteen principalities covered about a third of the territory of Ottoman Kurdistan.

This feudal and imperial relationship was respected by both sides well into the nineteenth century, when a specifically Kurdish literature and culture bloomed. Yet during this same period, sometimes referred to as the golden age of Kurdish feudalism, Kurdish society was practically cut off from the outside world. Each Kurdish tribal leader's horizon extended no further than his own frontier. Quarrels over supremacy and precedence set one tribal ruler against another and hindered any unity among the principalities (McDowall 2004: 38–48).

At the beginning of the nineteenth century, as the Ottomans' grip on their European provinces began to slip, they sought to recruit ever more troops to bolster their failing campaigns. They turned to Kurdistan as an important source of manpower. This move, however, began to be regarded by some Kurdish princes as an infringement of their privileges. Kurdish territory also became the theatre for the Russo-Ottoman wars (1823–30, 1877–8) and the Persian–Ottoman wars (1821–3), bringing a level of death and destruction which provoked Kurdish hostility and outrage towards the Ottomans. In addition, outside influences such as Western penetration into Kurdistan in the form of missions, consulates, and schools also began to impact negatively on the Kurdish tribal leadership's sense of privilege. In the course of the nineteenth century, over fifty insurrections broke out, during which Kurdish feudal leaders defended their ancient privileges by refusing to pay tribute or to furnish the sultan with soldiers for his military campaigns elsewhere. The 'states' of Baban, Soran, Hakkari, Bahdinan, and Bohtan, for example, all fiefdoms at the heart of Kurdish feudalism, were the starting points for the main insurrections. These uprisings failed because they were disjointed and because the sultan, with greater ingenuity, was able to play one Kurdish leader off against another.

After nearly a century of feudal revolts the Ottoman court changed its approach and sought to actually control and integrate the Kurdish ruling class into the broad system of state rule. Many of the sons or nephews of those Kurdish leaders who had led revolts were appointed to important posts in the Ottoman government. One was appointed as aide-de-camp to the sultan himself, and the son of another disaffected Kurdish leader became president of the Ottoman Senate in 1908 and was later appointed president of the Council of State. In addition, the sultan created a special Kurdish cavalry force recruited on a tribal basis. These regiments, the Hamidiyyeh, were originally set up in areas bordering on the Russian Caucasus (Erzurum, Bitlis, and Van) where the Kurds had not systematically rebelled and where the Armenian nationalist movement was in full swing. Finally, in 1892, Sultan Abdul Hamid set up two special schools in Baghdad and in Constantinople for the children of tribal leaders among the Kurds and the Arab Bedouin. Although these schools were short-lived, they had an enormous impact on the formation of a limited but effective Kurdish and Arab tribal intellectual presence in future generations.[7]

Kurdish identity evolved dramatically at the end of the nineteenth century. Up to the very end of the century, when nationalist and secessionist movements generally gripped the European part of the empire, few Kurds regarded themselves as anything other than members of their particular religious community (*millet*). The Kurdish peasantry continued to struggle with the demands of feudal landlords or pastoral tribal leaders. In many urban settings, local Kurdish workers and artisans had to deal with the demands of their *aghawat*, the local Kurdish power brokers and leaders. The latter, in turn, had to show respect and pay taxes to their hereditary princes (*beys* or *pashas*). The struggle to maintain distance and independence and remain outside state control, which had been part of Kurdish (and Bedouin) tribal ideology and activity, gradually came to be integrated into the nationalist movements emerging from the urban power centres. These struggles coloured the way in which Kurds and their militias responded to the end of empire.

With the exception of the Arabian provinces, no other part of the Ottoman state was as weak and poorly managed as Ottoman Asia, that part of south-eastern Anatolia and northern Iraq which was home to the Armenians, Assyrians, and other syncretic religious communities as well as the Kurds. The mountainous terrain as well the general unwillingness of its nomadic peoples to submit to central authority made anything other than local governance in this region very difficult.

The Kurdish tribes, like the Bedouin in Arabia, saw themselves in opposition to central authority. They were unaccustomed to following any orders other than those of their own leadership. They were part of an alternative system of social organization based on mobility and the fluidity of boundaries between tribes. From the time of the golden age of Sulayman the Magnificent (1520–66), the Ottomans struggled, not so much to control the Kurds, as to keep them from causing trouble. As long as the Kurds did not disrupt trade or attack settled regions, the Ottoman authorities often were content to leave them alone. Kurdish (and Bedouin) tribal practice of demanding tribute from settled villagers did not raise pronounced objection from the Ottomans until late in the nineteenth century, when tax was desperately needed by the state and the Kurdish practice of collecting tribute was undermining official state tax collection.

After the 1877–8 Russo-Ottoman war the state attempted to impose its authority over these traditionally rather autonomous

Kurdish regions. Sultan Abdul Hamid II attempted to bring the Kurdish tribes under his control by using their strengths to his advantage. The creation of the Hamidiyyeh Cavalry in 1891 was one example. He provided them with arms, uniforms, and some training. They were used for the first time in the repression of the Armenians between 1894 and 1896, which ended in a series of massacres in which tens of thousands of Armenians were killed. These same troops were used against the Kurds of Dersim when they rose up against the sultan. Under the command of Ibrahim Pasha, they were also put into action against Arab nationalists (Kendal [Nezan] 1980: 34). When Abdul Hamid was deposed fifteen years later the Hamidiyyeh was renamed, re-uniformed, and more centrally integrated into the formal standing army as tribal regiments of light cavalry. The new Ottoman government of the Young Turks adopted a more practical approach, bringing these Kurdish regiments under regular military control. But the home region, south-east Anatolia and the Syrian provinces, was never controlled. The lack of even an effective police or gendarmerie meant that Kurdish tribes were able to continue to extract tribute from settled society, and Armenian revolutionaries were able to organize themselves and manage smuggling networks to move weapons and ammunition into the region (McCarthy 2001: 66).

During the First World War, and despite the exhortations of the Ottoman sultan and the Grand Mufti to 'holy war', many pastoral Kurdish tribal leaders took a neutral position (Ahmad 1994). Other leaders took advantage of the situation to make a break for secession or to be on the winning side. A number of Kurdish tribal sections from the region of Dersim joined the Ottoman army at the beginning of the war, but later switched sides, joining Armenians, other Kurds, and Russian forces in attacking Ottoman convoys and pillaging local villages. In Van, one Kurdish leader attempted to set up a major Kurdish revolt.

The Kurds in Kurdistan could not have stayed aloof for long as their traditional lands were the scenes of a devastating struggle between three armies: the Ottoman, the Russian, and the British. For four years between 1914 and 1918 these armies clashed in many Kurdish districts, engaging in fierce battles that shifted the balance of power between combatants and caused huge disruption, death, and homelessness in many parts of Kurdistan. After a few months of fighting more than 15,000 Kurdish horsemen had deserted the ranks of the Third Army. In border regions it was not unusual for Kurdish soldiers, tribesmen, and their leaders to go over with their arms to the Russians (Ahmad 1994: 91). In other areas, Kurdish tribesmen mounted surprise attacks on Ottoman troops, sometimes looking for arms and ammunition for themselves or in cooperation with the British. In the territories initially conquered by the Russians in north-east Anatolia, Kurdish pastoral tribes generally made peace quickly with the occupiers. However, skirmishes between Armenian militias and Kurdish tribesmen continued throughout the war. Many of the Kurdish tribesmen who were fighting alongside the Ottoman army in the campaign against Persia in 1915 deserted and joined in the general pillage and rampage being carried out by the tribes in the region near Van.

Along the Russian front, Kurdish tribesmen and their leaders were being alternately wooed and chased away, while the Armenians and other Christian groups were by turns victorious or victims of massacres. The Russians never developed a coherent policy towards the Kurds, probably because Kurdish aspirations were bound to clash with those of the Armenians. As McDowall writes: 'It suited Russia in its policy with both Kurds and Armenians to encourage dissidence in order to weaken the Ottoman hold on the region, but not in order to permit either Armenian or Kurdish independence. Russia wanted eastern Anatolia for itself' (McDowall 2004: 102). The Russians had a continuing and serious interest in the Kurds, both hidden and declared. Their long-standing imperial goal was to push southwards into Ottoman Armenia and Kurdistan towards the Persian/Arabian Gulf, as well as to gain access to the Mediterranean through the Dardanelles Straits.

The British on the other hand were determined to push as far north and east as possible from the mouth of the Shatt al-Arab to meet up with Russian forces and squeeze the Ottoman armies between them. The day after the Ottoman Empire became an official combatant in the First World War, British forces attacked southern Iraq and occupied Basra. After this rapid occupation, and perhaps as a result of it, the Ottomans were able to raise a force of 10,000 men, including many Kurds, to fight against the British invaders. In April 1915 Ottoman units battled the British at Shu'aiba, suffering defeat and serious losses. Many of the Arab and Kurdish fighters left the battlefield then and returned to their homes. By March 1917 the British had entered Baghdad. After the Russian October Revolution of 1917, the British sped up their northward drive beyond Baghdad, later to engage in fierce battles to take Mosul and then Kirkuk before the signing of the Armistice of Mudros on 30 October 1918 on board the HMS *Agamemnon* on the island of Lemnos. The British were seeking to consolidate and protect their oil interests—partially in Kurdistan—as had been negotiated and agreed some years earlier in the secret Sykes–Picot Agreement.

A year into the First World War, secret talks had begun between Britain and France regarding the division of the Ottoman Empire. Early in 1916 Sir Mark Sykes, the British foreign minister, and his French counterpart, François Georges-Picot, travelled to St Petersburg, where they sought the cooperation of the tsar. At the start, Russia made it clear that, in addition to its desire to control the Dardanelles and Constantinople, it also wanted all of Ottoman Kurdistan and Ottoman Armenia. After lengthy bargaining with the French—who also had claims to the same area—an agreement was reached whereby Russia would have the northernmost Armenian regions of Erzurum, Trabzon, Van, and Bitlis up to a point on the Black Sea to the west of Trabzon. It would also control the Kurdish regions to the west of Van and Bitlis. The British had established claims to Mosul province as part of their plan for control of the oilfields and the outlets in the Middle East. They also pushed to acquire parts of Persian Kurdistan, even though Persia had remained neutral throughout the war years. The Sykes–Picot Agreement was followed by another round of negotiations and secret agreements. Italy, which had been excluded from these discussions, lodged a protest with its allies and managed to join in the division of spoils in November 1916. Early in 1917 Russia and France reached another secret agreement whereby, among other conditions related to Europe, France pledged to support Russia's claims to Constantinople and the Dardanelles Straits. These secret agreements—many of them contradictory—were setting the stage for one of the most dramatic land claims in colonial history, dismissing and at the same time toying with the aspirations and destinies of the Arabs, the Armenians, and the Kurdish people.

Before the war ended, however, Tsarist Russia had come to an end with the October Revolution of 1917. The new Soviet state withdrew from the Allied consortium and dissociated itself from the treaties of the previous regime. It recalled its troops from the battlefields and abandoned every area they had conquered. On 8 November 1917 the new Soviet government denounced the colonialist secret diplomacy and pledged to publish the texts of the Great Power treaties in its possession. After six weeks it released a number of these publications in the Soviet press. One of these included clauses of the Sykes–Picot Agreement. The Sharif of Mecca, still trusting British loyalty and friendship, asked for clarification from the British government, as these revelations completely undermined his own correspondence with Henry McMahon, the British high commissioner in Egypt, regarding the status of the Arab provinces after the war ended. The British, in an official letter sent by the Foreign Office via Cairo to Sharif Hussein, tried to dismiss the matter as a mere 'Bolshevik game' aimed at corrupting relations between the Arabs and the Allies.

The Kurdish intellectual response was relatively muted, as was that of the Armenians and Assyrians. Many of the region's political leaders believed the British Foreign Office assertion that the 'Bolshevik game' was aimed at destroying the relationship between the Allies and themselves. The Allies quickly altered their political statements, sometimes in direct contradiction of the contents of the secret agreements. In January 1918 the British prime minister, David Lloyd George, asserted that his country had been forced to participate in the war 'in defence of the rights of the peoples'. Three days later the US president, Woodrow Wilson, announced his famous Fourteen Points before Congress. Point Five recalled:

> ... the necessity for free, open-minded and absolutely impartial adjustment of all colonial claims based upon ... the interest of the populations concerned ... [having] equal weight with the equitable claims of the government whose title is to be determined.

The twelfth point related specifically to the Ottoman Empire and stipulated that:

> The Turkish portions of the present Ottoman Empire should be assured a secure sovereignty, but the other nationalities which are now under Turkish rule should be assured an undoubted security of life and an absolutely unmolested opportunity of autonomous development. (Snell 1954)

For their part, the British devoted considerable energy to bringing the Kurds round to their 'side' by promises of liberating oppressed peoples and granting them the right of self-determination. In both Kurdistan and Mesopotamia the British forces of occupation invested significant time and energy in the publication of two newspapers, *al-Arab* and *Tigeyashteni Raste*, which carried much of what was written by Woodrow Wilson. Many Kurdish intellectuals pinned their hopes on Wilson's Fourteen Points and wanted the USA to be more actively involved in determining their destiny at the end of the war.

After the Armistice of Mudros in October 1918, the Kurdish elite prepared to present their case to the Paris Peace Conference, which lasted for more than a year (January 1919 to January 1920). They were represented by a small delegation, led by Sherif Pasha, a high-ranking Kurdish Ottoman military figure and diplomat. For many at the Paris Peace Conference the 'Kurdish question' was connected to the 'Armenian question'. Some time was spent discussing Armenia and which Mandate it would come under. President Wilson sent a special commission, led by James Harbord, to consider the Armenian question. Harbord visited Asia Minor, and also some Kurdish regions. His recommendation, made in October 1919, was that one state should have a Mandate over all of Turkey and the Trans-Caucasus. The British put pressure on the Americans to accept the Mandate over the whole of Armenia, Constantinople, the Dardanelles, and the Caucasus. However, the USA rejected these proposals, and Great Britain and France renewed their deliberations. British interests in Kurdistan were acute, particularly as the Kurds were considered a vital element of British military borders to the north of Baghdad. They were unwilling to see Kurdistan shared with the French. These opposing positions among the Allies resulted in the inclusion of a number of awkward and contradictory articles into the Treaty of Sèvres regarding the Kurds.

The treaty was signed on 10 August 1920 in Sèvres, near Paris. The signatories included Britain, France, Italy, Japan, Belgium, Greece, Romania, Poland, Portugal, Czechoslovakia, Yugoslavia, Hijaz, and Armenia on the one hand and the Ottoman Empire on the other. Part III of Section III was devoted to the Kurdish question and consisted of three articles (62–64). These articles set out a timetable first for local Kurdish autonomy, followed, a year later, by the right to petition the

League of Nations for an independent Kurdish state. However, the ambiguity of the language in many of these articles, as well as the recognition of the overlapping interests of the French, British, and Italians in Kurdistan, meant that whatever optimism there may have been regarding Kurdish rights to self-determination was unfounded. The Treaty of Sèvres was, to use the words of William Eagleton, 'a dead letter from the moment it was signed, for history was written otherwise by Mustafa Kemal and finally by the Treaty of Lausanne in 1923. By then it was clear that within Ataturk's Turkey there was no place for an Armenian or Kurdish nation' (Eagleton 1963: 12).

The Treaty of Sèvres proposed to strip the Ottoman Empire down and confine it to just north-western and north-central Anatolia, with Constantinople remaining as its capital. Although the sultan's representative signed the treaty, the remnants of the Ottoman army, regrouped under the command of Mustafa Kemal, refused to accept these terms. Mustafa Kemal initiated a campaign for an independent Turkish state including all of Anatolia. An active local resistance to the French occupation, aided by the former Ottoman soldiers under the command of Mustafa Kemal, rapidly emerged (McCarthy 2001: 138–41). On 21 October 1921 the French abandoned their claims to Anatolia and signed a treaty with Mustafa Kemal's government. The French left Anatolia in December, taking 30,000 Armenians with them to their Mandated states of Syria and Lebanon. By August 1922 the Turks had retaken most of western Anatolia occupied by Greek forces and the following month they entered Izmir on the Mediterranean coast.

In October 1923 the Nationalist government of Mustafa Kemal agreed a new treaty with the Allied Powers at Lausanne. In the negotiations at Lausanne, the Turkish Nationalist government representative, Ismet Pasha, accepted British and French rule in Palestine, Syria, and Iraq. He also grudgingly agreed that the status of the Kurdish province of Mosul, which the Turks viewed as an integral part of Anatolia, could be decided by the Council of the League of Nations.[8] Kurdistan was divided between Iran and three newly created states carved out of the old Ottoman Empire: Turkey, Iraq, and Syria.

In Turkey, 4 million people had been lost between 1914 and 1922—nearly 20 per cent of its pre-war population of 17.5 million. The religious and ethnic character of the state had also changed massively with the flight and expulsion of Christians (mainly Greeks and Armenians) and the in-migration of Muslim refugees (mainly Bulgarians, Muslim Greeks, Albanians, Kosovars, Tatars, Circassians, and other Transcaucasians). The Kurds largely remained in their homelands, although much of Kurdistan was now divided and occupied by the British and their allies. In British Mandated Iraq, the British first depended upon Kurdish and Assyrian levies to support their occupation. However, as the Kurds grew increasingly restive, this auxiliary army of nearly 7,500 Kurdish and Assyrian men became almost entirely Assyrian by the late 1920s.

After the defeat of the French and the Greeks in Anatolia, Mustafa Kemal and his Nationalist government set about restructuring modern Ottoman society in order to create the Turkish Republic. Although many Kurdish intellectuals worked alongside him in this effort, many others, mainly tribal Kurds, were uncomfortable with the reforms he was instituting. Mustafa Kemal was determined to alter the language, education, form of government, clothing, place of religion, and even 'self-identification' or citizenship of the people in this new state. In order to do so, he needed to wipe out any persisting beliefs that the state could be a multi-ethnic one. Mustafa Kemal decided to focus on reform and the creation of a homogeneous Turkish citizenry.

The greatest breaks with Ottoman tradition were in the realm of religious and cultural norms. Mustafa Kemal was determined to break with the past. In 1922 he abolished the Ottoman Sultanate and in 1924 the Islamic Caliphate. Religious groups continued to provide welfare and education, but the *millet* structure was abolished. The Sufi brotherhoods were outlawed, and oriental symbols were discouraged, such as Muslim religious clothing, veils for women, old-style peasant clothing, and the fez. In the place of the *millet*s and Islam came the state (McCarthy 2001: 201–11). Mustafa Kemal, now renamed Kemal Atatürk, believed it was essential to develop Turkish nationalism for the state to survive through the twentieth century. He had no interest in continuing with the Ottoman traditional of ethno-religious identity. The problem was that most of the inhabitants of Anatolia were descendants of Turks who had arrived long ago from Central Asia and others who had been added to this mix: Circassians, Abkhazians, Laz, Kurds, Arabs, Bulgarian and Greek Pomaks (ethnic Slav Muslims), and

Sephardic Jews. Atatürk needed to formulate an inclusive nationalism to integrate all these peoples. There was no room for minorities; all the population of Anatolia had to assimilate, speak Turkish, and accept the secular state (McCarthy 2001: 212–13). Non-Turkish ethnic expression was suppressed. Atatürk's main antagonists were the Kurds. Some Kurds accepted this assimilationist Turkish ideology. They became 'ethnic Turks' and went on to be full partners in the governing of the Turkish Republic. For most Kurds, however, this assimilationist nationalism was repugnant. On 1 November 1922, three months after the successful conclusion of the War for Independence, Mustafa Kemal declared to the National Assembly that 'the state which we have just created is a Turkish State' (Kendal [Nezan] 1980: 37). The Kurds were quick to rise up in protest, and the next two decades saw constant revolts against the Turkish state in Kurdistan.

Kurdish Separatism and Nationalism

In January 1923 Kemal Atatürk proclaimed his intention to create a modern Republic of Turkey. In the name of that fraternity between Kurds and Turks, which the new government had adopted as one of its slogans, the Turkish Republic called on the British to hand back the old *vilayet* of Mosul. The British, however, issued a declaration which solemnly recognized the rights of the Kurds in British Mandated Iraq to form an autonomous Kurdish government within the frontiers of Iraq.[9] The British hoped to obtain international confirmation of Mosul as within the Iraqi frontiers, and thus secure for Britain the rights to exploit the oilfields of southern Kurdistan.

In the negotiations at Lausanne in 1922–3 to replace the now defunct Treaty of Sèvres, the Turkish representative, Mustafa İsmet İnönü, and his British counterpart, Lord Curzon, as heads of the two countries' delegations, each claimed deep concern for the interests of the Kurds. In fact, the real bone of contention was simply a border dispute between the Republic of Turkey and the Arab Kingdom of Iraq (represented by the British Colonial Office). The negotiations were inconclusive on the issue of the Kurds other than a few articles insisting on respect for the linguistic and national rights of Turkey's non-Turkish minorities. More significantly, the Treaty of Lausanne, which superseded the Treaty of Sèvres, recognized Turkey as a new power and furthermore stipulated that the Turkish–Iraqi frontier was to be fixed along 'a line to be determined in conformity with the decision of the Council of the League of Nations' (Article 3 note 2 of the Treaty of Lausanne).

Shaykh Said's Revolt

The first Kurdish rebellion in the newly created state of Turkey began fermenting towards the end of 1922, when a few Kurdish deputies founded a Committee for Kurdish Independence in Erzurum with links to the main towns in Kurdistan. A number of Kurdish religious leaders joined the movement the following year, distressed by Atatürk's plans to abolish the Caliphate as the Islamic foundation of the new state. On 2 March 1924, on the very day that the Islamic Caliphate was abolished,[10] a government decree was issued banning all Kurdish schools, associations, publications, and religious fraternities in a move to assimilate the Kurds into the Turkish state. The break between the Atatürk government and most of the population in Kurdistan was complete. From 1925 to 1939 there were constant revolts and peasant uprisings in Kurdistan. The first major revolt or insurrection was that of Shaykh Said, who was determined to create an independent Muslim Kurdish state. Within the space of a few months he and his partisans were able to take control of one-third of Kurdistan in Turkey and besiege the city of Diyarbakir, while other Kurdish units were liberating the region north of Lake Van. The Turkish government sent the bulk of its armed forces, 80,000 men, into the region and, with the approval of the French government in Syria, was able to send fresh troops along the northern Syrian railway and thus encircle the Kurdish forces besieging Diyarbakir. The uprising was eventually put down in April 1925; some of its leaders were taken prisoner, and others sought refuge among the followers of powerful Kurdish tribal leaders in Syria, Iraq, and Iran. In September 1925 Shaykh Said and fifty-two of his followers were hanged in Diyarbakir (Kendal [Nezan] 1980). Thousands of Kurdish peasants were killed and hundreds of villages were burnt to the ground. This wave of repression resulted in tens of thousands of Kurds fleeing to Syria, Iraq, and Iran.

SYRIA

Over the years, the Kurdish national movement's centre of gravity has shifted. It first emerged in Turkish Kurdistan between 1925 and 1938. Then it moved to Iraqi Kurdistan from 1943 to 1945, when Mustafa Barzani led a revolt in Barzan. This was followed by a brief Kurdish flourishing in 1946 when an autonomous democratic republic was set up in Mahabad in Iran. A year later the small Kurdish republic had collapsed, and Barzani and his best fighters forced their way through northern Kurdistan and took refuge in the Soviet Union, where they stayed for eleven years (Vanly 1992: 163). Between 1961 and 1975 the centre of Kurdish resistance was once again back in Iraq.

The whole of the twentieth century has been one long series of Kurdish revolts and uprisings in a struggle for self-determination—if not actual separatism. During and after each uprising in Turkish, Iranian, and Iraqi Kurdistan, Kurds have fled across the frontiers of these nation-states to reach safety and to regroup among close kin or other Kurds. Movement back and forth, clandestine but carefully regulated by Kurdish fighters (*peshmergas*) across the little-patrolled Turkish, Syrian, Iranian, and Iraqi borders, has been common. Only in Syria was there no uprising or revolt. Instead, Syria became a place of exile as well as a political refuge for its Kurdish leaders and political parties such as the Kurdish Democratic Party (KDP), the Patriotic Union of Kurdistan (PUK), and between 1980 and 1998 the Kurdistan Workers' Party (Partya Karkari Kurdistan (PKK)).

Beginning in the 1920s and continuing on throughout the twentieth century, Kurdish forced migrants have entered Syria to seek asylum among well-established Syrian Kurdish communities. The following section focuses on the integration of Kurdish refugees and exiles among Syria's indigenous Kurdish population over the past century, beginning with the 1925 Shaykh Said revolt. It examines the way in which these forced migrants found new places to live and regroup. It examines the factors that gave Kurds in Syria space to integrate yet maintain their Kurdish language and culture. Despite the vagaries of recent political fortunes in Syria, many Kurds, even those who became stateless (*bidoon*) by a political act in 1963 and then experienced arbitrary return of citizenship in 2012, had managed to keep their cultural and linguistic heritage alive. The discrimination they face is, in part, discretionary, and is often overcome by using social and political networks as well as local patronage systems. As a country which has been receiving Kurds for most of the past century, Syria offers an opportunity to examine the notion of migrant integration without assimilation, as well as citizenship and statelessness in an authoritarian state.

Kurds in Syria: Stateless among Citizens

Kurds are found throughout the Syrian Arab Republic, although their greatest concentration is along the northern borders shared with Turkey and Iraq—those parts of Kurdistan ceded to the French Mandated Syrian state in 1920. Damascus alone has a population of 300,000 Kurds, most of whom live in Salahiyya and Harat al-Akrad (the Kurdish quarter) in the foothills above Damascus. This area was first settled in the twelfth century by the families of the Kurdish soldiers under the command of Salah al-Din al-Ayyubi during the Crusades. There is a similarly large Kurdish population in Aleppo. The most densely Kurdish populated area of Syria is in the 'Mountain of the Kurds' (Kurd-Dagh) to the north and west of Aleppo. Most of these inhabitants trace their lineage back even further than the Kurds of Damascus. Here, some 360 prosperous Kurdish villages represent the westernmost region of Kurdistan. Further east, where the Euphrates river enters Syrian territory, there are 120 Kurdish villages in the Ain al-Arab region. However, the largest Kurdish population in Syria is found in the Jazireh, which shares a long border—280 kilometres—with both Turkish and Iraqi Kurdistan. During the Ottoman era this region was shared by competing, and, at times hostile, Bedouin and Kurdish pastoral tribes. Today it is made up of predominantly Kurdish villages—more than 700—and Christian towns, most of which were settled during the French Mandate period between 1920 and 1946. Large groups of Christian refugees (Assyrian and other Eastern Church refugees from Kurdistan) also were settled in the region. Qamishli, created by the French on the railway line, became an important settlement point, as did Hasake, which became the provincial capital in the absence of Mosul, which was now separated from the surrounding terrain by an international border.

In the early decades of the twentieth century, however, the Kurdish ruling *aghawat* class in Syria were deeply tied into the former Ottoman system, and generally did not welcome the Arab Revolt against the Ottomans led by the Sharif of Mecca, nor the arrival of his son, Faysal, as the new ruler of Syria in 1918. As a member of the Syrian Congress of 1919, Abd al-Rahman al-Yusuf, the leader of the Damascus Kurds, opposed Syrian independence and quietly strengthened his contacts with the French before they had actually overthrown the Kingdom of Syria in the summer of 1920 (McDowall 2004: 468). A few years later, when the French needed troops to put down the Great Arab Revolt of 1925 led by Arab and Druze fighters, France deliberately recruited auxiliaries from the Kurds, Armenians, and Circassians to crush this uprising. Many of these Kurds were recent arrivals fleeing after the Shaykh Said revolt in Turkey.

The connection between the Kurdish *aghawat* and the French authorities has entered into local myth, and even nowadays it is mentioned in the narratives of the Kurds. One of my elderly interviewees in the old Kurdish quarter of Damascus told me:

> There is an old proverb which says: 'An Arab can never be stingy; a Kurd can never be subservient; and a Cherkess can never be generous'. A Kurd is known for never being weak or compromising. That is why the Kurds were so appreciated by the French. They knew that Kurds are straight, honest people. Omar, Agha Shamdin, a most important Kurdish public figure from this quarter, used to be visited often by high-ranking French officers. They knew that he was held in greatest respect by the whole community. His requests of the community were met as one. The French knew that the loyalty of the community to Agha Shamdin could be also loyalty to them. (Yusuf, Harat al-Akrad, Damascus, April 2006)

When the pan-Kurdish independence party Hoyboun was founded in 1927, it seems the French allowed it to operate as it caused Arab nationalists some disquiet. The following year one of Hoyboun's leading members, Prince Jaladat Badr Khan, published a Kurmanji Kurdish journal, *Hawar*, and developed the use of Latin script as better suited to this Indo-European language. Also in 1928, a petition was submitted to the Constituent Assembly of Syria seeking official permission to use the Kurdish language alongside other languages in Syria and to permit it to be taught in the three Kurdish regions of Syria. These demands were no more than those required by the League of Nations when it awarded the *vilayet* of Mosul to British Mandated Iraq in 1926. However, the French refused to accept this petition. Some Kurds continued to embrace a Kurdish nationalism agenda, but most Kurds in Syria worked within the broad movement for Syrian independence.

Today most of Syria's Kurds have full citizenship, and the same rights and opportunities as other Syrian nationals. They are very aware of being Kurdish, and fully understand the complexity of their relationship with the state. Some urban and affluent Kurds are in positions of power or influence, and speak Arabic in public rather than Kurmanji. Other Kurds, however, particularly the more recent migrants, do face open discrimination (Yassin-Kassab and al-Shami 2016). The latter group represent perhaps 10 per cent of the total population of Syrian Kurds. However, since 2004 international political scrutiny has focused on this section of the Syrian population.

I was born in a Christian village in Jazireh. My mother was originally Christian. She was born in a village in Turkey. After the trouble and famine of the 1920s her family fled with others. A Turkish Muslim family took her in and brought her up. They married her to a son of theirs, but she couldn't stand it. She met my father and they both came to the Jazireh where they got married. My father was born in Turkey. His father had been an officer in the Turkish army. After Shaykh Said was executed, he didn't want to continue serving in the Turkish army and left for Syria. He came with the brother of Shaykh Said, Abdul Rahim. After first arriving in Jazireh he settled in Harat al-Akrad, in Damascus, and stayed for eighteen years. Then he moved back to Jazireh to be able to encourage Kurds to be aware of their national identity. ... The Syrian authorities did not approve of my father's activities; he was arrested and subjected to great humiliation.

I have six daughters and one son. We all speak Kurdish at home, but in school all my children learn Arabic. Some of my children speak it so well that no one would guess that they are Kurds. But it is forbidden to learn Kurdish in schools. Teaching Kurdish is carried out by political parties and involves only adults. We are not members of any party. But my son can read Kurdish. He studied French literature at the University of Aleppo. So he can read Kurdish because it is written in Latin and he can write it. My father-in-law advises us not to be affiliated with any party Kurdish or Arabic. He believes that parties will destroy the unity of the Kurdish nation. There are now fourteen to fifteen Kurdish political parties in Syria.

(Um Luqman, Kafer Janneh, Syria, April 2006)

Official Syrian government discrimination against the Kurds did not emerge until the late 1950s, and was partially in response to the instability and uncertainty faced by its neighbouring governments in Turkey and Iraq with regard to their own Kurdish populations. Paranoia took hold, perhaps fuelled by the growing Kurdish separatist movement in Iraq as well as the discovery of oil in 1956 and 1959 in the Kurdish heartland of Syria. Tensions were heightened between 1958 and 1961, when Syria joined Egypt to form the United Arab Republic. Kurds were accused of undermining the Nasserite pan-Arabism, and a number of leaders of the Syrian Kurdistan Democratic Party (KDP) were arrested on the orders of President Nasser (Nazdar 1993). Furthermore, the large representation of Kurdish intellectuals in the Communist Party of Syria (CPS), which was led by a Kurd, Khalid Bakdash, did little to assuage the concerns of the Syrian government. The year after the end of the United Arab Republic Syria turned inward, and took a decided look at its northernmost province, where so many Kurds lived. Its concerns focused on the growing Kurdish 'foreign' elements in the region, and led to the commissioning of a study of its population. Official numbers between 1954 and 1961 indicated a 25–30 per cent increase in the population of Hasake over a seven-year period. This province, once a lawless area controlled by Kurdish and Bedouin tribes, became, after French Mandate pacification, a fertile agricultural region with great potential as the next 'breadbasket' of the country. The Syrian government was understandably concerned by its rapid population growth. Indeed, as one British diplomat put it: 'It seems doubtful if the Damascus government could easily control the area if Kurdish dissidence from within Syria's borders should disturb the uneasy tranquility'.[11]

In August 1962 the government promulgated a special decree (no. 93) authorizing an exceptional population census in the governorate of Hasake. The stated purpose was to establish who had entered the country illegally from Turkey over the previous few decades. All non-Arab inhabitants had to prove, by documentation, that they had been resident in Syria prior to 1945. As a result of that census some 120,000 Kurds were stripped of their citizenship. The official justification for the enactment of this measure was that these were 'alien infiltrators' from Turkey who had recently crossed 'illegally' into Syria and hence had no entitlement to citizenship. Many of these now stateless (*bidoon*) people had actually fled into Syria from Turkey in the 1920s and 1930s and had bona fide citizenship papers granted during the French Mandate. The local designation for these people stripped of their citizenship papers was *ajanib* (non-citizen foreigners) on their new, red identity cards.

They could now no longer vote, own property, or hold government jobs. But the men were still expected to do military service. Those who failed to take part in the 1962 census or who were born from marriages between the *ajanib* and Syrian citizens were in a worse situation, as they could not even be registered. These unregistered persons or *maktoumeen* (those who are muted) do not exist in official records and face even greater discrimination and hardship than the *ajanib*. Sources estimate that there are currently 200,000 *ajanib* and *maktoumeen* in Syria. Others put the figure higher, with 200,000 *ajanib* and 100,000 *maktoumeen* (Montgomery 2005: 80). These stateless Kurds not only cannot vote, as is the case for Palestinian refugees, but they are not allowed passports and have no travel documents. Thus they cannot leave the country. Their entitlement to education and health care is discretionary; the local village or urban neighbourhood *mukhtar* (mayor) has the power to grant or deny such access. As individuals without a standard Syrian identity card, they have difficulty travelling internally on public transport, and cannot even stay in hotels.

We are quite comfortable. Our children all went to school; we have made a lot of Arab friends. I am proud of my Kurdish nationality, but this has not interfered with my respectful relations with the Arab community in which I live. I do wish to see my people liberated from any kind of colonialism. I would like to feel free to do what I feel like doing without fear of being questioned. For example, I would like to feel free to speak my language and hang the Barzani picture on the wall of my home. Also I would like to see all Kurds have identity cards. ... The husband of my daughter doesn't have one and their children are not registered. He [Um Luqman's son-in-law] was born here. The identity cards held by the Kurds were taken away from them in the census of 1962. They were withdrawn from them in order to deny the existence of Kurds in Syria. For example, I have six sisters. They all have identity cards but their husbands don't. My son-in-law doesn't have one although he was born here and his parents came about the same time as mine. Some cards have been restored. It is completely up to the mukhtars *of the village to determine who would have his identity card restored. The* mukhtars—*some are Arab and some are Kurds—are like feudal lords. ... The husbands of my six sisters have the red identity cards. They are a kind of refugee. They have no right to own property, to travel outside of Syria or to hold a government job.*

(Um Luqman, Kafer Janneh, Syria, April 2006)

In the fifty years since such discrimination became widespread in Syria, there has been limited organized Kurdish political agitation to address this inequitable and discriminatory policy (Allsopp 2015). Part of the reason may be the disunity among Kurds in Syria, where traditional ties of loyalty to family and tribe are paramount and where political parties have been cautious and have preferred to curry favour with rather than antagonize the government. A considerable number of Kurds in Syria have fought in Kurdish uprisings in Iraq and Turkey, as well as in the Syrian uprising, defending their populations from the depredations of the Islamic State group (IS). Furthermore, a substantial number of Syria's Kurds see themselves as part of a multi-ethnic Syrian nation. Many live in and work in the major Syrian cities, serve in the Syrian army, and feel an attachment to the wider Syrian community. Amongst the most celebrated contemporary Kurds in Syria are Ahmad Kuftaro, the Mufti of Syria between 1964 and 2004, and Khalid Bakdash, the last leader of the Communist Party of Syria. Other Kurdish religious leaders are authorized by the state to follow public careers, such as Shaykh Muhammad Said Ramadan al-Bouti, who has a popular religious TV programme and publishes books in Kurdish (Pinto 2007: 265). Thus, any Kurdish campaign for restoring the citizenship of stateless Kurds in Syria (many of whom are probably recent migrants with strong links to family in Turkish or Iraqi Kurdistan) needs to be negotiated in such a way as not to undermine either their own sense of Kurdishness in the Syrian 'Arab' Republic or the Syrian state's support for Turkish and Iraqi Kurds. Although in 2012 the Syrian government offered to return citizenship to those Kurds who lost their right to carry papers in the 1960s, not all have taken up the offer.

> *I was born in Qamishli in 1969. My father was born in Turkey, but it was my grandfather who brought him here when he was five or six years old. My grandfather had to leave Turkey on a personal matter, escaping a revenge crime. He chose to go to Qamishli because it was close to the border and there was a Kurdish community already there. He was the first member of the family to come. That was in the 1950s. He settled in a mixed Kurdish and Arab village where the community gave him mattresses and such things to get started. He had three sons with him and they all stayed here and got married. My father worked on the farm. I went to school until Grade 9. I could have taken the official Grade 9 certificate but I felt it was useless. There is no chance for the 'bidoon' to get a government job. We don't have Syrian identification cards. My little boy who is doing very well at school has started to consider leaving school because he knows that he will not be able to get a job. He will not be able to travel outside Syria. The red identifica-*

tion card we have states bluntly: 'Not valid for obtaining travel documents for travelling outside the country'.

I was born here in 1969. My family was in Syria when the census was conducted. But the census was not done properly. My grandfather's uncle and his family, for example, who came to Syria later than my grandfather, were granted Syrian citizenship and Syrian identification cards, but we were not. This was because documentation of who lived here and how long they had been here was based on the mukhtar's whims and interests rather than on actual facts. When asked, as the local official in charge of the village, about a person, it was his personal connection to that person that determined his ability to gain citizenship. If he said that a certain person had been in the country long enough to be eligible for citizenship, that person would then be considered as such. If not, he wouldn't. The mukhtars cheat and the data they provide is not fact-based. Because my birth was actually registered in 1969, I got my red identification card. But my children are not registered and cannot get even a red card. This is because their mother is a Syrian citizen and holds a Syrian identification card. In such cases, marriage between a Syrian and an ajanib [red card holder], the marriages may not be registered and neither are the children. They say this year there may be a new law allowing registration of marriage between a Syrian and an ajanib. This will in turn make it possible to register the children.

(Abu Alaa, Damascus, April, 2006)

In the wake of the 2003 Anglo-American invasion of Iraq and the Iraqi Kurdish political gains in the territory adjacent to the Syrian Jazireh, Kurds in Syria—citizens, and *ajanib* and *maktoumeen*—have become restive. In 2004 Kurdish riots erupted throughout the country. This outbreak of ethnic violence was the worst the country had seen in several decades. Some sources recognized that although the disturbances were fuelled by popular frustration in the Kurdish community, the riots 'were not an entirely spontaneous eruption, but a politically timed initiative to pressure the Assad regime in the face of heightened Syrian–US tensions and Iraqi Kurdish political gains' (Gambill 2004; also see Lowe 2006; Montgomery 2005).

It is clear that the Syrian Kurdish community began to experience a political re-awakening after the Syrian government, pressured by Turkey, agreed to end its support for Abdullah Öcalan's Kurdistan Workers' Party, the PKK.[12] In 1998 Turkey massed 10,000 troops on Syria's northern border, and demanded that the PKK be expelled and Öcalan be handed over. Syria and Lebanon had been the home base of the PKK since at least the 1980s. Within a very short time after the

PKK's formal withdrawal, Kurdish activists in Syria began to be more open in their criticism of the regime's policy regarding Kurdish assimilationist aspirations. After the death of the Syrian president, Hafez al-Asad, in June 2000, Kurdish activists felt particularly emboldened, as did many other civil rights advocates. It was the time of the 'Syrian Spring' when a liberal ambiance, fuelled by the American push for 'democracy and human rights', pervaded the country. Political organizations met publicly and shops began to openly distribute Kurdish books and music. Private Kurdish language classes proliferated. In 2002 Bashar al-Asad, the new president, visited the predominantly Kurdish province of Hasake. This was the first time a Syrian president had done so in more than forty years. In December that year a new, younger generation of Kurds and their sympathizers emerged as the Yekiti (Unity) Party, a pro-KDP group, and staged a sit-in demonstration outside the parliament building. They delivered a statement calling on the Syrian regime to 'remove the barriers imposed on the Kurdish language and culture and recognise the existence of the Kurdish nationality within the unity of the country' (Gorgas 2007).[13] Slogans such as 'Citizenship for Kurds' and 'End the Ban on the Kurdish Language and Culture' were prominently on display and were captured on Syrian television. Security forces broke up this gathering and arrested a number of the activists. However, Kurdish books, newspapers, and music tapes and CDs continued to circulate freely. The Kurds and other social groups, striving for greater civil liberties, continued their agitation for several months. At times this was permitted, while at others the activists were arrested. The Asad government seemed to play with this new generation of Syrian Kurds.

On 12 March 2004, in Qamishli, fans of a visiting Arab soccer team arrived at a stadium and began shouting ethnic slurs and chanting pro-Saddam Hussein slogans. When fans of the Kurdish team responded with chants praising President Bush, the two sides began to scuffle. Security forces opened fire on the Kurdish crowd, killing six people and setting off a mass panic. This sparked a riot by Kurdish residents of the city. The unrest quickly spread to nearby towns, where protesters torched the offices of the Ba'ath Party and vandalized photos of the Syrian president and his late father. In the days that followed, the violence spread to Ain al-Arab, Aleppo, and Afrin in the Kurd-Dagh region. Protests also reached the Kurdish neighbourhoods of Damascus. In an eight-day period 40 people were killed and 400 injured, and over 2,000 Kurds were arrested.[14]

The outbreaks of violence among Kurdish communities in 2004, and the typically heavy-handed response from the Syrian security forces, shook many Kurds as well as the regime. For nearly fifty years, Kurds in Syria, both newly arrived and long settled, had accepted the intransigence of government with regard to their community aspirations. The Syrian government's support for the three separatist movements—the KDP, KUP, and lastly the PKK, which was provided with a home base as well as refuge—meant that Syrian Kurds, in their 'gratitude' for Syrian support for their struggle against Turkey, were largely inhibited from further agitation for cultural and linguistic rights in Syria. Yet all the while, many Kurdish youth organizations ran informal courses teaching the Kurdish language as well as literature (Pinto 2007: 261). However, once the PKK had been closed down in Syria, and furthermore, after a Kurdish Regional Authority had been established in Iraqi Kurdistan, many Syrian Kurds, particularly the youth, began an active, and at times violent, agitation for the rights of all Kurds in Syria to be recognized as citizens. This was at the same time that the Syrian government, concerned by the Anglo-American occupation of Iraq and disconcerted by the 'separatist' presence of the Kurdish Regional Authority in the north of Iraq, began to view its own Kurds with suspicion as possible enemy collaborators should there be an American-led attack on Syria (Gunter 2014). Given such political positioning, it is not surprising that Kurdish youth in Syria have taken a militant and uncharacteristically violent stance in the Syrian armed conflict, and that many have set their minds on the creation of a semi-autonomous Kurdish region in northern Syria, Rojava.

Alongside their ongoing participation in the Syrian armed conflict, Kurds have managed to maintain and keep alive their language and culture, their poetry and prose, music and dance songs, through family efforts as well as community projects and associations. Their interests in Syria are not so much separatist (unless the aspirations of those who support Rojava is for more semi-autonomy within the state), but rather to advance their own political, cultural, and social agenda to formalize their integration in the country by having the citizenship claims of all

141

who entered the country prior to 1945 recognized. They are also seeking a reasonable process for acquiring citizenship for those who have entered the country more recently. Citizenship, as well as the right to formally and publicly maintain their own language and cultural traditions through private education if not state schools, is a key priority for most Kurds, and is especially promoted by the more militant Kurdish organizations. Not having to constantly adjust to the shifting Syrian political landscapes, which at times aggressively outlawed Kurdish language and culture and at other times tolerated it, is now being demanded as a basic civil and human right. The unpredictable but regular closing down of Kurdish bookshops in Damascus and Aleppo between the 1950s and 1970s, and the concurrent destruction of their publicly sold music cassettes and records, need not be part of the future of Kurds in Syria (Pinto 2007: 262). What the future will hold is unclear, but one thing is certain: Kurdish aspirations for full citizenship, and recognition of their unique language and cultural expression, will never again be in question.

I work in the construction business here in Damascus and live in a village where I rent a house from an Arab acquaintance. My sisters live with me and we all speak Kurdish at home but we don't know how to write it. It was forbidden to teach Kurdish in schools. Recently, I heard, that Kurdish schools have been allowed in Turkey and Iraq. For me (and for my father), citizenship is vital for the future of our children. Even if they finish their studies as lawyers or doctors they cannot get government work. The red identification card, which I can get for them after the registration of my marriage, will [still] not allow them to work or to travel or to own property. I am doing all I can to encourage my son to finish his studies. I even promised him to smuggle him out of Syria, if necessary, when he gets his baccalaureate. If I had two wishes, I would ask for Syrian citizenship and the teaching of Kurdish language in the schools. It is not much to ask to learn to speak, read and write one's own national language.

(Abu Alaa, Damascus, April 2006)

Like the efforts to promote multi-ethnic nationhood in the last decades of the Ottoman Empire, the Kurds in Syria are struggling for recognition as Syrians and as Kurds in a state which was once unofficially multi-ethnic but formally aspired to pan-Arabism. As before, the future depends not only on how the current armed conflict is played out internally, but on the regional and international scene as well. After decades of either subduing or ignoring Kurds in Syria while at the same time supporting Kurds in Turkey and in Iraq, the Syrian regime now relies on its Syrian Kurdish fighters to defend Syria's north-eastern borders from the depredations and provocations of IS. At the same time, it is maintaining a pragmatic realism as to how to prevent rewarding such action with acquiescence to future Kurdish territorial demands. Whatever the outcome, the Kurds in Syria have found a voice and strength from these international uncertainties. They are not imagining a homeland, they are living it. Their homeland is in the places where their communities live, in their strong kinship ties and patronage networks, in their language and culture. For many, the Kurdish homeland is in part of Syria, and Syria is part of Kurdistan. The pivotal issue for most of my informants was the desire to be recognized as 'Syrian' but with the right to speak their Kurdish language in public, to teach it to their children and to listen to it on TV as well as to promote and play Kurdish music. It is a rejection of the periodic Syrian assimilationist policies while at the same time a common calling for the basic human and cultural rights of all Kurds in whichever state they choose to live.

5

PALESTINIANS RETURN TO THEIR 'MOTHERLAND'

I was a passenger in a car that was being driven by another summer school partici-
pant to Edinburgh for a weekend break from our very busy Oxford schedule. As we
drove along the large freeways of the country, I saw a sign that said 'Welcome to
Scotland'. I blinked. How is that possible? I asked myself. I am crossing a national
border and no one is stopping me to look at my travel documents. This is the first time
in my life I am not interrogated at a national border, and my Palestinian identity not
causing me anxiety and distress in the frontier or border zones between states.

(Adnan, Oxford, 2001)

I first met Adnan during the last phase of his engagement with both
Palestinian activists and researchers. It was 1999 and I was in Damascus
seeking permission to conduct a study of Palestinian refugee youth in
Syria. I had been to the University of Damascus and requested a meeting at the Faulty of Arts graduate studies programme to try to find a
collaborative partner. There, I had been met by the dean and the full
academic staff. None were willing to take part in the study and all were
sceptical that I would be able to get permission to conduct such a study
in Syria. In confidence, one of the academic staff members—a
Palestinian—told me it would be nearly impossible to get permission
to do research in Syria unless I could persuade the Syrian Women's
Union to cooperate. I dutifully approached them and was directed to
their sister organization, the Palestinian Women's Union. A meeting
was set with Samira Jabril, its president. On arriving at its premises in

the informal refugee camp of Yarmouk in Damascus, I was ushered into her office and found there, already waiting, Dr Adnan Abdul-Rahim. Approaching sixty years of age, with a full head of silver-grey hair, he had the look of an absent-minded professor about him, but his eyes were alert and his voice cultured and measured. I explained the purpose of my study, and Adnan immediately agreed to take part. Under Samira Jabril's guidance, research permission was simply assumed. The Syrian authorities were not going to interfere with our work as long as it remained focused on Palestinian refugees and was championed by a Palestinian organization in Syria.

Adnan's life (1942–2013) epitomized the special relationship Syrians and the Syrian government have had with Palestinian refugees, from the first few years of their dispossession from Palestine up until the seizure of the Palestinian Yarmouk quarter of Damascus in 2015 several years into the armed uprising in Syria. His life course as a refugee child, a United Nations Relief and Works Agency (UNRWA) teacher, a Palestine Liberation Organization emissary, and finally a respected academic and development aid practitioner, was only realistically possible in Syria, where treatment of Palestinian refugees had once been considered the best within the Arab world. As a child of six, he fled on foot from his home town of Safad in his summer school uniform of shorts and shirt, holding the hand of his older sister. Such an image of a young refugee child running is one that is burned on the minds of many: the vulnerable and doubly powerless child and refugee swept up by the catastrophe of armed conflict. Adnan's life then followed a fairly common path: Red Cross tents in Lebanon, train journeys across into Syria, numerous rented apartments in Homs, and finally, the extended family pooling its resources and settling permanently by jointly buying an apartment in the Baramki quarter of Damascus. Then education in UNRWA schools, until he was able to enter a prestigious government high school in Damascus. There, from graduation, his life followed the trajectory of the Palestinian refugee 'elite'. He interacted with UNRWA and became a teacher in its schools; he was present at the birth of the Palestine Liberation Organization (PLO) and became politically engaged with it, and later with the resistance movement. Through a PLO fellowship he spent four years in Hungary gaining a Ph.D. in sociology. When he recognized that the Oslo Accords were going to unravel, he commenced an active engagement with international researchers, putting the sociology of Palestinian refugees in Syria on the academic map. At his untimely death in 2013 his three sons had dispersed further from Palestine. His youngest had been shot by a sniper the year before; his middle son had emigrated to Sweden to join his Swedish partner; and his eldest son was unable to take up a scholarship opportunity abroad in 2014 until he completed his two-year military service in the Syrian army. Adnan had long recognized that Syria was his home, if not his 'homeland', and that his sons' futures would become as precarious as his had been.

How did this tragedy of Palestinian displacement and statelessness come about? And how was it that Palestinians in Syria were granted nearly all the rights of citizenship, unlike the situation of Palestinians in the other states where the United Nations operated a special agency for Palestinian refugees? We know that within a few short months in the spring of 1948, more than three-quarters of a million people in Palestine were forced from their homes, and in many cases pushed over borders into neighbouring states. It was an exercise in ethnic cleansing which had begun nearly a half century earlier and which was now culminating in the *Nakba* (the Catastrophe), as Palestinians called this dramatic upheaval (Pappé 2006). The same period of time in the same physical space was described by others as the War of Independence and the birth of the state of Israel. This 1947–8 war was a struggle which came to a climax as armed Jewish militias occupied most of Palestine and forced the indigenous people to flee. More than 750,000 Palestinian people were evicted from their homes and places of work and took refuge in camps hastily set up by the Red Cross and other humanitarian agencies in the West Bank, Gaza, Lebanon, Syria, Jordan, and Egypt.

Unusually, instead of bringing this humanitarian emergency under the mandate of the existing United Nations International Refugee Organization (IRO), which held the dual mandate for protection and humanitarian relief, a special agency was set up the following year in December 1949, the United Nations Relief and Works Agency (UNRWA), to manage Palestinian refugee camps and provide health, education, and humanitarian aid. Prior to that, the legal and political protection of these refugees was assigned to a special United Nations commission, the United Nations Conciliation Commission for Palestine

(UNCCP), set up by General Assembly Resolution 194 (III) in December 1948. The UNCCP was composed of representatives of the United States, France, and Turkey. Its goal was to provide protection and facilitate durable solutions, including return, for persons displaced as a result of the 1947–8 war. The UNCCP was charged to intervene with Israeli authorities to arrange the return of certain categories of refugees based on humanitarian considerations, including family reunification, property safeguarding, the abrogation of discriminatory Israeli property laws, and facilitation of Palestinians to access blocked savings accounts in banks inside Israel. In 1952, after four years of effort, the UNCCP reached the conclusion that it was unable to fulfil its mandate due to the lack of international political will to ensure the right of Palestinian refugees wishing to go back to their homes and villages.

The largest number of Palestinian refugees today is found in Jordan, with over 2.1 million registered with UNRWA. Syria acknowledges somewhere in the region of 560,000, and in Lebanon figures of about 460,000 are registered with UNRWA. In the West Bank more than 37 per cent of the population—792,000 Palestinians—is made up of refugees, and in Gaza 1,300,000 Palestinian refugees make up 75 per cent of the total population. In total more than 5 million Palestinians remain stateless and refugees in the Levant (UNRWA 2017).

The Palestinian refugee problem remains poorly and often only partially understood despite its dramatic scale and longevity. In order to understand why this situation has remained marginalized and unresolved for more than half a century, one must come to terms with the way recent Palestinian history is intertwined with the emergence of Zionism in the late nineteenth century and the final decades of the Ottoman Empire. This history requires a brief focus on the migrations, forced and otherwise, at the end of the nineteenth century and early decades of the twentieth, as the empire was finally dismembered at the close of the First World War, and the League of Nations awarded various European states guardianship, or Mandated authority, over the former southern Arab territory of the empire.

Who Are the People of Palestine?

For some, the Palestinian people are regarded as the direct descendants of the biblical Philistines, Canaanites, and Hebrews. It is generally accepted that the Ottoman conquest of Syria in the early sixteenth century brought security and stability to the region after a period of several centuries of disorder during Mamluk rule. Palestine was part of the southern Syrian provinces of the Ottoman Empire. The first hundred years of Ottoman control generally opened Palestine up to interregional trade, stimulating economic and population growth (Hütteroth and Abdelfattah 1977; Lewis 1954). However, as that century drew to a close, the region began to suffer a decline. In 1583 the governor of Ajlun reported that the province, 'once inhabited and cultivated has at the present day become desolate and ruined' as a result of the growing strength and depredations of Arab nomadic pastoral tribes (Johns 1994: 25). Encouraged by the lack of central Ottoman authority or presence in the area, these Bedouin tribes moved into agricultural areas and demanded protection money (tribute or *khuwa*) from the settled farmers. Some gave in to these demands, but others packed up their own movable property and left for nearby towns and cities. Others took up a form of semi-nomadic pastoralism combined with agriculture, which allowed them to keep themselves from abject poverty by avoiding the tax-farmers while paying what protection money was required to Bedouin tribes (also see Lancaster and Lancaster 1995).

By the mid-seventeenth century, Jerusalem and Hebron were said to lie on the 'frontier of Arabia, where rebellious Bedouins disturb the peace' (Johns 1994: 26). For the next two centuries, Ottoman authority in the southern Syrian provinces declined, villagers were abandoning their settlements, and tax collection was both more difficult and more oppressive. The absence of permanent Ottoman authority in the region did not necessarily leave a vacuum behind, but rather a succession of local urban tribal elites grew up and operated in a manner resembling the pre-Crusader Syrian city-states (Johns 1994: 28). Whether due to Bedouin tribal rivalries, or local contestation among urban notables and elites, it is clear that the region suffered a general downturn in agriculture over these centuries, which was not reversed until some time in the middle of the nineteenth century.

Up until the middle of the nineteenth century, Ottoman authorities in Constantinople (Istanbul) regarded the southern Syrian provinces— largely the region known as Palestine—as very much a frontier zone;

it extended from the Hauran to the Hijaz, and was crossed once a year by the Pilgrimage caravan to Mecca. It was perceived as a zone of trouble, with power struggles between the Bedouin tribes and the sedentary communities. It was also a region in which—as with Anatolia in general—the population was either stagnating or decreasing and tax income to the coffers of the sultan was limited (Karpat 1974). Over the next few decades the Ottoman authorities sought quick solutions as well as significant political and economic transformation in the region so as to reverse the decline in tax income and be able to invest substantially in its development (Rogan and Tell 1994). The first Ottoman district governor was posted to the region in 1851, and established a strong military presence and an effective single-source tax collection to replace what was, in effect, double taxation by both the Bedouin and government tax collectors. Eventually the Ottomans established administrative and military units at a number of points: al-Salt, Karak, and finally at Ma'an. Once these security measures were in effect, the government turned its attention to resettling the areas radiating out from these urban centres and posts. With effective resettlement, the state could expect that proceeds from taxes on agricultural produce would render the district self-supporting and certainly go some way to covering the costs of mounting the annual Pilgrimage to Mecca (see Barbir 1980: 122–5).

The first wave of settlers consisted of local Palestinian farmers encouraged to move out from older settlements to establish new villages. The next wave—lasting for most of the last quarter of the nineteenth century (from about 1878 to 1906)—was largely of Muslim refugees from the European Ottoman lands lost to Russia. These were Circassian, Chechnyan, and also Turkmen refugees, generally grateful to the Ottoman state for providing them with new lands upon which to rebuild their shattered lives. They became loyal subjects of the sultan, driven to succeed in agriculture and ready to defend themselves against any Bedouin claims to the land on which they had built their villages.

During the period of economic stagnation in the first half of the nineteenth century, particularly in the agricultural sector, the Ottoman government sought advice from a number of international agricultural experts. These specialists encouraged the Ottoman state to find and train adequate manpower to cultivate land. The mid-century was an important psychological turning point in Ottoman relations with Europe. This was manifested in the 1856 Treaty of Paris which drew the Ottoman Empire into the Comity of European Nations, recognizing it as an equal to the European states, despite its different religion and its numerous wars in the past (Karpat 1974: 59).[1] The empire now looked to Europe to rejuvenate its agricultural backwater. Bringing in Palestinians to farm the lowlands and encouraging Circassian and Chechnyan forced migrants from the Balkans and the Caucuses to take up farming was important for the revival of Ottoman fortunes in the southern Syrian provinces.

As described in chapter 1, the following year (1857) the Ottoman government issued a decree on immigration and settlement which declared that immigration into the Ottoman state was open to anyone who would agree to give his full allegiance to the sultan, and to respect the country's laws. In addition, the decree stipulated that 'settlers will be protected against any infringement of the religion they profess and will enjoy religious freedoms like all other classes of the Empire'. It promised to give settlers the best arable land it had at its disposal free of charge, and to exempt them from taxes and military services for a period of six to twelve years depending upon where they decided to settle—in the Balkans or in Asian lands (Karpat 1974: 60).

The decree was translated and published in a number of European journals, and Ottoman embassies and consulates in Europe were swamped with inquiries. Of the more colourful requests was one from the Comte d'Haussonville, president of the Committee for the Protection of Alsace-Lorrainers, inquiring about land to establish French colonies in the Ottoman Empire similar to the German colonies founded in Jaffa and Haifa. The British consul in Cyprus proposed settling 300 Irish families on the island. And a group of 2,000 families of German origin living in Bessarabia informed the Ottoman consulate in Odessa that they too wished to settle in Turkey (Karpat 1974: 61).

Although this decree of 1857 did not immediately create interest among the Jews of Europe, several important personalities as well as the British government were interested. In 1846 Isaac Altarass, a French merchant, and Moses Montefiore, a British financier, had both discussed the settlement of Jews from Russia in Palestine. In 1847 the British consul in Jerusalem put forward a plan to transfer British consular protection to those Russian Jews in Palestine who had outstayed their 'one year Russian sponsorship/permit'. As the persecution of Jews in Russia notched up in intensity, small groups of Jews began to flee, some into Moldavia and Wallachia, which were still part of the Ottoman Empire until 1878, and others came directly into Anatolia and the Syrian provinces of the empire. The Sublime Porte welcomed individuals and small groups of Jewish settlers, but larger groups specifically requesting the right to settle in Palestine were often turned down. The Ottoman authorities were concerned to maintain the multi-ethnic and multinational basis of their state and thus insisted on wide dispersal of the refugees and migrants, both Muslims and Jews. But Jewish interests were very much focused on Palestine. Karpat cites one of many letters he found in the Ottoman archives, from Rabbi Joseph Natonek of Budapest, dated 21 October 1876 and addressed to Sultan Abdul Hamid.[2] Natonek requests permission to settle Jews in Palestine, arguing that such settlement would rejuvenate the area. The Ottoman government replied to Natonek by stating that almost all lands in Palestine were now occupied and that the 'autonomy' he proposed for the Jews was not compatible with the state's administrative principles.

The Ottoman position was clear. Individuals of any religion or nationality could immigrate, but there were restrictions on mass settlement—that is, the state would not permit one ethnic or religious group to establish its numerical superiority in any one specific area. The ideal of a multi-ethnic and multi-national state remained supreme in Constantinople.[3] Several decrees were issued to this effect in 1884, 1887, and 1888. However, proposals for mass settlement of Jews from Europe and Russia continued to flow in.[4]

By the 1890s Jewish requests for permission to immigrate to Palestine in the southern Syrian provinces had turned into facts on the ground. Large groups of Russian Jews began arriving at Ottoman ports without passports or visas. One group of sixty-five Russian Jews who were issued with visas at Odessa and travelled directly to Palestine created a stir in Constantinople. In 1891 the Ottoman Foreign Ministry issued a rebuke to its consulate in Odessa and sent a circular to its representatives in St Petersburg and Athens reminding them that individual immigration was permissible but not mass immigration. Despite these restrictions and regulations some groups found ways around them, as some Jews from Georgia and Bokhara in Central Asia found their way to Batum on the Black Sea and from there on to Palestine. Many of these immigrants settled in Jerusalem, transforming the ethnic character of the city by the end of the nineteenth century.[5]

In 1868 the Jewish (Oriental and European settler) population of Palestine was between 12,000 and 15,000. In 1882 the number had nearly doubled to 23,000–27,000 and represented about 6 per cent of the total population. By 1900, after the period of intensive Jewish emigration from Russia (1881–1900), the total Jewish population of Palestine had reached about 60,000 out of a total population of 500,000.[6]

The End of Empires at the Beginning of the Twentieth Century

Palestine was an integral part of the Syrian provinces of the Ottoman Empire for over four centuries. Its fortunes, like those of the empire itself, waxed and waned as central political power and economic strength also rose and fell. Only towards the end of the nineteenth century was internal economic reform doomed, as Europe began to look enviously at the potential for trade and raw material which the Arab provinces of the empire could provide. As the empire began to crumble prior to the end of the First World War, European powers started to vie for control of the Arab provinces. By 1915 Great Britain was eager to secure Arab support in opening a southern front in its war against the Axis powers. Its losses at Gallipoli made Arab involvement on the side of the Allied powers seem critical to the successful waging of the war.

Between July 1915 and March 1916 Sir Henry McMahon began to correspond with the Sharif of Mecca. Their exchanges resulted in the McMahon–Hussein Accords whereby Great Britain agreed to recognize and support the independence of the Arabs, should they rise up and revolt against the Ottomans. Responding to British overtures, the Sharif of Mecca, Amir Hussein, issued a call to the Arab people to revolt against Ottoman rule and to fight on the side of France and Britain. Yet, however strong the aspirations of the Arab people may have been for single-state 'nationhood', France and Britain had other plans and were simultaneously engaged in secret negotiations with regard to these territories. A few months later, in May, Sir Mark Sykes, secretary to the British War Cabinet, revealed a contradictory agreement with France and Russia which would have the Arab lands of the Ottoman Empire divided up so that France would take the territories that would emerge as Syria and Lebanon, Britain would take control of what would become Iraq and Transjordan, while Palestine was to be placed under international administration with Russia agreeing to the management of Jerusalem (Tannous 1988: 62–3). The Bolshevik Revolution in 1917, however, undermined that agreement, when Russia withdrew from the war and divulged to the rest of the world the—until then secret—Sykes–Picot Agreement, outlining a Franco-British division of the Arab provinces into zones of British (Palestine and Mesopotamia/Iraq) and French (Syria and Lebanon) control.

The Emergence of European Zionism

Zionism emerged in the dying days of the nineteenth century as a modern political movement. It was also a movement which categorically turned away from earlier Jewish efforts at assimilation in Europe and Russia. In 1897 the World Zionist Organization was established in Basel in Switzerland, as the brainchild of Theodor Herzl, who became its first head. In his book *Der Judenstaat* (1896) he had proposed the establishment of a Jewish state in Palestine or Argentina, as a means of solving what was then known as the 'Jewish question': the lack of a state for Jewish people in an era of nation-states, and in the context of the growing persecution of Jews in Europe. After some internal debate, Palestine, through its close association with the Old Testament, became the focus of this colonial or pioneering effort. It was Herzl's argument to Western powers that such a Jewish state would be like a 'rampart of Europe against Asia, an outpost of civilisation as opposed to barbarism' (Herzl 1896, chapter 2).

Prior to the establishment of the World Zionist Organization, most Jewish immigration to Palestine had been unsystematic and largely financed by wealthy Jewish bankers and merchants such as the French banker Baron Edmund de Rothschild. Between 1882 and 1899 nineteen Jewish agricultural colonies had been founded, of which at least nine were financially supported by Baron Rothschild (Margalith 1957: 144). Once a better-organized and systematic operation of immigration had been establish by the Jewish Colonization Association (a spin-off of the World Zionist Organization) Lord Rothschild (Lionel Walter Rothschild, second Baron Rothschild, a leader of the Zionist movement in London) was able to persuade the British foreign secretary, James Balfour, and the British political establishment to support the establishment of a home for the Jewish people in Palestine.

In 1917—less than a year after the Sykes–Picot Agreement had been signed setting out the Anglo-French post-First World War division of spoils—the Balfour Declaration was revealed. On 2 November 1917 Balfour sent Lord Rothschild a letter pledging support for the establishment in Palestine of a 'national home for the Jewish people'.

Foreign Office
November 2, 1917

Dear Lord Rothschild,

I have much pleasure in conveying to you, on behalf of His Majesty's government, the following declaration of sympathy with Jewish Zionist aspirations which have been submitted to, and approved by, the Cabinet. 'His Majesty's Government view with favour the establishment in Palestine of a national home for the Jewish people, and will use their best endeavours to facilitate the achievement of this object, it being clearly understood that nothing shall be done which may prejudice the civil and religious rights of existing non-Jewish communities in Palestine, or the rights and political status enjoyed by Jews in any other country.' I should be grateful if you would bring this declaration to the knowledge of the Zionist Federation.

Yours sincerely,
Arthur James Balfour

With the close of the First World War the League of Nations was established. In its Covenant, signed by all parties in 1919, the Palestinian people were recognized as an independent nation placed 'provisionally' under British Mandate. However, in 1922 the League of Nations formally issued the British Mandate over Palestine and incorporated the Balfour Declaration in its articles, perhaps not recognizing the fundamental inconsistency that now existed in them. On the one hand the British Mandate required Great Britain to act as 'custodian' (in Article 22 of the Covenant) to the Palestinian people who were 'not yet able to stand by themselves' as an independent state. On the other hand, the incorporation of the Balfour Declaration into the League of Nations Mandate for Palestine (Articles 2, 4, 6, and 7) clearly contra-

dicted significant parts of the original Covenant. These articles allowed
Great Britain to consult with the Jewish Agency (a powerful, autonomous para-state structure representing the World Zionist Organization)
on matters pertaining to land, Jewish immigration to Palestine, and
settlement, without referring to or consulting with the indigenous
Palestinian people of the former southern Syrian provinces of the
Ottoman Empire who constituted over 90 per cent of the population
of that region. The outcome of the First World War was, in effect, a
betrayal and massive humiliation for the Arabs of Greater Syria. Instead
of attaining independence and being united as one Arab nation, the
population was unnaturally divided into five sections (Lebanon, Syria,
Iraq, Transjordan, and Palestine). The lines on the map were largely
drawn by Sir Mark Sykes, a great supporter of Zionism.

The Arab Response

In July 1919, fearing that the promises made by their ally, Great
Britain, were about to be reneged upon, Arab nationalists convened the
First General Syrian Congress in Damascus, with delegates from the
entire East representing Muslim, Christian, and Jewish communities,
and restated their fervent desire for unity and independent statehood.
These delegates demanded

> full and absolute political independence for Syria [including Palestine] and
> a rejection of its dismemberment, a desire for a constitutional monarch,
> disapproval of any tutelage of a mandatory power and rejection of the
> Balfour Declaration of the Zionists for the establishment of a Jewish com-
> monwealth in that part of southern Syria known as Palestine.

These demands were presented to the American King–Crane
Commission which had begun its inquiry just the month before.

Henry Churchill King and Charles R. Crane had been sent by the
American president, Woodrow Wilson, on what was intended to be an
inter-Allied fact-finding mission to determine whether the region was
ready for self-determination and what, if any, nation(s) the local peoples wished to see take on a mandatory role. However, France refused
to take part, and Great Britain withdrew its nominated representative,
both fearing that the outcome of this mission would undermine the
Sykes–Picot Agreement. In the end the mission was solely an American

initiative to reveal the circumstances and conditions in the Arab provinces of the former Ottoman Empire. It quickly became clear to this commission that a new Arab nation had come into being, one which had widespread popular support and which was based on a common history, language, territory, and culture. The desire of the people in this state for independence and unity was clear to the commission. It was also clear to King and Crane that the people of Palestine—that coastal region of south-western Syria—clearly identified themselves as part of this Syrian nation. They also saw that the majority of the people in this Arab state of 'Syria' were against the formation of a Jewish state. The only way to establish a viable Jewish state, they reported, would be with armed force.[7] They advised that Syria be recognized as one state and that the League of Nations Mandate be over the entire Syrian Arab region (contemporary Syria, Lebanon, Jordan, Israel, the West Bank, and Gaza). They also recommended that Amir Faysal be appointed the head of such a constitutional monarchy and that America be the Mandatory power for a specified period of time.

Needless to say, the recommendations of the King–Crane Commission, which were filed in August 1919, were rejected by both Great Britain and France, and in April 1920 at San Remo the Allies proclaimed the establishment of the French (Syria and Lebanon) and British (Iraq, Transjordan, and Palestine) Mandates, dividing up what was generally recognized as Greater Syria. As British and French troops entered each of the Mandated territories, they were met with riots, mass demonstrations, prolonged nationwide strikes, and armed insurrections.[8] Initially these demonstrations and struggles were of a pan-Arab character, with support for Palestine as part of the Syrian Arab nation. Even though this struggle in Palestine was originally part of the general Syrian Arab struggle for national liberation, it was not long before the weight of the British occupation and the intensity of the Zionist settler project began to isolate Palestine from the rest of Syria and the Arab world in general. In some ways, after 1920 Palestinian Arabs found themselves, for the first time in history, a distinct unit shut off from their Syrian brothers (Barbour 1969: 94). Muslim and Christian Palestinian leaders who had attended the first two meetings of the General Syrian Congress in Damascus of 1919 agreed to hold a third meeting in Haifa once the British Mandate had been imposed.

This, the Third Palestine Arab Congress of December 1920, was the first independent Palestinian political event. As a result of this congress, the first Palestinian organization, the Arab Executive, consisting of twenty-four Muslim and Christian leaders, was established. This traditional, largely feudal, organization was unable to separate out Zionism from British policy or to see that the two were, in fact, inextricably tied to each other (Zogby 1974). Over the next ten years the Palestinian Arab Congress issued renewed demands for the British to halt Jewish immigration and slow down or prohibit the transfer of property from Arabs to Jews. It also demanded the establishment of a democratic government in Palestine with proportional representation—the largest proportion naturally going to Arabs in accordance with their greater numbers (Waines 1971a: 226). The British high commissioner, however, was intent on 'equal representation'; that is, 50 per cent each between Arabs and Jews, a proposal which the Arab Executive consistently rejected. The Palestinian Arabs became increasingly paralysed by the growing political and economic chaos in the country. Finally, in August 1929, the Arab population rose up and attacked a number of Jewish settlements, killing many and burning their synagogues. The Arab Executive appealed to the masses to return to their homes and to assist in the restoration of order.

Over the next three decades the Jewish percentage of the population of Mandated Palestine was to alter dramatically. In 1918 the population of Palestine was estimated at 700,000 people, of whom 574,000 were Muslims, 70,000 Christians, and 56,000 Jews. The growing anti-Semitism in Europe in the 1930s was pushing ever-increasing numbers of Jews to immigrate to Palestine. In a three-year period between 1932 and 1935, for example, the Jewish population of Palestine doubled.[9] By 1944 the number of Jews in Palestine was as much as 400,000 out of a total population of 1,700,000. Between 1946 and 1948 this number had increased to 700,000, or about a third of the total population of about 2,115,000 (Farsoun and Zacharia 1997: 79).

This rapid influx of Jewish immigrants into Palestine caused considerable pressure on the Arab population as well as serious local economic dislocation. The large sums of Jewish capital flowing into the country brought about inflation, and at the same time higher pay scales for Jewish workers. In some trades the salaries for Jewish workers were 400 per cent higher than those for Arabs (Waines 1971a: 225). These problems were made worse by the rising rural–urban migration of peasants who were being forced off their lands.

Most of the land purchase in Palestine during this period was by the political agencies of the Zionist movement, such as the Jewish National Fund and the Jewish Colonization Association, and took the form of land acquisition from mostly absentee Arab landowners. The land, however, was inhabited mainly by Palestinian tenant farmers, and this constituted a problem for the Jewish Agency. Clearing the land for the newly arriving Jewish settlers became an important goal. Josef Weitz, for example, the director of the Jewish National Fund's Land Department, wrote in his diary on 20 December 1937:

> Among ourselves it must be clear there is no room for both peoples in this country. … And the only solution is the land of Israel, or at least the Western land of Israel (Palestine), without Arabs. There is no room for compromise on this point. (Quoted in Morris 1987: 27)

By 1941 30 per cent of all Arab families employed in agriculture had been uprooted in this way and were made landless. Many of these dispossessed peasants flocked to the cities to look for work (Kanafani 1972: 51–2).

The 1936–1939 Palestinian Rebellion

The long-simmering Palestinian resistance, marked initially by the 1929 uprising, finally erupted into a peasant-based national rebellion between 1936 and 1939. One of the first acts of the British forces was to cut communication lines between Palestine and the other Arab regions (Kalkas 1971: 244). By 1938 the British were so concerned with the extent of pan-Arab support for the Palestinians that 'Jewish labourers were employed by the Government at the cost of 100,000 pounds Sterling to build a barbed-wire fence around the northern and north-eastern frontier of Palestine. This fence was intended to separate the Arabs of Palestine from the Arabs of Lebanon and Syria' (Barbour 1969: 192).

Among the Palestinians realization dawned that British military institutions were cooperating with the paramilitary Jewish organizations such as the Haganah, the Irgun, and the Stern Gang by providing them with military training and arms. The Haganah had originally been created to protect the Jewish colonies and enclaves that were springing up in Palestine. In 1936 one British officer, Orde Wingate, who was later to have a notorious career in Burma, became 'enchanted by the Zionist dream. He decided actively to encourage the Jewish settlers and started teaching their troops more effective combat tactics and retaliation methods against the local population' (Pappé 2006: 16). Wingate succeeded in attaching the Haganah to the British forces during the Arab Revolt so that they could better learn what a 'punitive mission' should entail. For example, in June 1938 a Haganah unit and a British company jointly attacked a village on the border between Palestine and Lebanon and held it for a number of hours.[10]

During this same period, the Palestinian Arabs recognized that they were being prevented from arming themselves or developing self-defence mechanisms against Jewish attacks. Palestinian resistance to Jewish colonization of their country was being met by the British Mandatory Authority with total abolition of civil law for Palestinians but not Jews. Palestinians were subjected to emergency law and military courts, and the discharge of arms or carrying of weapons was punishable by death (Tannous 1988: 230).

During this period of military clampdown on Palestinian society, the Syrian Shaykh Izzedine al-Qassam came to Palestine to organize the Palestinian fight for independence against the British. On 2 November 1935, in the first organized operation led by him near Haifa, he was killed. His death sparked a protracted Palestinian rebellion, which was to last three years. Qassemite armed bands began their offensive against the British authorities and the Zionist colonists in April 1936. The Jews in Palestine rose in anger, and Tel Aviv was filled with violent anti-Arab demonstrators who demanded the formation of an all-Jewish army. This in turn outraged the Arab community, and the violence spread. Arab national committees were set up in nearly every city and village, and calls were made for a nationwide strike. In an effort to salvage their leadership, the Arab Executive merged with representatives of the local strike committees to form the Arab Higher Committee (AHC). This committee met in May 1936 and called on all Palestinian organizations to continue the national strike until the British allowed Palestinians to form a national government based on democratic representative governance.[11]

This Palestinian resistance to what they perceived as the colonization of their land was met with repression and the abolition of civil law by the British: mass arrests, forced opening of businesses closed by the strike, collective fines and confiscations against villages suspected of harbouring 'guerrillas', and widespread demolition of homes belonging to suspected Palestinian supporters. The British army of occupation was also increased to 20,000 men. But the Arab strike continued. Palestinians were then subjected to emergency laws that declared all Palestinian political organizations 'illegal'. At the same time, the British continued to arm and train Zionist Jewish settlers and paramilitary organizations (Tannous 1988: 238).

In a desperate effort to end this dangerous turmoil the British government sent a commission to Palestine to study the Arab grievances, report on the causes of the revolt, and make recommendations that might solve the problems. This was the Palestine Royal Commission headed by Lord Peel (known popularly as the Peel Commission). Peel arrived in Palestine in November 1936. After two months in Palestine, during which time the AHC refused to speak to him, he returned to Britain, and released his report in July 1937. The Arabs hoped that this long-awaited report would affirm their call for representative, democratic government and a halt to Jewish immigration. Instead, the Peel Commission reaffirmed the League of Nations British Mandate and 'national home for Jews' policy. The commission suggested that a solution to the violence would be the creation of a partitioned, racially divided state. The north of Palestine would basically go to the Jewish state. There would be an international corridor around Jerusalem, and the Arab state was to include the south and mid-east of Palestine.

This report was regarded as a deep betrayal by the Arabs, and the national strike and violence continued. The British responded initially by outlawing the AHC and the other national committees, and arresting, sentencing to death, or sending into exile the Arab leadership. However, the rural revolt continued to grow. By mid-1938 the rebels were in control of 80 per cent of the countryside as well as the older parts of Jerusalem, Nablus, and Hebron (Kalkas 1971: 247–8). At this point the British unleashed a massive campaign of repression. In addition to the 20,000-man occupation force already in place, they brought in squadrons of the Royal Air Force from Cyprus and Egypt and supplied hundreds of

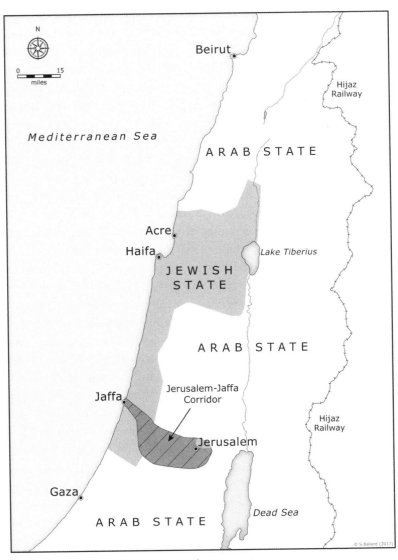

Map 8: Peel Commission

Jewish settlers with further arms, organizing them into 'night squads' to attack Arab villages. By 1939 the British Mandatory Authority was able to restore order, with 6,000 Jewish auxiliary police helping to suppress the last embers of the Arab revolt (Khalidi 2001: 26).

Following the 1936–9 rebellion, the British called for a conference of Arabs and Jews to discuss how to proceed in Palestine. The St James Conference or Round Table Conference of 1939 brought together Arab representatives from Palestine, Egypt, Iraq, Saudi Arabia, Transjordan, and Yemen. The MacDonald White Paper of 1939 which emerged at the end of the St James Conference set out key provisions which appeased the Arabs of Palestine but which severely compromised the British commitment to the Balfour Declaration of 1917. Its key provisions were:

1. It was not British policy that Palestine should become a Jewish state (contrary to the fundamental principle in the Balfour Declaration of establishing in Palestine a 'national home' for the Jewish People).
2. Neither was it British policy that Palestine should become an Arab state (contrary to the McMahon–Hussein Accords of 1915).
3. The establishment of an independent Palestine state in which Arabs and Jews share a government within ten years.
4. Jewish immigration to be limited to 75,000 over the following five years, so that the number of Jews in the country would not exceed one-third of the total population.
5. Transfers of land from Arabs to Jews to be severely restricted.

The Arab Higher Committee rejected the White Paper because it did not explicitly include a commitment to the independence of the Palestinian people. The Jews of Palestine were outraged at what was seen as British betrayal. In 1942 600 Jewish delegates met in New York to express their opposition to the White Paper. The delegates demanded the establishment of a Jewish army, their own flag, and unhindered immigration to Palestine. More importantly, the Jewish delegates called for a change of policy within the Jewish Agency and the Haganah. Zionist armed attacks were now to focus on British as well as Arab targets. The most infamous of these included, in November 1944, the assassination of Lord Moyne, the British minister of state in Cairo, by the Stern Gang led by Yitzhak Shamir, as well as, in 1946, the blowing up of the King David Hotel in Jerusalem by the Irgun, under the leadership of Menachem Begin. It was not long before the British came to perceive the conflict in Palestine as an economic and political burden, and, early in 1947, the British government declared the Mandate unworkable and announced the imminent withdrawal of its troops, handing the conflict back to the United Nations to find a solution.

The UN Partition Plan and the Declaration of the State of Israel

In 1947 the United Nations dispatched a commission of inquiry, the United Nations Special Committee on Palestine (UNSCOP), which proposed the partition of Palestine, and on 29 November 1947 the United Nations General Assembly, in Resolution 181, passed what was known as the UN Partition Plan. According to this the Jewish state was to comprise 56.4 per cent of the territory while the area allocated to the Palestinian Arab state was 42.8 per cent. Jerusalem was to become an international zone. At the time that the resolution was passed, Jews owned 7 per cent of the total land area in Palestine and constituted nearly one-third of the population. Palestinian Arabs owned the rest of the land and formed two-thirds of the population. Palestinians and other Arabs were outraged and rejected the UN resolution (Farsoun and Zacharia 1997: 111).

The day following the rejection of the UN Partition Plan, armed conflict spread throughout Palestine. The Palestinians entered the fighting with a deeply divided and ineffective leadership, exceedingly limited finances, no centrally organized military forces or administrative organs, and no reliable allies. The Jewish population, on the other hand, were politically unified, had centralized para-state institutions, and were exceedingly well led and well armed. The outcome of the 1947–8 war was a foregone conclusion. The Palestinians had larger numbers, but the Jews had more important advantages. As Khalidi succinctly summed up the situation, the Jews had a 'larger and more diversified economy, better finances, greater firepower, superior organisation, and considerable support from the United States and the Soviet Union' (Khalidi 2001: 30).

In March 1948 David Ben-Gurion, the de facto leader of the Jewish people in Palestine, put into effect Plan Dalet, with the aim of capturing, evacuating, and 'cleansing' Arab villages, neighbourhoods, and towns. In April 1948 one event in particular sent shockwaves through-out Palestine and the rest of the Arab world: the Irgun and Stern Gang massacre at Deir Yassin village. The exact number killed and women raped remains contested; but most sources give a figure between 120 and 300 deaths in a village of 600 people. Shortly thereafter, the Arab states formed the Arab League to consider intervention in Palestine with their regular armies (Farsoun and Zacharia 1997: 114). The Arab League agreed to intervene once the British Mandate had officially ended. A volunteer force was quickly put together with Syrian, Iraqi, and Lebanese individual volunteers and small military units. Most of these Arab states had only just achieved their independence from the French or British Mandate and were not prepared for international campaigns. Egypt was still in a semi-colonial relationship with Great Britain. Lebanon and Syria had only just been granted a grudging inde-pendence from France, in 1946 and 1943 respectively. By the time the small and irregular Arab armies decided to intervene, most of the major cities and towns in Palestine had already fallen to the Haganah and other Jewish militias. Among the Jewish fighting force, there were 52,000 men in the Haganah, 14,000 in the Jewish Settlement Police (which had been trained and armed by the British), and 27,000 Second World War veterans, as well as numerous paramilitary groups.

Only the Jordanians had a professional army, the Arab Legion, with a viable capacity to defend the Palestinians. And Jordan's King Abdullah was alleged to have given orders to his British-commanded Arab Legion to secure only the part of Palestine—the West Bank—allotted to him in secret talks with the Zionist leadership. Whatever the truth of the matter, one of the few triumphs in the Arab military history of 1948 was the Jordanians (with the help of an Iraqi contingent) success-fully repelling repeated Jewish attempts to occupy parts of the West Bank throughout the second half of the year (Pappé 2006: 43).

The Palestinians were defeated by the Jews in their struggle to keep their homeland and, on Friday 15 May 1948, Ben-Gurion declared the establishment of the state of Israel. Henceforth, 1948 marked two contrasting historical experiences. For the Zionists it was the culmina-tion of the dream of creating a Jewish state, as a means to defeat European anti-Semitism. For Palestinians it was the time of expulsion, exodus, and destruction of their land and society.

The Palestinian Exodus: Stateless, without Right of Return, and little Protection

> *I was born in Safad, Galilee in 1941. It was a town built on a hill. I remember that we lived near the Jewish quarter. My mother used to take us to the Jewish physicians because she trusted them. . . . One day there was a quarrel between an Arab and Jew about some clothes in a shop. The Jew was killed. Then instead of cooperation which used to distinguish the relations between the Jews and the Arabs in the town, everybody took care of themselves, they didn't mingle. Of course the war began outside Safad and in other villages. When these villages were controlled [by the Jews] we were protected by Jordanian troops and some Syrian volunteers. Then, one day the Jordanian troops pulled out without telling any of the inhabitants they were leaving. The local defenders were very poorly armed and realized they couldn't put off an attack. There was no defence. . . . So we left. . . . We went from one end of the country to the other. We didn't stay long there either. Maybe one night and then they took us to Homs where we started our life in Syria. . . . We thought we were going to go back to Safad in one week's time. We were promised, just get out of town until the Arabs regain it. When we left the fighting in Safad we thought that after one week we could come back. I remember I left in short trousers. We took no papers, not even our birth certificates. Nothing. Because we were promised that we were going back home soon.*

(Adnan, Damascus, October 2005)

By the middle of 1948 nearly three-quarters of a million Palestinians had fled their homes and villages in Palestine. The official Israeli historiography claimed that the Palestinian refugees fled due to enticement and encouragement by Arab governments. This claim was later refuted by Israeli historians who found no evidence to show that either the leaders of the Arab states or the Mufti (religious leader) ordered or encouraged the mass exodus of April 1948 (Morris 1992; Shafir 1999; Shlaim 1988). In June 1948 David Ben-Gurion put forward a plan for preventing the refugees' return to their homes. This plan was formalized and adopted by the Israeli Cabinet in the same month. Arab governments, on the other hand, refused to integrate Palestinian refugees in their host countries, maintaining that this would threaten their right of return. The Arab states wanted Palestinians to be repatriated and allowed to return to their homes in Palestine. Thus, they pressed for the formation of a separate specialized organization to meet the short-term and long-term economic relief of these Palestinian refugees.

PALESTINIANS RETURN TO THEIR 'MOTHERLAND'

On 16 September 1948 the UN Mediator in Palestine, Count Folke Bernadotte, submitted his recommendations to the UN General Assembly reaffirming Palestinians' right to return to their homes, to restitution, and to compensation. A day after this submission he was assassinated by the Stern Gang. Nevertheless, the widely quoted UN Resolution 194, based on his recommendations, was passed on 11 December 1948. Resolution 194 established the UN Conciliation Commission for Palestine (UNCCP). It was mandated to provide protection and facilitate durable solutions for those displaced. Its early activities included intervention with Israeli authorities to permit the return of certain categories of refugees, reunification of separated families, recommendations to safeguard the rights and properties of refugees, intervention to abrogate discriminatory property laws and facilitation of refugee access to blocked savings accounts and assets in banks inside Israel. One of the sub-organs of the UNCCP, the Economic Survey Mission, called for the establishment of both short- and long-term economic relief for the Palestinian refugees. This included the creation of a new mechanism, the UN Relief and Works Agency for Palestine refugees (UNRWA), which was duly established in December 1949 by UN General Assembly Resolution 302. Six months later, in May 1950, it took over the humanitarian relief operations in the Jordanian-controlled West Bank, the Egyptian-controlled Gaza Strip, Jordan, Syria, and Lebanon. The mandate for UNRWA was short. All relief and works operations were to be terminated by the middle of 1951, as it was expected that those refugees wishing to do so would soon be able to return to their homes in accordance with Resolution 194. Those not willing to do so were entitled to resettlement assistance. UNRWA's mandate has been extended on a regular basis year after year due to the lack of durable solutions for these refugees.

Palestinian refugees are a creation of the League of Nations and its successor, the United Nations. That is, their plight, their statelessness, and their liminality are the direct result of the misinterpretation of the Covenant of the League of Nations, the misadministration of the British Mandate, and the decision of the United Nations to partition their homeland and create two states. Unlike many other refugee situations, that of the Palestinians is characterized by numerous UN resolutions and recommendations relating to their case.

167

Palestinians in Diaspora

Upon their expulsion, Palestinian refugees sought shelter in neighbouring countries, primarily in the West Bank and Gaza (which had fallen under the control of Jordan and Egypt respectively), Lebanon, and Syria. The majority of Palestinians believed their expulsion would end in a matter of days—at most a few weeks. Most had not carried their belongings with them and many had left their doors open, while others took their keys. To this day, many hold on to the keys to their homes as a symbol of hope and resistance to exile. Others dream of returning to their villages and towns of origin. In the majority of cases these places of origin are less than 100 miles from where they now live, in refugee camps, middle-class urban neighbourhoods, and poor squatter settlements on the edges of Arab cities.

Most Palestinian refugees settled into particular sites in the adjoining countries in the 1950s and remain there to this day. As conflicts involving Palestinians in the Occupied Territories and in neighbouring countries flared up, more Palestinians arrived to swell refugee numbers in these states. The social and political conditions of Palestinians in the countries in the region differed in relation to rights to citizenship, their proportion within the entire population of the country, and their access to employment and housing.

Today they generally form a politically, socially, and economically disadvantaged group within the region and within the countries they live in, and many of them survive in conditions of poverty. With the exception of those living in Jordan, none of them had full rights to citizenship until 1995, when the Palestinians living in the Gaza Strip and the West Bank had the right to Palestinian passports issued by the Palestinian Authority.

In Syria, however, Palestinians have been treated with greater respect and sympathy than in some host countries, often being integrated into the social and political body of the state. Early in the 1950s the Syrian government issued a series of laws gradually paving the way for their integration into Syrian society while preserving their separate Palestinian identity.[12] In addition, Syria signed the Protocol for the Treatment of Palestinians in Arab States (Casablanca Protocol) in 1965, guaranteeing the following civil rights: they have rights to own land, commercial property, access free education and health care, and are not barred from any profession; they have the same rights as citizens, barring the right to vote or run for political office. These 'freedoms' amount to what is commonly called 'temporary protection' in international law. Hence the outbreak of violence in Syria after 2011 hit Palestinian refugees in Syria particularly hard, and their efforts to remain outside the conflict between state agents and opposition groups failed spectacularly in 2015 with the siege of Yarmouk, the largest settlement of Palestinians in Syria.

Palestinians in Syria

The majority of Palestinian refugees who came to Syria were poor, illiterate peasants. They left their villages and towns in the northern part of Palestine. Passing through Lebanon (due to the geography of the region), they were then transferred by the International Red Cross to Syria and distributed around the major Syrian cities. In 1948 these Palestinians numbered about 100,000, and were first given shelter in mosques, schools, former army barracks, and tents until the Syrian government offered parcels of land to UNRWA to establish refugee camps. The Palestinian refugees in Syria enjoyed similar civil rights to Syrian citizens from the earliest years in all things covered by the law, while preserving their original nationality (Brand 1988: 623; UNRWA 1992: 139). Today the Palestinian refugee community in Syria numbers just over 500,000. UNRWA statistics show that among refugees, children and young people up to fifteen years old represent nearly half of the population (46 per cent). Recent UNRWA reports show that 68 per cent of the Palestinian refugees in Syria were originally from Galilee and 22 per cent from Haifa and other coastal areas in British Mandated Palestine. Currently Palestinian refugees in Syria live in ten UNRWA refugee camps and three residential areas in major urban centres. The largest Palestinian settlement, known as Yarmouk camp, is located near Damascus and hosted one of the largest groups of Palestinian refugees prior to the siege of Yarmouk in 2015. Although exact figures are not available, UNRWA and UNHCR estimate that about 80,000 Palestinian refugees have fled the country while another 200,000 have been internally displaced within it. Palestinian refugees in

Syria hold a particular attachment to the country based in part on the historical association of Palestine as part of southern Syria, but also on account of the favourable legal and social status they enjoyed from 1948.

Josephine's story

Josephine was born in al-Ramleh in Palestine in 1926. She married when she was fourteen years old to a Syrian who was chosen for her by her stepfather. She had nine children; four were born in Palestine and five in Syria. In al-Ramleh, her husband owned two big houses; one was rented and the other was used as a family house. When the Nakba of 1948 occurred, her husband was in Damascus while she was resident in the family home in al-Ramleh. Her husband was supposed to be returning within a short time, but the war started and she was alone in the house without news of him. The Jewish militia who took over the town announced that all men and women should gather in the town's square. She was confused because her husband was away and her children were young, so she decided to hide with her children at home. One morning in early June, she heard somebody knocking at her door. Her children started to cry. She looked out of the window and saw more than twenty soldiers carrying guns; she did not know if the soldiers were British or Jewish militia. She opened the door and their leader approached her aggressively asking her what she was doing in the house. She was very upset, lonely, and confused. She didn't know what to do, where to go, and who to turn to. The soldiers told her that they would return the next day.

She had a sleepless night. At about five o'clock the next morning the soldiers returned with a lorry full of Palestinian women and children all crying and praying to God and to Jesus Christ to help them. She saw the Star of Zion on the doors and the sides of the vehicle. The soldiers pushed her and her children into the vehicle. They drove them away; she did not know where they going. After a few hours, they were dropped off in the mountains. She spent the night in the mountain and the next morning they walked till they reached an area called al-Bira in Palestine. She could not cross the border because her husband had their passports. After a month, they left al-Bira and fled to Amman with many other Palestinian refugees. In Amman, they were given shelter in a church where they remained for some time.

She crossed the Jordanian / Syrian border illegally and went to find her relatives in al-Midan district of Damascus. She stayed there for a while and then, with her relatives help, rented a house in the old city. After two years her husband came back to Damascus and the family was at last reunited. Once her husband was settled they moved into a much larger house in al-Joura quarter in old Damascus. Although the family was happy in this new house, still they considered that their stay in Syria was temporary and that they would soon be returning to Palestine. Recently, her husband died and now most of her children are married and live near her. A year ago, one of her sons died leaving her to look after his family. Although Josephine is well off, she still dreams of going back to Palestine.

(Josephine, Damascus, 2000 (HH20,G1,F))[13]

Sa'ada's story

Sa'ada was born in Palestine in 1914; she was brought up and lived in al-Qabba'a, near Safad. She was married at the age of fourteen years, and she gave birth to three children. She divorced her husband when he was jailed; her brother-in-law then took custody of the children. Then she worked as an agricultural labourer and sold green thyme. A year later she married Khalil who was already married with five children and a sick [paralysed] wife. She lived with her new husband's family and gave birth to two more children.

In 1948 the Zionist forces attacked her village (al-Dallatah); many people were killed and injured and hundreds of men were arrested. Sa'ada fled the fighting in her village. She left behind everything she owned and sought refuge in the Hauran in Syria. In 1952 her husband died leaving her with two young children. She found work again as an agricultural labourer. In time she left the Hauran and went to Damascus to search for people from her village. She managed to get work in the agricultural gardens of the Ghouta on the edge of the city. She had then only a one-room shelter at the very top of Mount Kassioun. After the end of her working day on the farm, she would gather some discarded onions, radish, and marrow in a bag and sell them in the market in order to have money to buy some cheese and bread and candles, to feed her children and to light their room.

Her children were provided with free schooling by UNRWA but she had to provide them with clothing and stationery. She could not afford the clothing and had to rely on some wealthy Damascene residents to provide her with second-hand shoes and clothes. In time, she saved some money and bought a room and made it habitable. Her children had to work during the school summer holiday in order to support their studies. One of her sons finished school while the other became involved in the Palestinian resistance movement.

Sa'ada shares her one-room house with her children and grandchildren. Today, they have electricity and water and the house is not so remote and isolated as it was in the past. Now, when her grandchildren make their way to school in the morning, they buy bread and sell it on in the neighbourhoods they pass to earn money to support the family. Although she has lived in Syria for many years and her children are grown up, she still feels alienated and she hopes to die and be buried in Palestine.

(Sa'ada, Damascus, 2001 (HH11,G1,F).[14]

171

Every refugee and forced migrant has a different story to tell; some are cushioned by wealth, such as Josephine, while others, like Sa'ada, are engulfed in a poverty so extreme that there is no escape. Of course, poverty and forced migration do not need to remain insurmountable variables. Many Palestinian refugees have managed to use the education provided them by UNRWA to break out of such cycles of despair and loss. But the sense of having been wronged, of wishing to return to their homes and villages, of taking up the livelihoods left behind under dire circumstances does not necessarily pass away. Although the political and social situation of Palestinian refugees varies broadly from one host state to another, there remain certain fundamental features in the development of individual and social identity which mark the Palestinians as unique. They are a people with a distinctive unassimilated Arab culture, dispersed over a wide region, variously discriminated against, yet on individual and family levels often well integrated into their host society. Nowhere is this more true than in Syria.

Palestinian Society in Exile: The Notions of Identity, of Place and Space

My name is Ra'isa. I was born in Gaza in 1909. But I come from Safad. My father was an accountant for the Hijaz railway. He started his job in 1914. At that time, Bilad al-Sham *[the Syrian provinces of the Ottoman Empire] was one country. My father moved us back to Safad when I was very young. Then, he developed a high fever and died. We were surrounded by family, the Khadra family. I studied at Safad until I finished elementary school and then I went to the Scottish College in Safad directed by Miss Mackintosh. In 1948 we were forced to leave Safad. As you know Safad is a mountainous city. We climbed down the valley and up the mountains until we got to al-Safsaf village, where we had some relatives. We stayed for the night, and early in the morning we took a truck that was used to move sheep and headed to the Lebanese border—to Bint al-Jbeil and then to Alma village where we stayed for a few days. Then we continued on until we got to Homs. We found a house to rent and stayed there for ten years. I was with my brother. He was a Law School graduate and found work with UNRWA as an official in charge of a district. In 1958 he was transferred to Damascus. The whole family moved to Damascus and we rented this house. I got a job as a headmistress of an UNRWA school in the Jewish quarter. Then I retired in 1972. I was always comfortable here. As a director of a school for Palestinians, I was well known and was committed to serving those whom I considered to be like my own daughters. I never felt as an immigrant in Syria. I always felt I was among my own people of* Bilad al-Sham. *It is, and has always been, one and the same country. ... At my age, and with all the Khadra family members around me, I would not go back to live in Palestine. I would say, no I wouldn't [Sister-in-law interjects: 'Auntie, what are you saying? If they allowed us to go back, we would go even if we have to live in a tent, it is our home country.']. Not me. Not at this age. My house is no more there, and the neighbourhood is not the one I knew. I would only get back to bad and bitter memories. I will never forget the experience of the exodus—how we walked down the mountain and all the way to the Tawaheen valley, and then up to the border village and finally the ride in a sheep truck.*

(Ra'isa, Damascus, November 2005)

Identity, status, and kinship ties are the themes that emerge from these narratives. The land is also important, perhaps even primordial, to Palestinian refugees, as they have all been abruptly severed from their roots. But between the generation that had to flee and the following generations born in exile a difference is emerging, one which distinguishes between space and place and which accepts notions of identity that are more fluid, and constructed around immediate social and cultural ties.

For many of the oldest generation who fled their homes in Palestine to reach safety away from the armed conflict, the physical space is no longer the place where their identity is grounded and nurtured. As Ra'isa states above, her house is no longer there, the neighbourhood is not the one she knew. Going back would only bring back sad and bitter memories. For her and many of the oldest survivors, identity and well-being is created and maintained by immediate family and friends, by Palestinian social networks and cultural ties in places of exile. The first generation remembers the physical spaces where their homes and communities were located. Some also have vivid memories of early challenges to those spaces by Jewish settlers during the British Mandate period in Palestine.

The second and third generation do not have original memories. Nor do they have experiences of contestation regarding their existence as Palestinians in the Mandated territory. The older Palestinians draw on their memories of belonging to an Arab nation (*Bilad al-Sham*) while the young hold on to the images and recollections of their original villages and homes as described by their care-givers. These narratives and descriptions are not that hard to construct into 'remembered memories', as the described landscape is often very similar to that which surrounds the Palestinian refugee camps or the neighbourhoods where Palestinian refugees live. The physical separation is often tens rather than hundreds of miles. In some cases the original villages can actually be seen, particularly at night, when the lights in the darkness make identifying villages of origin much easier.

For the second generation, that group of Palestinians generally born in the first few years after the *Nakba*, identity is more problematic. Exposed to significant hardships while the camps were largely still of cloth tents, and experiencing variable levels of pity and discrimination, the second generation is most adamant that the return to the homeland is fundamental to developing a sense of worth and dignity by ending the exile into which they were born.

The third and fourth generations share more than youthfulness. For many, the composite collective memory of their grandparents' or great-grandparents' forced migration emerged in internal contradictions within their own narratives. The past was as their parents had told them, but the present and their place in it was contested and showed clear elements of multi-vocal social memory (Chatty 2007). They belonged to the past but they also belonged to the country which hosted them. Yet their identity as Palestinians remained fundamental. For many of these youth education was the key to the future, the weapon with which they could fight for their 'right to return'.

Whether rich or poor, whether living in refugee camps or in the middle-class neighbourhoods of the major cities of the Arab world, Palestinian refugees have found a medium to express their cultural coherence and their social reality. That medium is education, both formal and informal, in which their common language, common history, and common culture both as Palestinians and as Arabs is reaffirmed. Wherever Palestinian refugees are found and whatever generation they represent, there are Palestinian cultural clubs and charities, Palestinian women's unions, Palestinian writers' unions and other professional bodies. For children and youth there are Palestinian kindergartens and nurseries as well as after-school clubs teaching Palestinian history, Palestinian music and dance (*dabka*). The Palestinian camps and the urban neighbourhoods are generally physically organized and named so as to remind their occupants of the villages and urban quarters left behind. Surrounded by kin and neighbours who fled together, making daily social contact with others like them, there is a physical reinforcement of 'Palestinianness' in the places they occupy today. And although identity has become multi-layered, particularly for youth, engagement in education and supporting the family remain particularly important features of Palestinian refugee society.

In closing this chapter about Palestinian refugees in Syria, I return to the reminiscences of Adnan and his conviction that Syria did right by him.

> I tried hard to organize my life, but it wasn't always under my control; it was not always in my hands. Not my decisions about my future; but I always held on to the thought that I must keep on studying because at that time most Palestinians thought that through education they could improve their situation; through education they could regain Palestine. They believed that education created miracles. It didn't happen of course, but this was the aim. You know, education was the only way to improve your life. I was convinced that education was the only way. Of course I would have preferred to be a citizen of a country somewhere in the world. And since I was born in Palestine I would have preferred to be a citizen of Palestine. But since I succeeded in making a life for myself here, I don't have a lot of things to complain about and I don't blame anybody, especially not the Syrians. They did not stop me from improving my life. I am satisfied now. I mean, I got what I was struggling for within the realm of what was possible. Even if I had come back as a child to Palestine, I don't think I could have done more with my life.

(Adnan, Damascus, 2011)

The integration of Palestinian refugees in Syria was smoother than in the other UNRWA operating states. In large part this was due to the recognition of Palestinians' historical connectedness with Greater Syria or *Bilad al-Sham*. Many Palestinian families already had long-settled family branches in that part of Greater Syria which became the truncated nation-state of Syria in 1946. Palestinians who arrived in Syria during the 1940s and after thus often had more resources, greater social, economic, and political connections, and faced far less discrimination in the modern Syria state than in neighbouring countries. One might say they were not so much strangers, but rather distant cousins; they already had family connections and a sense of belonging to a place that was not so strange or different, either in geography, economic activity, or social connections. Thus their integration into the modern Syrian state was effectively less trouble than that, for example, of the Kurds who fled the modern Turkish Republic in the 1920s seeking to live in a state where their ethnicity would be recognized.

6

THE MAKING OF A COSMOPOLITAN QUARTER

SHA'LAAN IN THE TWENTIETH
AND TWENTY-FIRST CENTURIES[1]

I was born in Bab Tuma. At the time my father was a teacher at Maktab Anbar. My father wanted to live in a modern—less conservative quarter. He moved us to Sha'laan in the 1930s. ... There were many French, Italian, and Greek families in the Sha'laan Quarter. ... Everything was available in Sha'laan. There were grocers and butchers. All the buildings you see here are new. Most of the houses were of traditional Arabic style except for the French styled ones such as this building on the corner and the houses on the right side of the lane you see on your way to Arnous. ... Present Sibki Park was not there. There was a farm where cows were raised and where we used to go with our grandmother to buy milk.

(Abu Wadi, 2008)

The rapid development of an area of orchards and farms on the outskirts of Damascus at the end of the First World War and during the period of the French Mandate is a perfect reflection of the dynamic migration—forced and voluntary—of people into Damascus and its transformation in the twentieth century. In recent decades this quarter, once officially known as Shuhada, has come to be informally called Sha'laan because of its close association with the Aneza Bedouin leader, Nuri Sha'laan of the Ruwalla tribe, who played a significant part in transforming it into an important political and economic centre of

Damascus. This quarter is approximately equidistant between the old city of Damascus and the important centuries-old village—now urban quarter—of Salahiyya in the foothills of Mount Kassioun along the city's northern rim. Sha'laan today retains certain unique features prominent in its early development: it is both a residential and a commercial district; it is home to a wide range of ethno-national groups including Circassian, Greek, Russian, Italian, French, and Armenian; it is religiously mixed, with Muslim and Christian believers. It has maintained its cosmopolitan residential and commercial dominance in the modern city of Damascus even though the city has spread far west with new, more modern residential quarters attracting many of the wealthy. How has this come about, and how has the quarter managed to maintain a vibrancy and international flavour into the twenty-first century?

This chapter explores the special circumstances which helped to develop Sha'laan into the cosmopolitan neighbourhood that it is today, even as other once-vibrant neighbourhoods in cities such as Aleppo, Homs, and Der'a have been devastated by the current armed conflict in the country. Focusing on a series of interviews with present and former residents of the quarter as well as merchants and shopkeepers, I set out to elucidate the features that its residents—often newly arrived migrants, exiles, and refugees—found so attractive in the past and still do today. The interviews reflect on life in the quarter from as early as the 1930s up to the present time. This interpretive chapter is based on these interviews. Some historical details may be partially or incorrectly remembered by the interviewees.

Sha'laan quarter certainly had a special appeal and convivial atmosphere. As one interviewee said, 'when we moved away from the area, we still returned to it all the time' (Usama, 2008). Those who were interviewed included forced migrants and settlers to the quarter in the 1930s, mainly exiled Palestinian leaders and their supporters as well as Armenian refugees and Circassian forced migrants, who were looking for cheaper accommodation than was possible closer to the old city or in the such suburbs as Halbouni, Afiif, or Arnous. Merchants and traders who came to the quarter in the 1940s and 1950s were also interviewed, including Armenians, who moved out of the largely Christian quarter of Bab Tuma and Bab Sharqi to develop their businesses in food vending, shoe production, and novelty shops—enter-

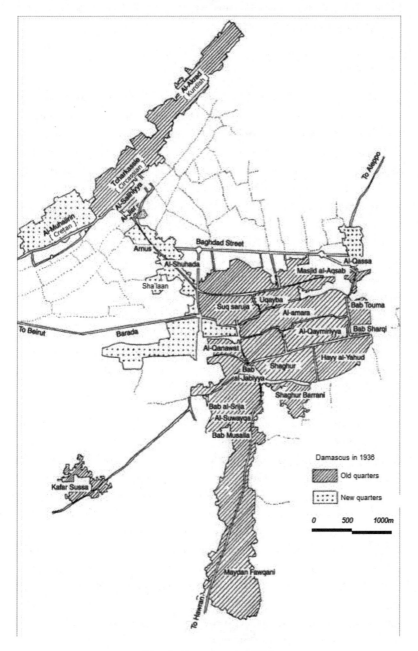

Map 9: Damascus in 1936

prises that they recognized would be eagerly supported by the residents of this modern quarter.

Background

The emergence of Sha'laan as a distinct district came on the heels of a major period of urban development initiated by the Ottoman state at the close of the nineteenth and early twentieth centuries; this included the establishment of a tram line between 1907 and 1913 linking the modern government offices in Merj just outside the walls of the old city with the ancient settlement of Salahiyya (Khairallah 1998). Prior to the establishment of this tram line there was only a horse and donkey track connecting the city of Damascus with Salahiyya and the Kurdish quarter, Harat al-Akrad. Over the next few years a number of important residences, government buildings, and schools were constructed alongside the tram line. There followed a parallel 'strip development' of several districts—Arnous, Shuhada, Afiif, and Jisr.

In 1919/20, as King Faysal of the short-lived Kingdom of Syria and his supporters withdrew from Damascus and moved to Baghdad to create the Kingdom of Iraq, one of the few large residences recently built in the gardens and orchards west of the tram line was bought by the ruler of the Ruwalla tribe, Amir Nuri Sha'laan. The amir had fought alongside King Faysal to support and secure the creation of the Kingdom of Syria as understood in the McMahon–Hussein Accords described in chapter 5. But his allegiance was to Syria and he was uninterested in moving to Baghdad. Instead, he purchased this villa and some adjoining farm land from Yassin al-Hashemi, who was planning to leave Damascus with King Faysal for the British Mandate of Mesopotamia (Iraq); al-Hashemi was to become Iraq's prime minister twice, once in the 1920s and again in the 1930s. This purchase, in some ways, marked the foundation and emergence of the quarter as a modern, ethnically mixed, cosmopolitan centre attracting migrants and exiles from near and far. The amir extended his residence by building three more villas, a mosque and gardens within the compound's walls, into which he moved his extended family. The Sibki family, which owned large tracts of apricot orchard and farmed wheat in the area, began to construct a number of hybridized two-storey houses blending traditional Arab with 'modern' European styles. The Shuhada Arch (or Sibki Arch) next to the tramline was the gateway to these gardens and farms watered by the Yazid tributary of the Barada river. The Sibki group constructed a block of four such houses close to the Sha'laan compound. These buildings were later rented to a number of important Syrian intellectuals, activists, and nationalists.

The French authorities, having completed the new Parliament building adjacent to the Salahiyya tramline in 1932 and established their army barracks and military hospital just behind it, followed by purchasing or commissioning residences for their army officers and administrative staff. They also built a large, modern French school for girls at the southern end of the quarter. These two near-simultaneous events, as well as an 'urban planning' map which set out to subdivide the quarter into sections and streets, seem to have initiated a major building programme which saw much of the adjacent farmland and fruit orchards turned over and converted into 'modern' residential buildings during the 1930s and 1940s.

With the withdrawal of the French from Syria in the 1940s, the residential blocks in and surrounding the quarter were increasingly inhabited by returnees (Syrians returning from periods of study abroad, often with foreign spouses), foreign nationals (many French businessmen), as well as successful middle- and upper-class professionals leaving the old city and seeking modern housing. Among the major players in the development of this quarter were members of the Sibki and Shanawani extended families. Both of these families made significant contributions to the development of Sha'laan and helped turn it into an important political and economic centre within Damascus. Amir Nuri, meanwhile, gave his name to the district quite by chance. In purchasing the former Ottoman residence, he established his compound as Beit Sha'laan, a centre of Bedouin hospitality with its open reception area (*madafa*) for visiting tribal members as well as the merchants and male residents of the quarter. He spent the last decades of his life at Beit Sha'laan, leaving an impression on the quarter not easily forgotten. One informant recollected that as a girl of ten she was entranced by the activity in front of Beit Sha'laan:

> *One of the most fascinating scenes that magnetized me was the sight of loaded camels as they approached, with their ringing bells, the large oval shape of the*

entrance of the Sha'laan House where some people were busy unloading the camels
while others rushed to pay respect to and take care of an elderly man [Amir Nuri]
who seemed to enjoy a certain status. ... There was always a group of ten to twelve
people at the door, which used to be kept open. And there was always some hay
outside the house where the camels used to wait while being unloaded.

(Watfa, 2008)

Both Amir Nuri Sha'laan and the Shanawani families built mosques in the quarter in the 1920s which are still important religious shrines today. The Sha'laan family, moreover, kept its guest room (*madafa*) open to the local traders and merchants. In the past, the family would invite all the quarter's residents to a meal in the *madafa* during Muslim religious holidays. Although the latter practice is no longer maintained, the *madafa* remains open on most evenings and the grandson of Amir Nuri continues to hold regular evening hospitality in the courtyard of this traditional house. The Shanawani family, on the other hand, a wealthy landowning family, were among the first to take advantage of the French Mandate land re-zoning scheme to convert some of their agricultural land and orchards into apartment blocks. Their legacy to the quarter is only a mosque which was built, some say, with stones salvaged from an old quarter just outside the walls of the old city that the French had bombed and burned in their effort to put down the Arab Revolt of the 1920s.[2] The Sibki family, who also constructed a number of apartment blocks and single-dwelling buildings, did not build a mosque in the quarter. But the sheer number of their buildings resulted in the district just to the north of Sha'laan becoming known locally as the Sibki quarter.

By the 1960s it was clear that a distinct area of the city locally recognized as Sha'laan was emerging as an established residential quarter just beyond a number of government ministries and the Parliament building, with its own places of worship—two mosques within the quarter and two churches at each end of the district. Government maps up to the 1960s, however, indicate that the quarter had no official name other than as a continuation of the adjacent quarter known as Shuhada. Similarly, the adjacent Sibki quarter was officially recognized as Zenobia Park. Thus neither the locally recognized Sha'laan contribution nor the Sibki influence on the quarter was acknowledged on government maps. Only in the 1970s, and later, was the quarter widely known as Sha'laan and its northern flank as Sibki Park.

THE MAKING OF A COSMOPOLITAN QUARTER

What emerges from the oral histories and recollections of the long-time residents of this quarter is a picture of an unusually vibrant, cosmopolitan residential and commercial centre constantly reinventing itself as waves of new settlers, exiles, refugees, and 'returnees' moved in, maintaining the cosmopolitan hue of its origins. In recent years the Sha'laan quarter has undergone significant transformation and is rapidly becoming one of the major shopping and entertainment centres for the city's youth as well as the young, rich elite. In the 1970s the integrity of the quarter was damaged when a major thoroughfare—Hamra Street—was cut through its eastern sector. The quarter recovered its primacy by reinventing itself, and at the close of the twentieth century it gathered a new clientele: the modern, educated youth of the city, attracted to its many new European franchised shops, cafes, fast-food eateries, and restaurants.

Sha'laan in the 1920s

Between 1918 and 1920 Damascus was the headquarters of the British general Sir Edmund Allenby, who entered the city with King Faysal and the troops of the Arab revolt against the Ottomans (Rogan 2015: 377–9). For the next two years King Faysal attempted to negotiate recognition of the Syrian Arab Kingdom by the West. The French, however, had landed in Beirut in 1919 and were determined to implement the Sykes–Picot Agreement which gave them a large sphere of influence over Greater Syria. In July 1920 French troops succeeded in destroying Syrian resistance at the Maysaloun pass and entered Damascus. In the same year King Faysal and his supporters were moved to Mesopotamia (Iraq) by the British to set up and administer a British sphere of influence there. The French required three more years to take complete control of Syria, and in 1923 were formally granted the Mandate over Syria by the League of Nations. This political decision was largely rejected by Syrians and several uprisings and revolts followed, with the Syrian Revolt (Druze Revolt) of 1925–7 as the largest and longest anti-colonial insurgency of the Mandate era (Provence 2005). With so much of its attention focused on consolidating its military hold over the country, French efforts to develop the city of Damascus did not begin in earnest until the late 1920s and early 1930s.

However, everyday life continued and, as the grandson of Amir Nuri recalled:

> The Beit Sha'laan was the only house in the area. Earlier we had another house in the Midaan Quarter. At that time the Midaan was the gathering point for Bedouin. It was not really considered part of Damascus, because it was outside the city walls. It was closely connected to the Hauran and the Bedouin grazing areas. The Bedouin used to come and sell their camels in the 'Sha'laan Market' in the Midaan, and buy whatever they needed from the Midaan. When King Faysal came to Damascus, my grandfather bought the Beit Sha'laan. Bedouin love to be on their own. He [Amir Nuri] bought the house because it was isolated and located in the middle of gardens and fields. He could have bought the whole area if he had wanted to. It was very cheap then.

(Amir Nawwaf, 2009)

Amir Nuri was never resident in the house for long. He would come for official meetings or to manage negotiations and draw up documents. Most of the time he moved between the Sha'laan house, his residence in 'Adra, and his tribe's grazing areas in the southern Badia (semi-arid steppe land of Syria). His immediate family, however, was moved into the Sha'laan house in 1920. The small expansion programme that the amir undertook—two further houses and also a mosque—was not the only activity in these gardens and orchards. Others were also establishing their presence nearby.

The Shanawani family also began to build in the gardens at about this same time. The eastern sector of the quarter was largely owned by them and had been divided into building plots, most probably under King Faysal's administration. Some time between 1922 and 1924 the Shanawani sold off a few of the building plots in order to pay for the construction of a second mosque: the Shanawani mosque. A few narrow passageways connected the Salahiyya tramline with this developing quarter around the Shanawani mosque. The simple Arab mud and wattle single-storey houses in these passageways were largely inhabited by Armenian refugees who had arrived in the city several years earlier. These alleyways came to be known as 'Armenian Lane'.

The quarter clearly had, at its birth, a mixed ethno-religious flavour. Yet it was under-populated; so much so that the one member of the Shanawani family recalls that the family patriarch is said to have gone to the old food market and given each porter one Syrian pound to wash and then go to pray in his mosque. At that time, no Friday prayers could be conducted unless there were at least twenty people attending (Mansour, 2006).

By the close of the 1920s there were several rows of housing running from Salahiyya to the west. The 'major' street where the most housing construction took place was along the pathway of the Yazid tributary, which was open in places and sometimes ran through the gardens of the homes built along its banks. This was to be known in later eras as the Hafez Ibrahim Street. Two mills were operating along this flowing water, one owned by and adjacent to the Beit Sha'laan and the other further to the east adjacent to a house owned by the Bitar family. With these flour mills came bakers selling bread as well as baking dough brought in by local customers, and small shops selling chickpea paste. As the resident population grew, the local farmers began to sell their produce—including milk—on donkey- and horse-drawn carts along these narrow streets.

Sha'laan in the 1930s

With the country largely pacified, the French Mandatory Authorities turned their attention to city planning and the construction of a modern quarter. The French military headquarters, the military hospital, and the Parliament building were all completed by the early 1930s just south and east of the Sha'laan quarter. The French Lycée of the French Laïque Mission was also built in 1930 with a capacity of 1,000 students on Baghdad Street, and commenced its 'civilizing mission' in 1932. Along the southern rim of the quarter they constructed the Ministry of Health building and supervised the construction of a Franciscan church and girls' school on land owned by the Shanawani family. In return, the family was permitted to put up a number of tall apartment blocks along the side of the Franciscan school. One informant suggested that the Shanawani were only able to put up the first of these blocks after the French had requisitioned what land they wanted for official buildings. Once these apartment blocks had been completed, the families rented them out to the foreigners flocking to this part of the city. 'Before we lived in those houses, they were let out to French officers. Our house, for example, was occupied by a French officer called Abel. Another tenant was a journalist from the Press Section of the French embassy. He stayed for years, until the early 1950s' (Mansour, 2006).

By the early 1930s, as well as the Sha'laan and Shanawani mosques, the quarter also had three churches: 'The Franciscan, the Latin church on the other side of the road. A little further up in the direction of Abu Roumanneh, there was a Russian Orthodox church for White Russians who had arrived in the 1920s fleeing the Bolshevik Revolution in Russia' (Bedros, 2009). These places of worship were significant indicators of the complexity of the identity of the local residents in Sha'laan.

Other informants commented on how the character of the quarter was coloured by its cosmopolitan residents.

> *I remember there were a lot of foreigners. The house next to us was taken by a Greek family. Um Elaine and her daughter, Despina, who was a student with us at the Franciscan. I also remember an Armenian family living in the house just before ours. There were many Armenians in the lane. There was an Italian family, the Montovanis. On the first turning on the way to the Franciscan church lived a French friend of mine and a school mate called Arlette Payees. In fact I did not have Arabic friends in the quarter. In the house across from ours lived a French Commandant who was the Director of the French Hospital.*

(Umaymah, 2009)

> *Sha'laan was self-sufficient. It had two butchers. ... There were two greengrocers. ... It was a quarter in which many French and Armenians lived. ... One of the original grocers started as a street vendor. He used to pull a horse-drawn cart down the street loaded with vegetables and call out in French 'Legume, Legume'.*

(Afaf, 2009)

It was not only foreigners who were drawn to the rapidly developing quarter. University students seeking lodging commonly found rooms in Sha'laan. So too did the Arab nationalists and exiles from the British Mandate of Palestine.

> *Some of the families who chose to live in Sha'laan were those who fled British oppression in Jordan or Palestine, such as the Abu-Labans, the Nabulsis, and the Kamals. Those families were forced to flee for political reasons. The narrow lanes of Sha'laan were occupied by such families or French families. The houses were small with little front gardens and rivulet / stream running through it. ... All the houses had rivulets. The water flowed with such strength that they had to be covered lest a child should fall in and be carried away beneath the next house.*

(Watfa, 2008)

Some local families were building or renting houses which combined both Arab and 'modern' styles, in keeping with the changing social networks and patterns of community living. One informant described his home in Sha'laan in the 1930s as:

> a mixture of Arabic and modern style. You got into the house through a small corridor. The kitchen was on the left and the bedrooms were upstairs. Downstairs there was a spacious reception room. In the court-yard there were kabbadeh and lemon trees. The river passed through the courtyard, but it was covered with iron bars. There were two flour mills nearby. One was just next to our house. The other was down by the Bitar house. The river continued its way to the parliament building.

(Abu Wadi, 2008)

These small houses did not provide enough room for some new residents, who chose instead to live in the modern apartment blocks being constructed by the Shanawani family.

> *We were fourteen people. We lived in a small house for a couple of months only. A new building was recently built across the road from the Franciscan school. The famous political figure, Abdurrhaman al-Shah Bandar, lived there. On the first floor there were two apartments. We pulled down the dividing wall to have one large apartment with ten bedrooms, two bathrooms and two kitchens. In those days we often had to accommodate revolutionary men coming from Palestine to give or receive arms.*

(Watfa, 2008)

To the north of the quarter another residential building project was rapidly taking shape. This was largely constructed by the Sibki family, who had built themselves a spacious sixteen-room multiple-storey residence at around 1900 on the street which followed the Salahiyya tramline. This building was later taken over by the French Mandate Ministry of Education.[3] Another large family house nearby was rented by the French Military 'Adjunct'. The new constructions in this area were all owned by the Sibkis and rented largely to the French. The Sibkis systematically 'opened a road, put up a building, and then rented it out. That is how Sibki 1, 2, 3... to 10 came into existence' (Suheil, 2009).

By the end of the 1930s the Sha'laan and the Sibki houses and orchards all came to be regarded as part of a single emerging cosmopolitan quarter self-sufficient in the provisions needed for daily life and within easy access of the important official agencies as well as the leisure industry. With the city under control and the West politically distracted by the looming Second World War, Damascus stopped expanding and instead consolidated its quarters and finished off its building projects by establishing parks for family outings and regularizing access to such activities as cinema, theatre, and dance.

Sha'laan in the 1940s and 1950s

The early 1940s was a period of great upheaval in Syria, and consequently there was little urban development. The French Mandate Authority was taken over by Vichy France in 1940, but within a year had been defeated by the Allied and Free French Forces. Syrian nationalists elected a new Parliament in 1943 and demanded recognition as an independent state (which the USA and the USSR granted in 1944). The following year Syria became a charter member of the United Nations and pressed for French troops to leave the country. Following two years of deep unrest in all the major cities of Syria, all French troops were pulled out by 15 April 1946. The Sha'laan quarter was home to many of the elite of the city as well as nationalists who fought for Syrian independence. The Ba'th Party, which at that time was only just gathering a following, opened an office in a three-storey building in the quarter (actually in one of the Sibki side streets), and people such as Badi al-Kasim, Jawdat al-Rikabi, and Jalal Farouq al-Sharif were often seen there (Afaf, 2009).

The Beit Sha'laan had become the centre of life in the quarter by this time. It sat directly on what became the main street of the quarter: Hafez Ibrahim Street. As one informant recounted, reeling off the names of notables in the quarter:

> Towards the west of the Sha'laan House was the Zahra's house. Abdul Qader al-Zahra was a doctor … as well as president of the Freemason Society in Damascus. Next to him was Dr Abdul Qader Radi … his grandchildren worked at the TV station and the surname 'Radi' often appears on the small screen. Following the Zahras was Samim al-Sharif's house … across from Samim's was the house of Abdullah Atef, the first Defence Minister after the French left Syria … Saki al-Arsouzik … Wahib al-Ghanem … Munzir al-Midani[4] … Temmirs … Nasib al-Bakri… Subhi and Badi' Sibki.

> (Afaf, 2009)

THE MAKING OF A COSMOPOLITAN QUARTER

By the mid-1940s Sha'laan had settled into a comfortable suburban community. Fatima, a young girl of seven when her family moved into the street registered as Hububi 3 in Sha'laan, recounted how, during the French bombardment of the Syrian radio station in 1945, she recalled seeing French soldiers and sandbags on the rooftop of a nearby building. Also living in her building was the Bekdash family—the same Bekdash who today have the ice cream shop in Hamadiyyeh Souq. Worried for the family at the time of the French bombardments, her mother sent her out looking for her father. She remembered dashing out onto Abu Roumanneh, which was empty at that time with no buildings except that of her aunt which was still under construction. Fatima recounted:

> We were friendly with the daughters of the shaykh of al-Haddadiyin [an elite Bedouin family] and we used to chat with them from across our balconies. It wasn't common for children to play in the street. At that time there was in the quarter, Abu Sa'id, the grocer, al-Tahawi, the butcher, Halfoun, whose children cooked sweetened cereal, at the shop across from the public fountain, and later Kanfash, the coffee store. ... There was also an Armenian dressmaker. And a textile shop run by a Syrian Jew. All the residents of Sha'laan shopped in his store on credit. He was a kind man and the prices at the shop were very reasonable. ... The grocer's, the butcher's, the bakery, and the fabric shop were all nearby.
>
> (Fatima, 2008)

By the end of the 1940s or early 1950s, the main Sibki farm—once a dairy farm—and adjoining lands had a compulsory purchase order placed on it. No one knows by how much, or even whether, the Sibki family were compensated. A public park, officially named Zenobia Park, was created some time around 1947, and the track that ran along the northern edge of the park from the Arnous Arch westwards towards Rabweh was named Mahdi Bin Barake Street. The name Zenobia never stuck, and the park today is known locally as Sibki Park. One informant recalled how he would walk along the park's northern edge when it was first opened, 'cross Rawda to Rabweh through uninterrupted green fields under shady trees. The old road to Lebanon ran through the fields with signboards telling the distance in kilometres between villages on the way' (Zuheir, 2008).

In the 1950s the Sha'laan quarter came into its own. Relatively reasonable rentals were available for the older Franco-Arab two-storey houses. Modern apartments were available to rent, although some building plots on the edges of the quarter could still be purchased. As returning 'native sons' sought accommodation for their often bi-cultural families, Sha'laan was more appealing than the traditional quarters of the old city, or even the Souq Sarouja of the more recent Ottoman period. It had become a 'busy and lively quarter' whereas Mazra'a and Abu Roumanneh were 'very new and dull' (Fatima, 2008).

Where there were people, more shops and services opened. One of the earlier shops in the quarter was opened by Kamal Zeitoun on the corner diagonally opposite from the Beit Sha'laan and called al-Zawiyya ('the corner'). Interviewing Kamal's son, Ziyad, revealed that the shop had been opened in this location in 1943. Previously the father had worked in one of the French Mandate co-operatives and learned his trade there as well as developing an idea of the kinds of foodstuff preferred by foreigners. Sensing a business potential, he came to Sha'laan and found a corner shop to rent. 'My father sold vegetables, fruits and dairy products. We made yoghurt, labneh, and milk. The shop next door made yoghurt from milk, and cheese. Everything was home-made' (Ziyad, September 2008). With business acumen reminiscent of that of the traders in the old city, the Zeitoun brothers began to procure items from the specialized markets in the old city for their customers, many of whom were foreign: *basterma* (pastrami) from the Bab Tuma quarter, spices and nuts from the Bizouriyya (spice market of the old city). They were also willing to create credit accounts for settlement at the end of the month. The quarter was becoming a cohesive community, one in which little effort was required to have the comforts of home from abroad.

One informant, an upholsterer, from the old quarter of Shaghour, recalled how he had opened his first shop with his brother in side street near Sha'laan called Armenian Lane in the 1940s and then moved his shop to the newly opened main street of Sha'laan (actually it was facing Sibki Park). He recalled that at about the same time a carpenter moved into the area, a real-estate office, a shoe-repair shop, and an Armenian shoemaker. He recounted how his customers came from all parts of Damascus but that he knew nearly every family in the quarter, many not originally from Damascus, including the Sheikh al-Ards, the Sadeq Malas, the Shanawanis, some Armenian families, including Albert

Karavian, who was the commanding officer of the Syrian Artillery Force, Rashid B'eira, Bader al-Lahham whose family ran a dairy-product shop, Jamal Atassi, Fihmi Sultans, the Christian Kalash family, the Circassian Aladdin Statis, the family of Siham Turjamn, the Attars, the Daqqers, the al-Sharifs, among others.

His recall of the shops along Hafez Ibrahim Street behind him was also good. Opposite the Beit Sha'laan public water fountain was a well-known shop that sold Arabic sweets: Halfoon's. Across from Halfoon's was a fabric shop run by a Syrian Jew. 'He always used to use the phrase "*bismillah*" [in the name of God] and "*allahumasalli 'ala Muhammad*" [May God pray for Muhammad] whenever he was dealing with Muslim customers' (Nazek, 2009). There was, Nazek recalled, the corner shop (al-Zeitoun) which specialized in dairy products, next to it a shop selling salted nuts, and also a shop for Arab sweets and cooked cereals. Opposite the mill adjacent to the Beit Sha'laan was an oven and bakery known for its nice thin bread; there was also a pharmacy, a dried-goods store, and a grocer who used the shop to cover up for his real trade in 'banned' goods. There were dressmakers and men's tailors, barber shops and the long-surviving Abu Steif's shoe repair. In all, Sha'laan had developed from an isolated and quiet hamlet nestled in apricot orchards and wheat fields to a bustling cosmopolitan residential area with a thriving commercial district to accommodate the needs of its inhabitants.

Sha'laan in the 1960s and 1970s

In the 1960s new modern residential areas opened up for the city's elite and wealthy foreigners. Malki and Mezze had been laid out, and building construction boomed. Although some commercial establishments followed, these shops often closed as customer density could not match that of Sha'laan and business could not have been as brisk. Ziyad Zeitoun recounted how when he started to work for his father in 1967 he learned where to source the diverse supplies. With a basket attached to his bicycle, he cycled through town to the airport, to the Bizouriyya in the old city, and collected stock. He got to know the agents for imported products, for example, Libby and Cole, where to buy and when to buy; some items could only be sold once a year at the International Trade Fair. Foreigners became important customers of the shop, but they were never the only ones. According to Ziyad they were able to stock a great number of different types of cheeses and meats—Roquefort, Camembert, Cheddar, Brie, Gruyère, Pastrami, Bresaola, and Salami—but they never lost sight of their local clientele.

By the 1960s and 1970s competition among these shops was keen. Two markets opened on Abu Roumanneh and in the residential areas of Jahez and Malki. 'Abu-'Ula al-Shatti opened a nice supermarket next to al-Jahez Park. All his customers were Americans. He was closer to the American School. He had more foreign customers than we did' (Ziyad, 2008). However, many of these shops stagnated as business and economic opportunities faltered or the customer base left the country. Some of the shops simply were unable to generate enough business in their isolated position. Sha'laan as a physically small area of tightly nested buildings and shops with its mixed Christian and Muslim population, local and foreign, rode out the economic stagnation of the following decades.

One shopkeeper who opened a new sort of shop, a 'novelty' business, in Sha'laan was Fayez. Born in Qanawat and apprenticed in sewing brassieres for another merchant in Salahiyya, he decided to open his own business and found rents in Sha'laan reasonable. He opened on Hafez Ibrahim Street in 1970, bringing with him his customers from Salahiyya.

> Sha'laan was a mid-way between al-Salahiyya quarter on Mount Kassioun and the old city. Salahiyya Street was a sophisticated area and had a lot of foreigners. Souq al-Hamidiyyeh [in the old city], on the other hand, attracted a lot of simple, local people. Sha'laan was a kind of extension of Salahiyya. My customers were quite sophisticated ... there were only three shops like mine. These shops sold a lot of items: clothes, underwear, and specific lines of lingerie. ... What you offer is determined by your customers. One has to be sensitive to customers' preferences. I started by selling locally manufactured bras and nightgowns. Then I noticed there was a demand for different brands of imported bras: Naturan, Triumph, Warner. I shifted completely to imported items.

> (Fayez, 2008)

Several similar shops opened on the same street during this era, nestling in among the carpenters, metal furniture shops, the cabinet makers, the music stereo shops, the grocers, the furnace bakeries, and the roasted-chicken shop and falafel makers. Over the decades in Sha'laan,

Fayez has developed close relations with his clientele, as have the other successful traders. He identified these relations as 'family-like', and stated that even a new customer, once in the shop, would soon feel at home. The quarter had character; it also had a soul. Local residents and those from further afield felt at home in these shops where the merchants knew most customers by name and had a finely tuned sense of both local and foreign clients' desires or needs. This quality, which perhaps emerged from the attributes of traditional quarters, was combined with a willingness to explore the foreign and the cosmopolitan. These characteristics are what made the quarter special.

Perhaps one of the most successful shops in Sha'laan has been al-Zawiyya. Now in its seventh decade of trading, it embodies the character of the quarter. The son of the founding owner expanded the business from a small shop with limited goods into one which supplies the major hotels in the city as well as several important clubs. The square footage of the shop has not changed, but the size of its customer base and annual turnover has grown immensely. The family has done this by intuitively understanding the needs of its customers as well as its neighbouring shopkeepers. Always willing to search for produce, take telephone orders, and deliver goods to individuals and companies alike, the Zeitoun family embodied the small community ethos as well as the entrepreneurial spirit which a multi-ethnic and cosmopolitan clientele demanded. As Ziyad Zeitoun points out:

> There are many more new customers in addition to our old ones and their offspring. However, a lot of our old customers have moved to Mezze, Dummar, Qudsia, and other suburban residential areas—Mrs Kallas, Mrs Sabbagh, and Mrs Daqqer. Some of these people still come to get items from our shop not regularly available in other shops.

> (Ziyad, 2008)

One reason for the success of this family shop has been its close eye to the requirements of its local customers. For example, in the 1970s Ziyad's father used to send his son to deliver groceries on order to Mrs Jamal Atassi in a wicker basket covered with green leaves, with the artichokes already prepared for cooking. That attention to detail led Ziyad to recognize the growing demand for ready-prepared fresh vegetables. About ten years ago he went into partnership with one of the producers. 'We provide the space outside the shop. A lot of TV documentaries are being made about this line of business in Sha'laan—peeled and cut vegetables, zucchini prepared for stuffing and the like. Women say that pre-prepared vegetables help a lot when you have a guest or emergencies' (Ziyad, 2008). Recognizing the changing clientele and demands on their time, the Sha'laan merchants are modernizing and adapting to the requirements of their heterogeneous constituency, as did their fathers and grandfathers before them.

Conclusion: Sha'laan in the Post-Ba'thi Era

Sha'laan came to life in a period of rebirth and regeneration. Its origins are closely linked to the early French Mandate period of forced migration, as well as to the local and regional resistance to the League of Nations notion that Syria (as well as Mesopotamia (Iraq), Transjordan, and Palestine) was not yet ready for full independence. The population of the quarter reflected these wider realities, with Christian and Muslim residents living side by side and often joining together in political positions. Circassians, Druze, Palestinians, Armenians, and Russians all found homes here, along with French military officers and administrators, Italians, Greeks, and other Europeans. Each decade saw a greater density of residence and accompanying services and trades.

In the last few decades of the twentieth century the quarter changed markedly again, adapting to meet the requirements of its contemporary residents. Gone are the laundry, the shoe repair, the butchers, the dressmakers, the men's tailors, the framers, the multiple ovens with their fresh bread. All these shops catered to a different era, when clothing could not be readily bought, when shoes could be repaired, when the comings and goings of daily life required the services of many skilled craftsmen. Gradually, and then in rapid succession, these traders and tradesmen began to disappear. In their place came the clothing and shoe boutiques, the French paste jewellery shops, fast-food shops, cafes, and restaurants. Even the Arab sweet shop has been replaced by a modern 'herbalist'. Sha'laan today has become the trendy centre of food, clothing, and music for a younger, elite, and cosmopolitan generation. It bustles in the evening and the shops do a thriving business. Its residents sometimes complain about the noise, but few move out of the quarter. Many more are looking to move in. As one informant recalled:

THE MAKING OF A COSMOPOLITAN QUARTER

I still remember the day I went with my mother, my sister, my uncle's wife and a female cousin to a wedding in Muhajiriin. The wedding was over at dawn and we simply walked back to our house in Sha'laan. We couldn't have done the same had we lived in Mazra'a; it was too cut off.

(Fatima, 2008)

Sha'laan was a quarter that grew and thrived with the arrival of any dispossessed social group. The impact of these newcomers on the quarter was not always immediate; it took time for some forced migrants to gather the resources to find a space to operate in the commercial and residential quarter. But Circassians, Bedouin, Jews from Central Europe, Armenians, White Russians, Kurds, Palestinians, and Iraqis have all made their mark on the quarter. Sha'laan may have been born in the French Mandate period. However, it has reinvented itself several times over, always managing to maintain its multicultural, convivial nature. Even in 2017, it still manages to be the bustling heart of a multi-ethnic, cosmopolitan quarter.

7

IRAQIS AND SECOND-WAVE ASSYRIANS
AS TEMPORARY GUESTS

When I first came here [to Damascus] from Iraq, I noticed the atmosphere of festivities. I am Christian but when I saw how [the Muslim] Ramadan was celebrated here, I was so surprised. In Barzeh [a mixed Christian and Muslim quarter of Damascus] shop owners used to keep the stores open until early morning. I was not working then, so I would wait for the evening to celebrate with everyone, Syrians, Iraqis, Palestinians, Somalis, and so on. For the Christian festivities, I would go to Bab Tuma. It was such a special atmosphere. Amazing! Now for Easter they have decorated the church with a white cloth from top to bottom. We don't have this back home [in Iraq]. We walk in the streets here and people offer you some special desserts for the festivities. It is fascinating. What more do you want? People enjoying and celebrating their religions and enjoying each other's company. So what more could we want? Water, electricity?

(Maha, Damascus, 2011)

Though I have lived and worked in Damascus for decades and thought I had a good grasp of its varied social groups and ethno-religious minorities, I first became aware of a significant Iraqi exile community in Damascus in the mid-1990s. I had been searching for contacts with the publishing world in Damascus and a few of my Syrian writer colleagues suggested we meet and chat about it at the Journalists' Club in the Afiif quarter of Damascus on the way to Salahiyya. At the club, engulfed in the smoke from the water pipes my colleagues were smoking, I was told that I should look up the new publishing houses opened by Iraqis, as

they were cornering the market in publishing works in European languages translated into Arabic. I was surprised by this information, and
the more I enquired the more I learned about this growing but well-
established community of Iraqis in Syria. On leaving the club I noticed
that the building opposite was the Iraqi Society Club. I was told it had
been established decades before. Suddenly I was coming across Iraqis
everywhere. When had they come, and how had they managed to integrate so smoothly into Syrian society?

Iraqis have been moving into and out of Syria since the foundation
of the modern state of Iraq as a League of Nations British Mandate. The
lines drawn defining the borders of British-Mandated Iraq, and French-
Mandated Syria, within *Bilad al-Sham* (Greater Syria) separated some
families, businesses, and other interests. During times of upheaval and
political crises the lines blurred, and politicians from both states often
crossed the borders to escape persecution or death in one country or
the other.[1] In the 1980s and 1990s Damascus was a place of refuge for
numerous political elites from around the developing world, including
Iraqis such as Nuri al-Maliki, prime minister in the post-Saddam
Hussein era from 2006 to 2014, and Iyad Allawi, the interim prime
minister in 2004–5 and vice president in 2014–15.

Over the past century there has been a steady trickle of Iraqis going
into exile or seeking asylum in Syria. That trickle built up in the 1980s
and 1990s under Saddam Hussein's harsh dictatorship, and eventually
became a massive influx in the mid-2000s. Why did this come about,
and how did the international humanitarian aid effort respond to this
crisis? How was that different from the local and national response to
all these temporary guests? In this chapter, I first describe the perplexing elements of the Iraqi humanitarian crisis which was unleashed in
the aftermath of the Western invasion to locate and destroy 'weapons
of mass destruction' in Iraq in 2003. I then back-track to give a more
detailed background of the widespread displacement within the region
in the late nineteenth and twentieth centuries and the 'deterritorialized' nature of belonging as a relic of the Ottoman *millet* system, which
has led to a willingness to allow Iraqis to integrate into Syrian society,
to make themselves 'at home' without assimilating or letting go of their
Iraqi identity.

Iraq and Weapons of Mass Destruction

In November 2002 the United Nations Security Council voted unani-
mously to back an Anglo-American resolution (Resolution 144) requiring Iraq to reinstate UN weapons inspectors. This measure marked a
key step in the race towards a war which began five months later, when
US air strikes launched Operation Iraqi Freedom on 20 March 2003.
In the intervening five months, a series of assessments from the humanitarian aid regime suggested that military action might displace more
than a million people within Iraq and across its borders. The UNHCR
and numerous international and national non-government agencies
(IGOs and NGOs) hurriedly made preparations to receive large numbers of Iraqi refugees in Jordan, Syria, and Iran. They negotiated the
establishment of reception centres and camps, stockpiled food and
non-food items, and prepared for the transfer of further materials
through ports in Jordan and Turkey. Yet, six months after the invasion
and the fall of the Iraqi regime, few Iraqis had fled their country. None
had fled into Iran, a few hundred had registered in Syria, and some
2,000 had arrived in Jordan. It seemed that the international aid community had misjudged Iraqis' attachment to their state. Camps were
dismantled, stocks of food and other items were removed, and the
international aid regime sat back (for more details see Chatty 2003).

Then three years later, in 2006, governments and international
agencies were caught off-guard as hundreds of thousands of Iraqis fled
their homes, seeking to escape a general collapse in social order manifested in a complete lack of security and deadly sectarian violence.
Although estimates varied widely, between 1 and 2 million Iraqis travelled to Jordan and Syria, settling largely in the cities of Damascus,
Aleppo, and Amman. Others moved to Cairo and Istanbul, and many
travelled much further. By 2008 the number of Iraqi applicants for
asylum in North America and Europe was more than double the combined total from both the second- and third-largest source countries,
Somalia and the Russian Federation (UNHCR 2009a).

In the states bordering Iraq, the UNHCR and other international non-
government organizations raced to set up reception centres and to provide emergency aid and measures for temporary protection in an environment where international legal protection for asylum seekers and

refugees was unknown. Despite concerted efforts and innovative pro-grammes, including mobile registration opportunities as UNHCR staff moved about the neighbourhoods where they knew there was a strong Iraqi presence, by the end of 2011 fewer than 200,000 Iraqis out of an assumed 1.2 million had registered with the UNHCR in Syria. Clearly there was a significant disparity in perceptions among the displaced Iraqis and the international aid regime regarding the solutions to their plight. For the United Nations, durable solutions consisted of voluntary return, local integration, or third-country resettlement. The displaced Iraqis apparently had different ideas of how to manage their exile.

Iraqi forced migrants now constitute one of the largest refugee populations worldwide. Nearly 5 million Iraqis were displaced by the Western military invasion to remove Saddam Hussein from power in 2003 and the sectarian breakdown and insecurity that followed (al-Khalidi et al. 2007). Approximately 2 million are labelled refugees, because they have crossed international borders, and 2.8 million are designated internally displaced persons (IDPs) within their own country. Sectarian and ethnic violence are the dominant characteristics of this displacement. The unmixing of neighbourhoods has rendered internal displacement a semi-permanent feature within Iraq, whilst those who have crossed international borders show little inclination to return except in very small numbers (Marfleet and Chatty 2009). Today Iraq is far from stable, and the Iraqi government has not been able to create the conditions for successful return, either for refugees or IDPs. The bombing of Iraqi churches in 2010 and thereafter also gave rise to further out-migration, as Iraq's Nestorian or Assyrian Christians—nearly half a million—came to be increasingly targeted by insurgents. Many made their way to the Christian neighbourhoods of Damascus, where they found a measure of security under the Syrian government's determination to protect the ethnic minorities in the country. Despite the armed conflict, escalating violence, and terror being experienced in Syria, return movement to Iraq has been limited and is unlikely to morph into a significant return movement to central Iraq. The majority Shi'ite government of Iraq has set up holding camps near the Syrian–Iraqi border to contain Iraqi returnees until after they have been vetted and judged as representing no threat to the current government.

Most of Iraq's forced migrants fled to Syria, with a smaller percentage to Jordan, Lebanon, and Egypt. Their refuge in these neighbouring countries is rapidly approaching the ten-year mark and is clearly defined as a 'protracted crisis' by the humanitarian aid regime. Evidence, so far, from all four countries suggests that the tolerance of their host governments will continue, even if grudgingly, in part because of the generous response at the local level among neighbours and hosting families (see Chatty and Mansour 2012). Often unwilling to return, and largely unable to emigrate to the West or to Europe, Iraq's refugees are in a perilous situation; largely Sunni Muslim and Christian (Assyrian), they are not welcome back in the newly created 'democratic', but Shi'ite-controlled, Iraqi state which emerged after the United States backed deliberations to write a new constitution and elect a new leadership. The protracted displacement which the Iraqis now face promises to become permanently 'temporary', much as the Palestinian displacement of almost seventy years has done.

Iraqis have surprised the West, first by their refusal to flee at the beginning of the 2003 invasion of their country, and then in 2006 by their mass flight as Iraq descended into sectarian violence, ethnic cleansing, and anarchy, which escalated with bombing of the al-Askari Mosque in Samarra in February of that year. That single event became the iconic image of sectarian violence and the 'unmixing' of people which followed. In both Syria and Jordan, Iraqis were not regarded as refugees by the host governments, partly because neither country was a signatory to the 1951 United Nations Convention relating to the Status of Refugees. Their reception and protection in these countries of refuge depended upon Arab solidarity, social custom, social networks, and kinship ties rather than any mechanisms of international law.

Many of the Iraqis seeking asylum were from the educated professional and middle class. A number managed to escape with savings which helped to ease their transition. Previous waves of migrations during earlier decades meant that some Iraqi social networks were already in place in the host countries. The residual cultural memory of the Ottoman *millet* system, which gave ethnic and religious minority communities a limited amount of power to regulate their own affairs, meant that Iraqi arrivals in these cities were generally tolerated if not actively supported. Also, memory of the pan-Arab aspirations in the region meant that Iraqis were seen as temporary guests and 'Arab brothers'.

In April 2009 the UNHCR declared that security in Iraq had improved to the extent that people displaced from most regions of the country should no longer be viewed as refugees. It also began to formally prepare for the imminent return of 'large numbers' to Iraq. The facts on the ground, however, were that many Iraqis kept their distance from the official agencies mandated to assist them. Despite a concerted effort by the UNHCR to register Iraqis as refugees in Syria, the majority have refused to come forward. The reasons can only be guessed at. Some Iraqis claimed to fear involuntary repatriation to Iraq if they formally register with the UN agency. Others were afraid of returning to a country where the mixed ethno-religious communities and the legacy of Ottoman tolerance had been wiped away. The targeting of Christians, particularly Assyrian and Mandaean communities, towards the end of the first decade of the new millennium clearly pointed to the continuing 'unmixing' of peoples in Iraq, even under the 'democratically' elected government of the newly created state.

The general consensus is that Iraqis have fled their country 'as a consequence of a conflict in which they have no stake but of which they were made victims' (International Crisis Group 2008: 1).[2] Compounding the real and perceived threats of violence and a deadly rise in sectarian terrorist acts, countless publications emphasize the widespread impoverishment within Iraq after years of sanctions as an important factor prompting out-migration. By many accounts, the Iraqi middle class has been under excruciating pressure. Sassoon highlights the dramatic decline in the number of doctors, academics, professionals, and artists, who had been targeted as groups, becoming unemployed and censored, and thus choosing exile over continued suffering (Marfleet 2007; Sassoon 2009).

Becoming Iraqi

Understanding why Iraqis have been leaving the country for decades— first as a trickle, then a steady stream, and finally in the late 2000s in a flood—requires a brief review of the country's modern history. The Kingdom of Iraq emerged from the Paris Peace Conference at the close of the First World War. In line with the secretly negotiated Sykes–Picot Agreement, the Allies entrusted the League of Nations, which they established, to give Britain administrative powers over the Kingdom of Mesopotamia in 1919. This region, between the Euphrates and Tigris rivers, consisted largely of the former Ottoman cities and hinterlands of Basra, Baghdad, and Mosul, which the British had invaded at the onset of the war. The population of this Mesopotamian Iraq immediately rose up in massive and violent protest, called the Great Iraqi Revolt of 1920. Gertrude Bell, who was a leading figure in the creation of the Iraqi state, reflected many of the views of her own time. In her memoirs she wrote that Iraqi people were mute and passive, and that they would favour benign British rule.[3] She went on to write that the 'vociferous minority' who called for independence should not be heeded, as then all would end in 'universal anarchy and bloodshed' (Burgouyne 1961: 104).

Many of the elite urbanite, tribal leaders and former Ottoman army officers in Baghdad initially rejected this colonial imposition and fanned the flames of uprising. After all, the other British war-time agreement—the McMahon–Hussein Accords of 1915—had promised the Arabs their own kingdom, of which Mesopotamia was an integral part, if they rose up in revolt against the Ottomans. They had done their part of the agreement, as witnessed by the triumphant entrance into Jerusalem and then Damascus of the conquering forces of General Allenby and those Arabs who had fought with Amir Faysal and T. E. Lawrence. The betrayal was seen as profound, and violence rapidly spread throughout the territory, forcing the British to bring in more troops from India. By 1921 much of the urban elite of Baghdad and leaders of the major Sunni Bedouin tribes acquiesced in British rule (Dodge 2003). In the same year, the British held a plebiscite and arranged for the deposed King Faysal of the short-lived Kingdom of Syria (1918–20) to be made king of Iraq. His brother, Abdullah, was made king of the British Mandated territory of Transjordan in same year. However, in the Kingdom of Iraq matters did not run smoothly. Opponents were exiled and Shi'ite and Kurdish communities were sidelined in this political transformation. Massive uprisings continued, and by 1922 the British, having brought what additional troops they could spare into Iraq from India, decided to supplement and partially replace their ground troops with Royal Air Force bombers (Dodge 2006). The continuous air bombardment of villages and towns as well as fleeing Bedouin and their herds of camels and sheep made for a theatre of 'shock and awe' in its time. One elderly tribesman speaking to a Special Forces officer in 1924 remarked: 'There are only two things to fear: Allah and *Hakumat al tayyarrat* [government by aircraft]' (Dodge 2003: 131). In 1925 Leo Amery, the secretary of state for the colonies, returning from a month-long tour of Iraq, wrote in his memoirs that the Royal Air Force was the backbone of the whole of the British occupation:

> If the writ of King Faysal runs effectively through his kingdom, it is entirely due to the British airplanes. It would be idle to affect any doubt on that point. If the airplanes were removed tomorrow, the whole structure would inevitably fall to pieces. ... I do not think there can be any doubt about that point. (Dodge 2003: 131)

By the middle of the 1920s the British turned to some of Iraq's ethno-religious minorities to help them police this unruly state. They relied heavily on the Assyrian Christian minority to make up the country's gendarmerie—a branch of the armed forces responsible for internal security. Neutral throughout most of the First World War, the Assyrians later took the side of Great Britain and made up the Iraqi Levies (Assyrian Levies), an armed force under the command of British officers. After a decade of unrest, constant civil disturbances, and unsuccessful efforts to subdue dissident factions, Britain declared Iraq unmanageable. It admitted that it could not turn the three former Ottoman provinces of Basra, Baghdad, and Mosul into a 'modern democratic state', and gave up its Mandate in 1932. But the British maintained a military presence in the country as well as a number of political advisers. This continued unwanted presence in the country did not help the situation of the numerous minority groups who had supported them. Among the urban elites a few went into exile, but it was the Assyrians, who had worked closely with them, who were the most vulnerable to reprisals. Thus, the first massive wave of forced migrants from Iraq in the 1930s was the Assyrians, who fled to Syria, Lebanon, Turkey, and the West. Those who did not flee the country tended to gravitate to the north of the state, a region roughly coterminous with the ancient state of Assyria. The newly independent Kingdom of Iraq then imposed its will upon the population by either sending individual politicians into exile, or moving entire communities from one part of the country to another. Dispossessing and relocating communities, mainly to the less densely populated northern regions, became fairly common for the next few decades, which were marked by armed coups (between 1936 and 1941 there were five).

Finally, in 1958, deep unrest saw the Hashemite kings of Jordan and Iraq form the Arab Federation, some say as a counter-measure to the union that had just been declared between Egypt and Syria (the United Arab Republic). But this was not enough, and later in the year a coup took place in Iraq that ended the monarchy and saw a wave of royalists fleeing the country. The Iraqi king and his family were executed, and those who were not quick enough to flee Colonel Abdul Salam Aref's regime were placed under arrest in a former hospital converted into a prison—Abu Ghrayb. Those who escaped the country made their way to Jordan, where they were welcomed by King Hussein, a cousin of the deposed family. The new republican leadership in Iraq continued the practice of dispossession and eviction on a larger and wider scale. Misconduct by an individual politician could result in an entire tribe or clan being exiled. The trickle of movement out of the country throughout most of the twentieth century then gained momentum after 1978, when Saddam Hussein came to power. His despotism and unpredictable behaviour caused many of the country's elite to seriously consider leaving. The decade-long Iran–Iraq War in the 1980s increased the out-migration from the country. But it was the aftermath of the First Gulf War and the sanctions imposed by the West in 1991 that saw a steady stream of Iraqis (hundreds of thousands) leaving the country in an effort to escape increasingly desperate circumstances. These waves were composed of members of the political, intellectual, and business elites.

Reports indicate that by 2003 there were over 300,000 Iraqis settled in Jordan. In Syria, Lebanon, and Egypt it is likely that there was a similar population of Iraqi exiles, though fewer than in Jordan. The presence of nearly 500,000 Iraqis in the region prior to 2003 was felt in business, and in the arts in particular. They formed solidarity networks for newcomers, helping to re-anchor recent arrivals without resorting to international aid. They were largely invisible to humanitarian assistance regimes, as they did not seek formal recognition, but rather relied on Arab notions of hospitality and traditions of giving asylum to settle and create new lives for themselves, all the while reinforcing pre-existing social, political, and economic networks across the borders of the Arab states.

The Nature of Refuge and Asylum in Post-Ottoman Syria

I am from Baghdad, the capital; I came in 2008 and have not gone back to Iraq since. The situation there [in Baghdad] has changed by 180 degrees. From what I hear and see the situation is hard. When we were in Baghdad there was no sectarianism. Since I came here [to Damascus] I felt safe. I always say this and I always mention it when in meetings [with international humanitarian aid staff]: Syria has provided the Iraqi people more than any other country. Syrians have hosted us, they have given us residency permits, and they have made us feel safe. There is cooperation between people. There are no problems here. We have felt safe up to now and we hope things don't change.

(Samira, Damascus, 2011)

A remarkable feature of the Ottoman Empire was the way that its organizing ethos was not based on territorial rootedness but rather on religious affiliation. Belonging was tied to social places rather than physical spaces. In other words, belonging in this region of the eastern Mediterranean, until the end of the First World War, was based on recognition of the superiority of Islam in the empire, alongside a tolerance of the *Ahl al-Kitab*—its Jewish and Christian communities. This tolerance was not just derived from religious tenets but emerged also from economic and political realism. European nineteenth-century economic and political interests in the Christian and Jewish communities in the Middle East, as well as Ottoman principles of self-governance for these ethno-religious groups, resulted in the mid-nineteenth century Ottoman reforms which formally legislated the establishment of protected communities, *millets*, whose religious and social affairs were organized from within the structure of the church or synagogue. It was the legacy of these *millets*, I have contended elsewhere, that shaped the way in which the migrants (forced and voluntary), exiles, and other dispossessed peoples were integrated without being assimilated into the fabric of the societies and cultures of the Middle East (Chatty 2013b).

The Ottoman *millet* system of administrative recognition of a wide range of ethnic and religious communities has been described in chapter 1. With the end of the First World War, this largely successful multicultural and religiously plural empire was rapidly dismantled. However, despite the forced migrations of millions of ethno-religious minorities (as well as Muslim majorities from the Balkans), which saw an entire empire on the move, the legacy of the deterritorialized aspects of belonging tied to the Ottoman ethno-religious *millets* laid the foundations for later elaborations of migrations. These were mainly circular and back and forth movements between relations, co-religionists, colleagues, customers, and creditors in the modern Arab successor states of the empire. This was particularly true of forced migrants from Iraq. With identity and security based on family, lineage, and ethno-religious *millets*, movement did not represent a decoupling, or deracination, but rather a widening of horizontal networks of support and solidarity that stretched throughout the former Arab provinces of the empire. Relatives, close and distant, were spread over a wide region far beyond the confines of the modern Iraqi nation-state, and could be called on for support, shelter, and security when needed.

Notions of hospitality, generosity, and the worthiness of the guest in augmenting individual and family honour are fundamental to an understanding of many societies and cultures. They are particularly redolent of Syrian society, and the Arab world in general, where notions of modernity are mixed with those of custom and customary principles of behaviour and action. Hospitality and generosity encompass notions of respect and protection as well as security. The family, the lineage, the social group, and the nation's reputation are in many ways hostage to correct behaviour with a guest or stranger; inappropriate behaviour might lead to disrespect, danger, and insecurity. Thus in Syria, Iraqis were welcomed as temporary guests, and as long as they behaved as was required of a guest (did not raise their heads above the parapet) they were treated like other nationals and allowed to go about their business of settling in, setting up a business, or engaging in circular migrations in and out of Iraq, without risk of detection or detention as 'refugees' or 'forced migrants'.

Contrary to the dominant discourse on hospitality in the West and in the humanitarian aid setting, where asylum seekers in the detention centres and refugee camps are placed in the middle ground between mere biological life and full social existence (Agamben 1998), the notions of hospitality and generosity in Syria and other Arab states have made it nearly impossible for the government to adopt a 'bureaucratic indifference' to human needs and suffering. Syria, like most countries of the Middle East, has no domestic asylum laws, largely because asylum is deeply rooted in notions of individual, family, and group reputation. The nation is regarded as the home, and the head of state is the head of the family. The nation becomes a house in which hospitality can be offered and received. The collective memory of a number of forced displacements of the past few centuries means that yesterday's guest is readily acknowledged as today's neighbour (Zaman 2016: 131). In this sense the host is thus someone who, or something which, has the power to give to the stranger (generosity) but remains in control (Derrida 2000). Providing hospitality (or asylum) in this region is seen as increasing the reputation of the individual, the family, and the nation for generosity. Thus customary law and a moral positioning to treat the stranger as a guest does not require national legislation to be implemented; the setting up of international humanitarian internment camps becomes problematic, if not repugnant.

Iraqis Redefine Movement and Migration in Search of Neighbourhoods and Homes

The Iraqi displacement crisis had reached a critical stage a year or two into the rapidly growing violent conflict in Syria after the Arab Uprisings of 2011. International humanitarian interest in Iraq had begun to decline. Yet the lack of security, continuing civil conflict, and economic uncertainty, alongside a muted 'return' policy by the current government, made it unlikely that there would be a mass Iraqi return any time soon. More likely, Iraqi exiles, refugees, and displaced people would remain in neighbouring states such as Syria under increasingly difficult circumstances. As their savings diminished and their circular migrations into and out of Iraq to make money or collect rents became more precarious, it was likely that Syria would become the site of permanent 'temporariness' and the base for irregular and long-distance migrations to keep in contact with family who had scattered over the face of the earth.

TEMPORARY GUESTS

My parents and my siblings are already abroad. So when I came here I registered immediately with UNHCR. It is now my third year. I did all the interviews and am waiting [to be resettled]. My brother is a naturalized American, and my mother needs a few more months to get it [American citizenship]. My brother and sister are in Canada. My uncles are in Michigan, USA. My other uncle is in Australia; my cousin is in Denmark. I keep in touch with all of them. If I am offered resettlement, I don't think I will resettle, I don't think I will take it because I am not married. And I am here with my father who is an old man. For me I think I will remain here in Syria for now [with my father].

(Samira, Damascus, 2011)

Iraqi refugees in Syria are urban based and largely from Baghdad. This is hardly surprising given that much of the sectarian violence in Iraq has occurred in the mixed Shi'ite and Sunni areas of Baghdad and other urban centres (Harper 2008). One Iraqi woman, Muna, expressed her connection to her Baghdad home and neighbourhood in terms of the vibrant social fabric:

> After we received threats, my brother told me that we had to leave because there was no one left from our family in Baghdad. You know, I don't have any family in Baghdad, but I still cried a lot. The scent of my country. My land. My friends. My neighbours. My neighbours are Muslim and I am Christian, they were crying as though I was their daughter, not just a neighbour. We were raised together. I was there for thirty years. I was born in 1979 in that house, with my neighbours, in my neighbourhood. I was crying and asking my husband, how could I not see my neighbours tomorrow?

(Muna, Damascus, 2011)

Although Syrian government records do not include the religious affiliation of Iraqis entering the country, the documents of the Syrian offices of the UNHCR suggest that 57 per cent are Sunni, 20 per cent are Shi'ite, and 16 per cent are Christian, with 4 per cent Sabaean–Mandaean (al-Khalidi et al. 2007). The Iraqis in Syria are on the whole well educated and constitute what was Iraq's professional middle class. A large proportion of them are relying on personal savings and remittances from Iraq, though some have managed to secure employment, both formal and informal, in Syria. Many undertake risky, but brief, visits to Iraq to keep their businesses operating, collect pensions and food rations, or check in on elderly relatives who have refused to leave.

This circular mobility is an important coping strategy for Iraqis and has baffled the international humanitarian aid regime, which often still regards 'refugeeness' as a one-way road (to resettlement).

Entry into Syria has never required a visa from any Arab, and Iraqis make full use of this anomaly in international border control. It was only during a brief period between 2008 and 2010 that a more stringent visa regime was imposed, partly at the request of the Iraqi prime minister, Nuri al-Maliki, who wanted to see more control on movement into and out of Iraq (Amnesty International 2008). By 2011 the visa regime was relaxed again and a one-month visa could be obtained by Iraqis at the Syrian border, then renewed in-country. In some ways this 'open' or tolerant visa regime has challenged the classical definition of a 'refugee' being completely removed from his home country. When reports from Iraq seem to suggest a reduction of targeted violence, a greater surge in circular migration emerges, and there is increased movement of Iraqis returning home for a specific reason: to check on relatives, to sell their assets, collect their pensions, and to assess the security situation first hand. Some Iraqis use this circularity of movement to find the optimal conditions for themselves and their families. One Iraqi left Iraq for Jordan and then decided to go back to Iraq and try to live there. Then he fled to Lebanon a year later. Further down the line he left Lebanon, fearing that he would be picked up by the security services as he had no papers. Now in Syria, he does not need papers, but he needs to keep his head down.

> *Iraq changed; it changed for the worse, not for the better. … I am trying to forget that Iraq is my country so that I don't ever go back. This is how I am thinking. Because honestly, I cannot live there [in Iraq] anymore.*

> (Mahmoud, Damascus, 2011)

Life in Damascus

Humanitarian aid agencies need refugees in order to operate. So when Iraqis did not come forward in the expected large numbers to register for assistance from the UNHCR, the Agency faced a serious crisis if not an existential one. With no previous experience of working in Syria, and with a government that had never had to struggle to assert its sovereignty vis-à-vis the international aid regime, it was not surprising

that clashes of culture and misunderstandings occurred as these international actors struggled to set up a meaningful presence in Damascus
(see Hoffmann 2016). Without refugees to protect, many a humanitarian aid organization's own mandate would come under scrutiny.[4]
Perhaps that was the push which made the UNHCR rethink and
rewrite its policy towards urban, self-settled refugees (see UNHCR
2009b). Or perhaps it was independently considering updating its previous position regarding the self-settled refugee as somehow irregular,
and outside the 'legal' framework of its mandate. Whatever the background, the UNHCR revised its policy and its programmes in 2010 in
view of the Iraqi response to displacement in Syria and in view of the
demands of the Syrian government that all aid to Iraqis had also to be
extended to needy Syrians. In addition to its concerted effort to create
mobile teams to seek out Iraqis to register as refugees, it also created
Syrian and Iraqi refugee volunteer teams to provide support in local
hosting community centres, and community drop-in centres. Muna
was one such UNHCR volunteer:

> I live in a popular neighbourhood where there are people from many dif-
> ferent countries. In our apartment building there are Syrians, Palestinians,
> Iraqis, and Somalis. Our relationship with them is all good. We don't
> bother them and they don't bother us and we are in good communications
> with each other. We help each other. There is an Iraqi neighbour who was
> a housewife with four children, two boys and two girls. One day her hus-
> band went out to work, it was informal, as Iraqis are not supposed to
> work, and she received a phone call that her husband had died. Imagine,
> she had no one. She did not believe it and thought that it was a joke. She
> went to the hospital and there he was, dead. So I helped her as a neighbour
> and an Iraqi. We were able to get funds to bury him though friends and
> UNHCR. And she stayed for one month after that waiting for him to come
> back every day at 8 pm. I started dropping by every day at that time
> because she would get into a hysterical fit. But thank goodness she recov-
> ered after a few months and life goes on. Of course she is grieving inside.
> That is what neighbours are for.

(Muna, Damascus, 2011)

Between 2005 and at least 2012, Syria was a haven and a refuge for
over a million displaced Iraqis. And while some Iraqis have now been
compelled to move on in response to the increasing instability and
armed conflict in Syria itself, a sizeable percentage of the 200,000 Iraqis

registered with the UNHCR as of 2011 continue to receive assistance in the government-controlled areas of Syria (UNHCR 2014). Many Iraqis who remain in Syria belong to minority Christian groups such as the Assyrians and are 'protected' by the state. Up until the present, there has been no mass exodus of Christian Arabs, Assyrians, or other ethno-religious Syrian or displaced group from government-controlled areas. Many of the displaced Iraqis mourn the loss of religious diversity within both Christianity and Islam in Iraq. Their continuing presence in Syria speaks loudly to their general ease of worship there.

> We were a family in Iraq, like any other family, a mother and father and future for kids. We were all university educated. I was a university student and I used to go and come back on my own. But now the displacement due to the occupation is huge. It changed everything. Everything is gone from Iraq. It is mass destruction. In one day, everything got turned upside down. Nothing. No home to stay in, no father and no mother, both separated to different areas. We never used to say Muslim, Christian, Sunni, Shi'a. My case is that my father is Sunni, and my mother is Shi'a. We didn't differentiate. Our friends were Christian, Muslim, Sabaean, Yazidi, and so on.

(Samira, Damascus, 2011)

Despite the brutality of the Syrian conflict and the extraordinary menace of the Islamic State group (IS) with its imported sectarian extremism, Syria remains a place of refuge and sanctuary. Providing asylum to the stranger is a clearly defined ideal in Syrian society, and one that is generally acted upon. It is mainly in the north-eastern sections of the country where IS has terrorized the Christian communities of Hasake and Qamishli that such ideals are hard to find in practice. Otherwise, across the country, in urban neighbourhoods, towns, and villages, Syrians have opened their homes to fellow Syrians displaced by the conflict in nearby areas. As Zaman identifies, a United Nations inter-agency survey conducted in 2013 in fifty-two neighbourhoods in the city of Aleppo found that of half a million Syrians registered as internally displaced, nearly 60 per cent were hosted by local charities and families (Zaman 2016: 5). In Damascus, local reports suggest that similar sanctuary has been provided to nearly 2 million internally displaced Syrians, including many 'stateless Kurds', swelling the population of Damascus from about 2 million to nearly 4 million over the past few years. This local response to provide for the stranger is not surprising, given the importance of sanctuary and the generosity in Syrian society. And despite the public emphasis on the Syrian Red Crescent and international agencies in the Western press, most of the humanitarian work at the local level in Syria is organized and managed by local grassroots organizations. Many of these voluntary groups have been complemented by the dynamism of the humanitarian initiatives run by the Syrian diaspora and the wider Muslim solidarity groups that have brought humanitarian help from the Middle East and Europe. The Iraqi refugee crisis in Syria mobilized these small, fragmented, informal charitable associations and local religious organizations, Muslim and Christian alike. Many had been operating with destitute Syrians in the country before the mass influx of Iraqis to Syria. With the displacement crisis many new groups and networks have been formed in Syria in response to local suffering (see Slim and Trombetta 2014).

The director of the Middle East Council of Churches in Damascus was interviewed by Tahir Zaman, and confirmed the conflation of religious with social and moral duty:

> As Syrian citizens, we have a duty to support and help the government indirectly and to alleviate let us say the burden and the tension, otherwise we would see people on the street starving and this would affect our society. We are a part of this society and we bear our responsibility. We believe it is not only the responsibility of the humanitarian agencies but also the churches.

> (Zaman 2016: 160)

Such outpourings of local-level charity, compassion, and support, as well as familiarity with social ideals and customs, have led many Iraqis to see their places of abode and their neighbourhoods in a familiar and familial light. Displaced Iraqis in Damascus have expressed notions of familiarity, neighbourliness, and home-like spaces in the community. Some of these have been recognized and elaborated on by agencies of the international aid regime, such as the establishment of a cohort of volunteer Iraqis who seek out and assist new arrivals, but others have emerged from the action of Iraqis themselves. As Zaman argues, Syria can be conceptualized as a familiar space for Iraqi forced migrants, wherein cultural practices, including religious ones, are sustained and realized through social and kin networks, and also mediated through new urban settings. These communal 'home-like spaces' are then produced and inhabited by the Iraqi forced migrants (Zaman 2016: 18).

These familial homes—the domestic dwellings, community organiza-tions, and the city—thus constitute key spaces that help Iraqi forced migrants reorient themselves in the wake of displacement.

Making a home is one of the most fundamental human acts, and among forced migrants is particularly vital as it is a 'remaking', often with limited—if any—resources. In the context of Iraqi exiles in Damascus it can be seen as a central 'emplacement' strategy, in which everyday experiences of Iraqis and their engagement with religious practices are re-calibrated as a practice of conviviality (Zaman 2016: 133). The home in Syria, as in any other authoritarian state, becomes the defining religious space—reinforcing the petty acts of daily life with the religious practice. The privacy with which religious obligations are gen-erally regarded is best expressed with the response I often heard when someone had overstepped the bounds of 'correct' behaviour and speech: 'That is between me and God'. Rules governing the etiquette of hospi-tality and privacy rights become part of a universal pattern of order and religious salvation. The city itself is thick with religious significance and practices. And a form of quiet religious activism in the neighbourhood mosques and informal Quran study groups for men and women has grown, perhaps because of a lack of government interest (Pierret 2013). Much the same occurred in Iraq under the secular dictatorship of Saddam Hussein. Thus for Iraqi refugees these practices are important, as they affirm Damascus as a familiar space.

When we consider Iraqi displacement and forced migration to Syria, we need to conceptualize Syria as a familiar receiving space where Iraqis can belong, rather than as a space of isolation and alienation (Chatelard 2011). Damascus is perfectly described by Ulf Hannerz (1996: 13) as a city which has especially intricate internal goings on and simultaneously reaches out into the wider world. It is a city that brings the home out into the neighbourhood and refreshingly makes community ties as important as familial ones. A common expression heard in Damascus is 'al-jar qabil al-dar wa al-rafiq qabil al-tariq'. This proverb of ancient origin advises people to choose the neighbour before the house and the friend before the road taken. For Iraqi refu-gees, the Damascene popular admonition to make neighbourly ties as important as domestic ones guarantees that the stranger, or temporary guest, will find comfort and ease from his distress (Zaman 2016: 145).

Damascus, and Syria in general, has occupied an important intersti-
tial place in the region. It is where ideas, people, symbols, language,
music, and goods from the Middle East and wider world have criss-
crossed for centuries. Iraqis arriving in Damascus find themselves at
home in the city and its residential quarters as they already possess an
understanding of the city and share its cognitive space.

> *[If] you speak to someone who is fairly family comfortable [in Syria], has work and
> a home—he doesn't give Europe a second thought. Do you know why? He tells you
> that he can go to the mosque and pray at his convenience. He can hear the* adhan
> *(call to prayer) as a Muslim. When it is Ramadan he feels that it actually is
> Ramadan and the same for 'Eid. In Europe you can't feel that it is Ramadan, 'Eid
> or another occasion. Isn't this something that affects a person? A Muslim is affected
> by such things.*

(Mu'tasim, quoted in Zaman 2016: 153)

Conclusion: Displaced Iraqis and the Gathering Storm Clouds

Iraqi exiles have regularly confounded the Western-based system of
humanitarianism. Iraqis did not flee their country when expected to,
nor have they returned at the rate it was assumed that they would, even
after the descent into armed conflict in Syria, their major hosting state.
They have eschewed the holding centres and containment camps set up
for them on barren borderlands, and have sought refuge and hospitality
from their Arab hosts in populous localities and urban centres of Syria
(as well as Jordan). The Iraqi rejection of camps as a response to refugee arrivals has caught the international community off guard, and has
since resulted in a significant and major rethink, at the UNHCR and
other refugee agencies, as to how to deal with refugees who do not
enter refugee camps. Only a few years ago, refugees who evaded camps
were criminalized for such acts. However, in 2009, largely as a result
of the Iraqi crisis, the UNHCR issued new guidelines to address the
bureaucratic requirements for effectively dealing with (protecting) the
self-settled, urban refugees.

Iraqi exiles and their hosts have largely rejected the contemporary
Western notion of the separation of the stranger or asylum seeker from
the rest of society. These acts have a resonance and clarity with the
historical context of the late Ottoman era, and its system of *millet*

communities spread far and wide over the Arab provinces. With the collapse of the empire and the imposition of British and French Mandates in the inter-war years, migration, forced and voluntary, characterized the region, creating widespread and large-scale networks of families, lineages, and tribes. Considerations of social capital, networks, and alliances then became significant when Iraqis came to decide the time and the route by which to flee. In addition, notions of hospitality and refuge operated at the individual and community level—not by government decree. Escape and exile—though by its very nature dangerous and insecure—was more easily converted into security and asylum in the public consciousness. The granting of hospitality was seen not only as a public good but also an act that enhanced the host's reputation. These social and ethical norms underpinned the success of Iraqi self-settlement and local community hosting in Syria.

More ominous, though, and reflected in the title of Sophia Hoffmann's book *Iraqi Migrants in Syria: The Crisis before the Storm* (2016), was the response of both the few large IGOs permitted to work in the country after 2007 and the young, educated Syrian hosts who were employed by these agencies. Prior to 2006, Syria had no official NGOs other than those set up by Asma, the wife of Bashar Asad. Her 'government/non-government organizations' (GONGOs) were set up to help address Bashar Asad's push to gradually 'move' from a centrally controlled socialist economy toward a more neo-liberal (if crony) form of capitalism, much as it seemed China had done. These GONGOs created the initial acceptance among the political elite of the country for non-state welfare provisions. They also created a small cadre of young, educated Syrians able to work alongside international staff. Once the Asad government had permitted the international humanitarian aid IGOs and NGOs to operate in Syria, the stage was set for a storm of massive proportions. These agencies brought with them hegemonic standards of aid delivery which relied on particular state–society relations and ideas of statehood which were very much at odds with the day-to-day reality of Syrian politics and relations between the citizen and the state.

The humanitarian aid regime's operational 'handbook' required the labelling and categorizing of people, on the basis of which they could then determine what rights each group was entitled to. To do so, they needed to build the capacity of their local Syrian counterparts, and imbue them with a sense of empowerment, agency, capacity, and democratic awareness. In some cases this meant lectures on civil disobedience in democratic societies. Initially the Syrian government had little interest in these activities, perhaps viewing them as focused training for Syrians in order to better liaise with the international agencies and their work with Iraqi refugees. But among the educated young Syrians working side by side with international aid practitioners, questions soon emerged. Why do some Iraqi refugees have rights that Syrian citizens don't have? Why does a 'gay Iraqi woman' get special treatment and prioritized resettlement, while a Syrian gay man—who is also discriminated against—has to remain in the shadows, out of the view of internal security services, for fear of being blackmailed or arrested, or, worse, 'disappeared'?

The question of citizen rights vis-à-vis the state were particularly perplexing in a society where the social contract between the individual and the state was built upon two fundamental principles: keeping your head down so that you were not noticed, and developing a social network and connections (*wasta*) to see you out of any unwanted attention or trouble. The Syrian citizen had no assurance of being able to travel, for example, even with fully valid travel documents. He could be stopped at a border crossing and refused exit without explanation. He had no fall-back, other than his connections. The Iraqi registered with the UNHCR, however, suddenly had rights and community support within the framework of the Syrian neighbourhood and community he inhabited which the Syrian citizen did not have.

Perhaps my most prescient encounter in Damascus at this time was coming across a crowd in 2010 that had decided to protect a young man being given a traffic ticket for alleged irregular parking in the old city of Damascus. This was a common ruse often used by traffic police to collect a little extra on the side. *Baksheesh*, they called it. The young man who was being ticketed felt he was not in the wrong and was protesting loudly. A crowd gathered around him and began to harass the policeman. 'Let him go,' they started to shout. 'He has done no wrong. He has rights, you know.' That was the first time I heard the use of a rights-based discourse by a crowd in the streets of Damascus. Where had this language emerged from? Clearly a new generation of young Syrians were aware of the language of humanitarian aid and were beginning to test the waters. The stage was being set for widespread sympathy for the Arab Spring erupting elsewhere in the Middle East and the massive storm in citizen–state relations that exploded in March 2011.

8

THE UNMAKING OF A STATE AS SYRIANS FLEE

Syria became home to the refugees who fled the armies of Ibrahim Pasha in 1839
Syria became home to the Circassian refugees in 1860
Syria became home to the Armenian refugees in 1914
Syria became home to the Palestinian refugees in 1948
Syria became home once again to Palestinian refugees in 1967
Syria became home to the refugees from Kuwait in 1990
Syria became home to refugees from Lebanon in 1996
Syria became home to refugees from Iraq in 2003
Syria became home to refugees from Lebanon in 2006

It will be written in the history books and generations will remember that Syria never closed its borders for those who fled their homes seeking safety and refuge

Syria has never asked any Arab for a visa to enter its lands whether it was a visit or a permanent stay

In Syria not a single tent was put up on the borders to accommodate refugees across the years, houses were opened, streets were vacated and cities were renamed to allow refugees to feel at home

Let it be written in the history books and let generations remember, that when a Syrian needed help and refuge, borders were closed and the world looked away.

Yaman Birawi, Facebook post, October 2015

In March 2011 I was in Damascus staying at the Danish Research Institute, Beit Aqqad, a fourteenth-century Mamluk residence that had only recently been opened after nearly a decade of careful restoration by Danish and Syrian architects and conservationists. I was there to run a two-day course on Palestine refugees and international law and was resting in the *liwan*, the vaulted portal of the institute's large interior courtyard. In one of those moments of complete serendipity, I recognized the young man crossing the courtyard. 'Chesa', I called out, 'What are you doing here?' Chesa Boudin had been an American Rhodes Scholar and one of my students at the Refugee Studies Centre at the University of Oxford a few years back. 'I am here with my mother, Professor Bernadine Dohrn, and Professor Lisa Wedeen from the University of Chicago.' Katherine Boudin, Chesa's mother, had belonged to the 1970s radical American group the Weathermen, as had his father, David Gilbert. They had both served time in a federal penitentiary on murder charges following a failed bank robbery. Katherine had driven the getaway car. On Katherine's incarceration, Chesa was 'adopted' by a fellow Weatherman, Bernardine Dohrn, who later became an adjunct professor of law at Northwestern University. Chesa had written about his unusual childhood in his statement for admission to our graduate programme. I had been deeply affected by his story and his intimate familiarity with the US prison system. Now he was here in Damascus with a law professor (Dohrn) and a political science professor (Wedeen), known for her important book about the Hafez Asad regime, *Ambiguities of Domination: Politics, Rhetoric and Symbols in Contemporary Syria* (1999).

'Yes, but what are you doing in Damascus now?' Chesa explained that he was accompanying his mother and Professor Wedeen on a speaking tour she was undertaking in Syria sponsored by the US State Department. And he went on to say that Lisa was speaking about civil disobedience. I remember thinking 'how odd'. What Syrian would attend such a talk when there was a palpable sense of unease in Damascus in the wake of the Arab Spring demonstrations around Tahrir Square in Egypt and the fall of Mubarak? The sister of a close Syrian friend had been staging demonstrations outside the Ministry of Interior for several months; occasionally she was arrested and released after a few hours and at others times she was held for a few days. The authorities were obviously playing with her—threatening her, but hesitating to be too brutal. She came from an elite political family and had strong connections within the educated pre-Ba'thi political nobility of the country. After her arrest for participating in demonstrations in February she had gone on hunger strike once she realized that the authorities were not planning to release her soon. Finally in early March she was released and 'advised' to leave the country for Lebanon, where she could conduct her Facebook protests reunited with her son. The city was also abuzz with news emerging from Der'a where some teenage boys had been arrested for writing anti-government graffiti on walls. The elders of the community were engaged in talks with the government for their release, and demonstrations in their support were growing daily. Their arrest and alleged torture provoked an immediate response from the tribal leaders and elders of this traditional town. In a delegation to the governor, the elders asked for the release of the boys, citing their youth and asking the governor to be forgiving. His response was to tell the elders to go back to the mothers of these young detainees and tell them to 'make more children'. This chilling threat, and the shocking disregard for the traditional respect generally accorded to the older generation, galvanized the population and turned what had been peaceful demonstrations calling for greater freedoms into ugly and violent mobs.

It wasn't easy to make sense of why the US State Department would have supported talks on civil disobedience at such a time. But perhaps following the logic of Lisa Wedeen's book, the notion of 'as if' could apply to Western liberal ideas of protest as well as to political rhetoric supporting reverence for the country's president. So, Syrian government permission for a series of talks on civil disobedience was granted to the US embassy as an 'as if' notion; except this time it was the Asad regime that was taking on the 'as if' role: 'We permit these talks *as if* we are a liberal, democratic state'. My take on all this was that a polite, but small, audience would attend these talks. For as much as the educated elite might have wanted to attend, memories of the regime's brutal crackdowns in the late 1970s and early 1980s and fear of its surveillance apparatus, as well as some ambiguous positioning in the light of the ongoing protests in Damascus and Der'a, would keep people away.

The next morning, Friday 18 March, we began teaching early. At our midday break, I asked the Beit Aqqad security guards how the previous evening's talk had gone. They told me it was packed out with no seating room left; people had spilled out into the courtyard to hear Lisa talk. I was really surprised. It was not what I would have expected from a Syrian audience living under the brutal fist of a regime that brooked no dissent beyond that permitted 'for show'. Perhaps it was the educated Syrian youth who largely attended, the 'millennials' born after 1980, who had no memories of the brutal past and who had come of age during the regime's attempt post-2000 to move to a neo-liberal economy (see also Abboud 2016). I was sure very few of the middle-aged or older generation of educated Syrians had attended. But I hardly had time to digest this information when the guards told me to come into their security room and watch the television. Al-Jazeera was reporting massive demonstrations at the Umayyad Mosque just a few hundred metres away from us, as well as reports that five people had been killed by security forces trying to disperse demonstrators in Der'a. The next day Der'a was reported to be sealed off, with no one allowed to enter.

The governor of Der'a—a cousin of President Asad—was quickly withdrawn from his post. But it was too late to stop the mass demonstrations in Der'a growing in strength. Syrian security forces are not given much training in crowd control or managing demonstrations peacefully. It was not long before the government resorted to force. In a region like Der'a, which has a strong tribal presence, force was quickly met by force. The more the government used lethal force, the more the demonstrators found means to defend themselves and their families. Certainly as early as April 2011, rumour was circulating in Syria that the Der'a demonstrators were being armed by Saudi Arabia. Throughout the country local coordinating committees sprang up, made up largely of educated young men and women who had gained some experience working with international agencies during the Iraqi refugee crisis in 2006–10. They took part in organizing peaceful demonstrations demanding government reform, greater freedoms, and dignity. As the government began to lash out at the protesters, some civilians began to arm themselves and march with the protestors to protect them from assault by government troops and military machinery. But they lacked a formal unified structure.

Demonstrations continued in Damascus and in Der'a. The government released images of guns, hand grenades, and bullets found hidden in a mosque and began a media campaign accusing foreign terrorists of running and supporting the agitation. Within a month thousands of soldiers were on the streets, backed up with tanks and snipers opening fire on civilians. Armed security agents were also conducting house-to-house sweeps in the search for activists, several of whom were 'disappeared' and have still not been found. By May demonstrations and clashes with regime forces had spread from Der'a to Damascus, to Homs, Hama, and Aleppo. The USA imposed further sanctions on Bashar Asad and six senior Syrian officials for human rights abuses; the Swiss government passed measures to restrict arms sales to Syria and banned thirteen senior Syrian officials from travel to Switzerland. By June details emerged of a mutiny by Syrian soldiers in the town of Jisr al-Shaghour, who refused to fire on civilians. By August a ferocious assault on the city of Hama left hundreds of protesters dead, and the USA, Britain, France, Germany, and the European Union demanded that Asad resign, saying that he was unfit to lead. In the wake of the Arab Spring in Tunisia and Egypt, many in the West misjudged the Asad regime's powerbase, and disingenuousness. The demonstrators were recast as terrorists by the government, and brutal force was deployed to kill, arrest, and 'disappear' any dissidents.

Backdrop to Syrian Forced Migration

By October 2011 the West's call for the overthrow of the Asad regime was met by resistance internationally, and a proxy war between numerous states was clearly emerging. In that same month, Russia and China vetoed a UN Security Council resolution that threatened sanctions against Syria if it did not immediately halt its military crackdown against civilians. They were supported by Iran and the Iranian-backed Lebanese Hezbollah in their defence of the regime. Turkey, Saudi Arabia, and Qatar, along with other Arab states, however, allied with the West to demand that Asad step down, and were openly supplying arms and funds to the numerous armed opposition groups that had formed in the country. By November, the UN human rights office reported that the death toll from the uprising was 3,500. And later that month the Arab League overwhelmingly approved sanctions against Syria to pressure the government to end its crackdown, an unprecedented move by the League against an Arab state.

On 23 December the nature of the uprising changed when two car bombs exploded near intelligence agency compounds, killing forty-four people in the first suicide attack since it began. Many analysts began to question how it was possible to penetrate these compounds; evidence has since mounted suggesting that it was the regime itself that had set off these explosions in order to substantiate a 'terrorist' enemy and thus justify its actions against the demonstrators and armed opposition. At about the same time the government released 755 prisoners, ostensibly in response to a Human Rights Watch accusation that the regime was hiding hundreds of detainees from the UN observers. Many of those released were former Iraqi soldiers who had been 'decommissioned' by the US administrator of Iraq, Paul Bremer,[1] in 2003 as well as others who had become radicalized in the intervening years. These largely al-Qaeda fighters had been defeated by an alliance of US General David Petraeus's Surge Campaign with local Iraqi Sunni tribal fighters. The battle-hardened Iraqi former soldiers and other radicals who fled Iraq after the successful Petraeus campaign were regarded as a threat to Syrian stability when they crossed over into the country between 2007 and 2008. Most were rounded up and put into Syrian prisons. Their release in December 2011 was seen by many as a cynical effort by the state to create and 'grow' a terrorist enemy.

By March 2012 the resistance in Homs crumbled, and the UN reported that more than 8,000 people had been killed by the government crackdown on the popular protests. The popular uprising was rapidly transforming itself into a civil war with government forces and shadow militias—called *shabiha*—opposing local protestors, now often supported by Free Syrian Army (FSA) units, and other armed groups, some more extreme than others. The armed conflict soon attracted radical extremists, Islamists, and other jihadists. These included fighters from Afghanistan, Chechnya, Jordan, Tunisia, and Western states. The more the violent fighting spread, the greater the displacement of Syrians and their families. Initially families moved from scenes of fighting to safety in other parts of the country. Such movement was labelled 'internal displacement' as Syrians, like many peoples before, looked for safety and sanctuary among kin groups or social networks. Initially many resisted crossing Syria's frontier zones to neighbouring countries. The Palestinian dispossessions of 1948 and later 1967 were a stark reminder of what happened when you crossed your country's borders; the displacement and forced migration of Iraqis after 2003 looked as if it was going in the same direction. Once you left your country, return was next to impossible.

By March 2012 a numbers game had emerged within international circles in reporting on the Syrian crisis. For Western aid practitioners and some scholars, the higher the estimated numbers of forced migrants the better; media appeals for humanitarian aid work best when numbers are high and assistance can be formally organized. Policymakers can better justify international condemnation when it can be shown that very large numbers of innocent people are being caught in the crossfire or are being deliberately targeted. For the Syrian government, on the other hand, the lower estimates of people displaced helped to maintain the official narrative of 'terrorists' and others randomly attacking the state. It played to the government position that this was not a popular uprising but rather a foreign plot to unseat the Ba'thi-led government. The state apparatus also believed that with fewer numbers fleeing, international interest might wane and the state's internal security service could then go about doing its work with impunity.

The facts on the ground were very hard to ascertain, with few journalists allowed into the country, and much of the information from the armed uprising emerging on YouTube and individual blogs. Verifiable reports from the specialist UN agencies showed small but significant numbers of people fleeing flashpoints of fighting between the state forces and local insurgents; they revealed a pattern of flight, local accommodation, and return whenever possible. At times people were fleeing to neighbouring villages and towns where they might have kin; at other times and in other places, they were crossing international borders. This pattern of movement had deep roots in the history of dispossession and displacement in the region. Though relatively small in numbers in the first year of the crisis, the flight of innocent bystanders in Syria was creating a grave humanitarian situation, which required international assistance and support to neighbouring countries outside the usual response of UN emergency assistance through formal 'refugee' camp structures.

Throughout the months that followed, the government took to accusing the protestors of being armed by foreign elements—the

Saudis, the Qataris, and the Libyans were the assumed bankrollers. The more force the government used, the greater the crowds, both peaceful and not so peaceful. Finally the government's apocalyptical warnings came true. The violent demonstrators became the rebel forces, some armed and protected by middle-class Syrians and others supplied from abroad. The armed defenders of local communities were increasingly joined by young conscripts who had absconded from the army, not willing to shoot their own people. They called themselves the Free Syrian Army, and set out to protect towns and villages from the government forces and internal security (see also Yassin-Kassab and al-Shami 2016).

When fighting broke out in Idlib in the north of the country in 2011, the Turkish government set up a refugee camp just across the border. At least 10,000 Syrians, men, women, and children, fighters and families, took refuge in the camp. Reliable estimates put the total number to have crossed the Turkish border in 2011–12 at 20,000. Many returned to the Syrian towns and villages in the Idlib region when the fighting stopped. With each fresh government assault on the province, the numbers crossing the border into exile increased sharply. The mobility and circularity of movement across the border surprised some humanitarian aid workers. However, this region of Turkey adjacent to Idlib was the Hatay province—once part of Syria under the French Mandate, but transferred to Turkey in 1939 in an effort to keep it on the side of the Allies in the Second World War. Many crossing the border had personal connections which they could tap into in their search for refuge. Such local hosting accommodation rendered the usual international efforts at number counting at formal refugee camps inappropriate and insufficient to assess the significance of the crisis in humanitarian terms.

In Lebanon a similar situation prevailed. The Bekaa Valley was the primary destination for many Syrians fleeing the fighting in Homs and the surrounding villages. The Bekaa, too, had been part of Syria until the French Mandate split it off to create a 'Greater Lebanon' in the 1920s. Thus, here as well, many Syrians had family ties and other links with local communities. The Lebanese government refused to set up formal refugee camps. If the displaced Syrians seeking sanctuary and asylum had been had been consulted, they too would have refused to be corralled in a fenced UN refugee camp. Instead, they sought refuge with host families, with landowners whose crops they had picked seasonally for decades, and with relatives throughout the country. This pattern of seeking sanctuary made it very difficult for international aid agencies to compile accurate numbers of displaced Syrians for fundraising campaigns. By mid-2012 there were 'guesstimates'; UN sources put the number of Syrians to have crossed the border into Lebanon from the north at somewhere between 7,000 and 10,000. These numbers were in addition to the nearly 500,000 Syrian migrants who largely made up the Lebanese construction and agricultural sectors. To make head-counting even more difficult, many Syrians who sought sanctuary in Lebanon regularly returned to Syria as news reached them that the fighting around their villages and home towns had died down.

The Jordanian border was also an important crossing area, particularly from the Der'a region. Credible estimates in 2012 put the number of Syrians who had crossed into Jordan at 10,000–15,000, joining another 80,000 Syrians already working legally in the country. Many were in the northern border areas and were being accommodated by local communities. By early 2012 rumour had it that the Jordanian government had asked the UNHCR to open an official UN refugee camp for Syrians between Mafraq and the northern border. It was clear from the circularity of movement and flight that the displaced Syrians had exhibited in this first year of the conflict that such an enclosed camp would be unpopular. Syrians were clearly seeking to maintain their mobility and thus their ability to return when they assessed that the situation permitted. Furthermore, many Syrians did not want to register and reveal vital information about themselves, for fear that it might compromise their ability to return if such data fell into the hands of the Syrian government. Registering with the UNHCR as a refugee in this conflict was tantamount to publicly taking sides, something many Syrians did not wish to do. Rather, they were seeking short-term refuge until they felt it was safe to return to their homes.

Contrary to some expectations, few Palestinian or Iraqi refugees in Syria fled during the first year of the uprising. UNHCR figures from 2012 for 2011 suggested that only 1,200 Iraqis returned to Iraq during those first twelve months. Both refugee groups kept a low profile. Most of the fighting in the first year of the crisis was not in areas with significant Palestinian or Iraqi neighbourhoods. Homs, Hama, and Der'a were not settlements with large refugee populations. But there were urban concentrations where unemployment had been growing, especially as impoverished Bedouin herding families from the north-east of Syria gave up their land in the face of a prolonged drought and came to the outskirts of these towns and cities in search of alternative employment to keep their families alive.

Until 2012 the crisis in Syria could not be called a 'refugee' crisis as such; rather, it was a humanitarian emergency, a human crisis of displacement and dispossession. Considering the scale of violence, the number of people crossing its borders during the first twelve months was relatively small, perhaps 50,000 in total. Syrians were crossing borders only when there was no other option—and for good reason. They had seen how Iraq's refugees had now reached a milestone of ten years in exile, and a label of 'protracted crisis' had been attached to their situation. They also had the experience of hosting stateless Palestinians burned deeply into their psyche. For Palestinians, the temporary flight from areas of armed conflict and fear of further massacres in 1948 had now turned into nearly a catastrophe of almost seventy years' duration. Most Syrians were keeping their flight to safety as short as possible. They were fleeing their towns and villages and seeking refuge in adjacent towns, villages, and neighbourhoods, waiting for the fighting to stop. Some UN figures suggested that between 2011 and 2012 as many as a quarter of a million Syrians had been displaced internally, but had not crossed international borders. Negotiations to open a humanitarian aid corridor into the country to disburse emergency assistance to all those who had fled their homes and were in temporary shelters were under way. But as hindsight reveals, government intransigence and suspicion of international sympathies meant that little if any aid would reach Syrians living in areas not under the control of the Syrian government.

Mass Flight to Neighbouring States and to Europe (2012–2015)

The descent into armed conflict between Syrian state security and the numerous non-state armed actors after 2011 resulted in the massive and sudden flight of nearly 2 million people across these modern borders. Syrians fleeing south to Jordan sought out familiar family networks; those heading west to Lebanon sought refuge with kinsmen, employers, or social contacts, and those crossing to Turkey largely entered the formerly Syrian Hatay province, or, in the case of Kurds, the Kurdish territory that was originally their homeland before the Shaykh Said rebellion, which saw tens of thousands of Kurds leave Turkey and flee into northern Syria in the 1920s. The frontier zones of Syria were endowed with significant social and economic networks dating back many generations (Chatty 2010b). Thus the enormous forced migration across Syria's borders had been largely determined by its recent 'neo-colonial' and late Ottoman history.[2]

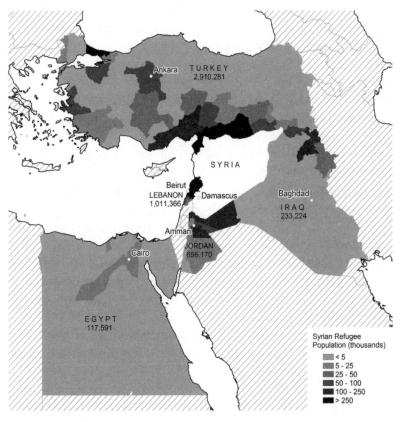

Map 10: Syrians in Neighbouring States

Reception in the host countries was complicated by what appeared to be a clash of expectations, perceptions of rights, and inconsistencies between international human rights and refugee law and local social norms and institutions (Chatty 2013b). Lebanon and Jordan had not signed the 1951 Refugee Convention. And although Turkey had, it reserved its interpretation of the Convention to apply only to Europeans. Furthermore, the UNHCR had not made a prima facie determination that all people fleeing Syria should be regarded as refugees as a group, as they had done for those fleeing certain parts of Iraq in the past decade. Those fleeing Syria had to apply individually to the UNHCR for Refugee Status Determination (RSD) in order to receive any assistance. UN estimates at the end of 2014 were that over 70 per cent of the Syrian refugees flowing across international borders were self-settling in cities, towns, and villages where they had social networks. In other words, only 30 per cent of the Syrian refugee flow was into camps. This included twenty-five camps in Turkey, three in Jordan, and none in Lebanon (ECHO 2015). The general rejection of 'encampment' by refugees in Jordan and in Lebanon was in stark contrast to what had happened in Turkey (Kirisci 2013).

By August 2014 about a quarter of the approximately 800,000 Syrian refugees in the country had actively sought out the 'non-standard' camps managed by the Turkish Disaster Relief Coordination Institution (AFAD) under the Office of the prime minister. These camps had been described as 'five-star' by international experts (International Crisis Group 2013). They did much more than give food and clothes; most camps had classrooms, hospitals, areas for recreation, sports, and religious worship, laundry and television rooms, meeting tents, and even hair salons. Psychological assistance was offered, and the centres were well guarded and safe. Access roads to these camps were paved. And some camps operated well-stocked supermarkets supplying food to the refugees, who used a per capita allowance put on credit cards organized by the World Food Programme (WFP). In contrast, an estimated 600,000 Syrians flooded into Jordan over a short period of time. This led to government fears that these refugees would destabilize the country if they continued to self-settle. The Jordanian government then abandoned its laissez-faire policy and determined that all newly arriving Syrians would be placed in

UN-sponsored camps. Thus, new arrivals after the summer of 2012 were rounded up by the Jordanian army as they crossed the border and handed over to the International Organization for Migration (IOM) for processing and entry into the UNHCR border camp at Za'tari. In Lebanon, an estimated 1,100,000 Syrians had crossed the border and were self-settled in thousands of small units throughout the Bekaa Valley and along the coastal cities of the country, making standard humanitarian relief mechanisms hard to deliver. The international aid regime persisted in recommending the establishment of official UN refugee camps in the country. But these requests have been consistently rejected by the government, for fear of creating another situation similar to the Palestinian 'problem' and the risk of massacres and other violent acts which might be directed at an unpopular population enclosed in a small place (White et al. 2013).

The same summer, an offshoot of the Iraqi-based al-Qaeda group the Islamic State in Iraq and Syria (ISIS) succeeded in taking over Syria's largest oilfield, al-Omar, as well as removing opposition groups from Raqqa. Government forces remained focused on defeating the opposition groups and ignored ISIS. After a number of Westerners it had captured were filmed being beheaded a US-led opposition coalition began targeting ISIS in Syria. By early 2015 the UN estimated that nearly 8 million Syrians had been displaced, some internally and others across national borders. For the next eight months or so increasing numbers of Syrians fled in the wake of ISIS advances, some into areas controlled by militias opposed to the Asad regime. When Russia began to launch air strikes in Syria to support the government forces, a fresh wave of Syrians fled, many of them middle-class professionals who had been staying to help keep the towns and cities they lived functioning. They were fleeing Russian and government bombardments as well as ISIS advances. This massive influx into neighbouring countries did not stop there. Many had the means to pay smugglers to get them to European shores; alternatively, they made their way to Turkey and then proceeded to follow the land bridge to Europe through the Balkans. For a few weeks, this mass of terrified and vulnerable humanity evoked a response of moral duty—especially after the photographs of a dead toddler, Aylan Kurdi, on a Turkish beach were flashed around the world. However, within a few weeks European borderland states started to close their doors, making it nearly impossible for Syrians to reach sanctuary in northern Europe, especially Germany, Sweden, and the United Kingdom. Containment of this dispossessed mass of humanity in Syria's neighbouring states was promoted by the European Union as an acceptable way forward under international law. As a sop to humanitarian principles, the UNHCR could identify the most vulnerable in the refugee camps it controlled, who could then be resettled in countries outside the region; a process which generally took two or three years to complete.

Reluctance to Flee: Bedouin Tribes and Local Coordinating Committees

By 2017 more than half of Syria's population of 23 million had been displaced. Figures released by the UNHCR in March 2017 confirmed more than 11 million displaced, with more than 7 million Syrians thought to be internally displaced while 4.9 million have crossed the state's borders seeking refuge and asylum. We know that more than 1.1 million have crossed into Lebanon, a small country with a population of only 4.4 million. Another 2.9 million have entered Turkey, which has a population of over 76 million. And at least 650,000 have sought refuge in Jordan among its population of less than 6.4 million. Why have some sought refuge across national borders while others have remained in Syria, even when fighting has destroyed their homes and neighbourhoods? Why have some who fled returned? And finally, why have so few of Syria's Christian minorities fled? In other words, why has there been no mass exit of Christians or other minority groups, as occurred in Iraq after 2003 (such as Assyrian Christians and Mandaeans); just the steady exit of people generally in family groups seeking sanctuary and security away from sites of armed conflict?

To answer some of these questions we need to look at the place of the ethno-religious and tribal social groups of Syria. In 2012, a year into the Syrian crisis, policy pundits in the USA and Europe began asking 'Is this the end of Sykes–Picot'? In other words, is the hundred-year-old secret agreement between France and Britain that shaped the contemporary state borders of the Middle East coming to an end? That very question was addressed in 2014 by Abu Bakr al-Baghdadi after he declared himself the 'caliph'—chief civil and religious ruler—of the entity known as ISIL (the Islamic State of Iraq and the Levant) or ISIS (the Islamic State of Iraq and Syria). His goal, he said, was to erase the borders of the modern nation-states of Syria and Iraq, and thus erase Sykes–Picot, which had established these boundaries. But the artificiality of these borders set up by the British and the French are only part of the story. The carving up of the region following the First World War cut across multi-ethnic communities and regularly ignored natural and social frontiers. With or without the Sykes–Picot borders, Syria's numerous multi-ethnic, religious, and tribal communities were responding to the crisis with integrity, internal social cohesion, and a unified defence, even if only at the local level. That community cohesion and defence was often led by the once marginalized Bedouin tribes of the region, the mobile pastoral herders of the vast swathe of semi-arid land that comprised 80 per cent of the Syrian land mass.

Although Bedouin tribes have been largely missing from contemporary Arab political discourses, there is convincing evidence that self-identification among the Bedouin of Syria has grown exponentially (Chatty and Jaubert 2002). They represent between 10 and 15 per cent of the population of Syria and their current involvement in the Syrian crisis must not be underestimated (Chatty 2010a). The Syrian Uprising has drawn Bedouin leaders, national and transnational, deeply into the conflict. Their voices and positions are largely, but not exclusively, on the side of the opposition to the Syrian regime. During the first few months of peaceful demonstration, the shaykh of the 'noble' Hassanna tribe was outspoken on the need for greater freedoms. In the later phase of the uprising he, as well as other leaders, joined the Syrian Tribal Council, which met in Amman and then later in Istanbul to find commonalities with the Syrian National Coalition. In July 2013 Shaykh Ahmed al-Garba, a member of the same family as the great Bedouin leader Ajil al-Yawar, was elected president of the Syrian National Coalition. Other tribal leaders and their followers, such as the Ageidat, have been particularly active in forming armed anti-Asad fighting groups at the local level and as part of a national tribal coalition. The Hadidiyin fought on the side of the opposition forces near Aleppo and Idlib, the Mawali near Hama, Aleppo and Raqqa, while the Beni Khalid had several battalions fighting with the Free Syrian Army near Homs and its suburbs; other Mawali tribesmen fought against the Syrian military in the vicinity of Ma'arat Nu'man. Yes, some other tribal leaders with previous close links to the security services in Syria and in Lebanon have remained loyal to the regime. The Baggara—a large confederation of 'common' (i.e. non-noble) sheep-herding tribes in the Jazireh east of the Euphrates river—have participated in armed activities both in support of and against the opposition. However convenient it would be to connect all the 'noble' transnational tribal Bedouin leaders and their followers with the opposition and its backers in Saudi Arabia, and the 'common' local Bedouin tribes with the regime, the lines are not clear-cut. The key point is that the Bedouin have been present and have participated in both the peaceful demonstrations of 2011 and the violence that followed.

Protests in Syria turned into violent confrontation with Syrian security personnel in March 2011 in the town of Der'a, and shortly thereafter in Homs and Hama. This string of towns had a strong settled Bedouin tribal presence. It was clearly evident that the Bedouin communities in these flashpoints resorted to armed self-defence when attacked by government agitators or troops. Some tribal leaders issued manifestos against the Asad regime (e.g. Al Hassanna); their followers formed brigades to defend their neighbourhoods and quarters in these front-line towns against the onslaught of the security forces. Throughout the zones of armed conflict along the string of cities and towns between Der'a in the south and Aleppo, Bedouin have formed armed neighbourhood defence units, keeping the local coordinating committees who struggle to provide services to the local population as safe as possible. They have come to represent the local-level defence forces of villages, towns, and urban neighbourhoods where their membership predominates. By these acts of defiance, they created pockets of relative safety and sanctuary for displaced Syrians from other parts of the country who have resisted going into the exile that crossing international borders largely suggests.

Seeking Sanctuary across Borders

The decision to leave one's country is never easy. For the majority of the 11 million Syrians who have been displaced, crossing the frontier into Lebanon, Jordan, or Turkey has not been an option, due either to inability to reach these zones or a determination to remain in Syria. Of the nearly 5 million who have crossed into neighbouring countries, most have fled to Lebanon, Jordan, and Turkey. These movements have not all been one way; many families moved back and forth between several destinations in their wish to find safety, especially for their children, but also to stay close to home. Some continued to move back and forth, visiting Syria to check on relatives left behind, or on property, or on businesses. Across the frontiers they found great variability in asylum; in some places local communities worked tirelessly to provide sanctuary, seeing the provision of asylum to the stranger as a duty; in other places the atmosphere was not welcoming, and the newly arrived Syrians were discriminated against and criminalized for seeking to work in order to feed their families. In Lebanon the UN was very slow to set up registration and minimal services; in Turkey it was largely kept away from actual service provision and only engaged with as advisers to the government. In Jordan the duty to be generous rapidly gave way to more formal UN refugee camps and services.

Syrians Seeking Refuge in Lebanon

Lebanon has over a million Syrians in the country; most of them have found sanctuary for themselves and their families from the violence, chaos, and anarchy in their homeland. Some wealthy Syrians have managed to move their businesses to Lebanon, and own property in the major cities. Some of these well-off Syrians have been active in setting up or contributing to national or local charities and non-government organizations, helping fellow Syrians to find sustainable livelihoods, or encouraging their children to attend school or take on specialist training. Others are in more desperate situations, and find themselves running out of savings and increasingly impoverished. The latter have become the target of discrimination; some of Lebanon's municipalities have set up curfews, meaning that many Syrians are afraid to go out at night, to work overtime, or to mix in any way with the Lebanese population. For the unskilled Syrians, these curfews have meant that older children are being pulled out of whatever schooling they had been entered into in order to work during daylight hours with their fathers.

SYRIA

Many of the Syrians in Lebanon were not new to the country but had been working for many years in the construction and agriculture sectors of the economy. The continuing armed conflict meant that the wives and children of these workers fled Syria and came to join their husbands and fathers. Their movements were largely progressive and in stages, first arriving in Akkar or the Wadi Khalid region of northern Lebanon and gradually making their way to join their spouses in the Bekaa, Tripoli, and Beirut. Those with jobs feared losing them once it was known that their families had joined them, contributing to the fear and isolation of many of these Syrians.

I was born and raised in Damascus; my husband in Hama. Even before the crisis the economic situation was not good. My husband went to Damascus to work and so I followed and rented a house there. He didn't have a lot of work; his work barely put some food on the table. Then my husband got a job offer in Lebanon so he went there. After a while the situation in Hama and Damascus deteriorated. The primary reason to stay in Lebanon is that there was no money at all in Syria. He came to Lebanon, stayed for a while and then he came back to Syria then went back to Lebanon; it was a very hard situation. My neighbour started giving me money. Even after my husband got a job in Lebanon, he didn't have money for commuting to Lebanon. He used to come and go, stay for a while and then go back to Lebanon. I think we came to Lebanon around the first year of the events in Syria, maybe 2011. It was before my husband had settled down properly in Lebanon; we came to Lebanon twice. First we went to Akkar; my husband's nephew was in Akkar. We were waiting for his nephew to help us find work for my husband, but I couldn't stay any longer so I went back to Syria. I came back for another fifteen days then went back to Syria again. This time I stayed there for nine months. I lived alone, in the same area as my family but I rented alone, I rented a furnished apartment in the beginning, but then there was a big explosion near us. It was very scary, and the neighbourhood used to horrify me, but I couldn't find another house. I couldn't even sleep, I was very distressed. My husband had no intention of bringing me to Lebanon, for him it was settled that he's working in Lebanon and I am in Syria. But after the explosion I told you about, the situation deteriorated badly. I got scared, a lot of things happen, the voices ... the voices, the screaming you hear, and the explosions ... especially after the explosion. God protected my three children; they were in school when the explosion happened. Even now [after three years] I haven't decided whether to stay in Lebanon. Deep inside I wish with all my heart to go back to my house [in Hama]. What's stopping us is work, not fear, not the situation, only work. You can be scared of everything, but you tell yourself whatever God wrote for you will happen, but we have children. We as grownups can endure anything, but it is about the children.

(Reem, Beirut, January 2015)

In the Bekaa Valley—where most Syrians had worked in agriculture—those who have sought sanctuary there with their families are accepting very low-paid work to provide their families with food. This has aroused hostility among the local poor and unskilled Lebanese, who see the Syrian workers as a threat to their own livelihoods, resulting in increased social discrimination and vigilantism. Many Syrians—despite their long association with Lebanon over decades, and often close kinship ties—have begun to feel frightened and cut off from Lebanese society. A response to this has been a growing movement among Lebanese local municipality leaders to provide both for the Syrians and for the Lebanese poor in their areas. These local-level community efforts to help Syrians survive until such a time as they can return to their homeland are being reproduced across the country. The take-up of local hosting community efforts to help Syrian families get up on their own feet is unevenly distributed across Lebanon and is a complex matter, which brings into play the sectarian make-up of the community, its economic and social ties to Syria in the past, its politics, as well as variable notions of duty, hospitality, and morality.

Not all those who sought refuge in Beirut were poor and unskilled. Many were well-educated professionals who reluctantly sought sanctuary in Lebanon. Some, like Marwan below, were well connected with the medical profession in Lebanon and had a relatively soft landing.

I am a medical doctor by training. I was born in Aleppo, and lived there my entire life. I practise medicine but also I do research on different topics especially on public health issues. And by in 2010, I considered myself to be a stable person, with a good family, good job, and would peacefully wait for my retirement. That was my last thought like that because in 2011 the revolution started in Syria. Between March 2011 till June 2012, Aleppo was quiet. Nothing there except, you know, peaceful demonstration from time to time but there was no armed group working inside Aleppo. In 2012, early 2012, a new phenomenon started in Aleppo; the kidnapping of people. And this was started by people who were called 'shabiha' (shadowy figures) at that time. Kidnapping people especially businessmen, doctors, intellectuals and asking for ransom. Then after that, another process started of kidnapping children, children of those businessmen and doctors. And at least two of my friends, two doctors, were exposed to this horrible experience. The daughter of one of them and son of the other were kidnapped. Of course for ransom. In August, late August 2012, I decided to leave because of that feeling of … 'I don't want to expose my children to this experience'. I was afraid, I was so nervous, you know, I used to go down with them at six o'clock in the morning, to be with them waiting for the school bus and then wait for them at the bus stop when they return in the afternoon. I would leave the hospital to go to the bus stop and wait for them to get off the bus. After a while, that made me, you know, so crazy.

But, my wife first refused to leave Aleppo.We had bought our dream house in 2011 just before the crisis and my wife was an architect and she spent almost a year to restore that old house to be something amazing, you know ... it was a big house and she restored it from scratch and we had a very, very good house and we thought this is our house for the rest of our life. Unfortunately, we just stayed there for only three months. So first, my wife refused to move; then she set a condition that we would move for two weeks only, thinking leaving Aleppo temporarily would be good for my mental health. After exactly two weeks, she asked me, 'So? What? It is two weeks now' and she went back. She took the children and put them in Damascus because it was safer there at that time and she went back alone to Aleppo and spent a month alone in our house. Then she realized that life couldn't go on like that. For a while she kept going back and forth between Beirut, Damascus, and Aleppo. Until she recognized that she had to remain in exile until things changed in Syria.

(Marwan, Beirut, December 2014)

But the triggers for flight and the forced movements to safety were never straightforward. Syrians engaged in a circularity of migration, trying to decide whether a move was necessary for the safety of the family or whether other options were possible. The close ties, economic and social, between Damascus and Beirut and Aleppo and Damascus made it possible for Syrians to move multiple times and to take advantage of quiet periods to determine the best place for sanctuary for themselves and their families. Lebanese authorities continued to keep the borders open for visitors, guests, refugees, and exiles for most of the period of the Syrian crisis. Even in 2017 the road between Damascus and Beirut remained open and taxis plied their trade, taking Syrians who could afford the fare back and forth between these two capital cities. Residence permits may still be bought, and those Syrians with means purchase them as necessary. Syrians in Lebanon fall under the same legal provisions as any foreigner. Those too poor to purchase permits to remain in Lebanon have had to either register with the UNHCR as refugees and hope to qualify for some support, or turn to the informal marketplace to find a way of surviving. However, in January 2015 the Lebanese government asked the UNHCR to stop registering Syrians as refugees. Entering the country as temporary workers or guests has also suited many Syrians. Remaining near to Syria was important to them so as to be able to return when conditions permitted.

Syrians Seeking Refuge in Jordan

There are over 600,000 Syrians registered in Jordan as refugees, but also many who were in the country before 2011, legally working and sometimes partners in businesses with Jordanians. Jordan's initial response to the flow of Syrians from the Der'a region after 2011 was open and generous. Most Syrians had kinship ties in northern Jordan or well-established social networks, and the hosting of this initial influx was positive. However, over time the Jordanian government began to show concern at the large numbers streaming across its borders and started to restrict access for some (unaccompanied male youth) or actually returned others (Palestinian refugees from Syria). The host community in Jordan is bombarded with information regarding the negative influence of Syrian refugees in the country—although this is not backed up by the studies that are emerging. At the same time, however, there is widespread acknowledgement that Syrians are skilled workmen, especially carpenters. Employment in the informal sector has created stress even though it brings in much-needed funding. Syrians who are working are fearful of possible arrest as they have no work permits—even though they are largely replacing Egyptians, not Jordanians, in the work force.

> *I am from Der'a. I used to be a nurse and my husband worked in customs and sometimes ran a tailor shop in our building. There were six brothers and they all owned in the apartment building; it had six apartments. At first the fighting in Der'a did not affect us, but after a year it moved into our neighbourhood and our building was hit. My brother-in-law's house which was next door was totally demolished and all his children were killed. So we grabbed our documents and our three children and ran away from the fighting. We also carried the men's father, he was very old, and nearly ninety, but we could not leave him behind. At the Naseeb border crossing we were taken to Za'tari camp where we were given two tents; one for us and one for my father-in-law. After ten days we managed to leave through 'bail' (Jordanian sponsorship). Thanks to the Jordanian wife of my sister's brother-in-law we found these two rooms after a few months searching in this unfinished building. … But our situation is very bad. My husband only finds day wage labour occasionally for 15 Jordanian dollars [US$21] a day. So we cannot ask the UN for assis-*

tance, but it is not enough to live on and we are always worried that he might get deported if he is caught working, because it is not legal to work in Jordan. ... We are just waiting for the conflict to end so that we can go back.

(Rana, March 2015, Amman)

Over time, security concerns began to override the duty to be hospitable, to be generous.

At the beginning you had a refugee crisis with a security component and it has become a security crisis with a refugee component. So in the early days it was 'these are our brothers' and so the natural generosity has now given way to more suspicion about who these people are and the security card is played all the time now.

(Senior international practitioner, Amman, 2015)

Furthermore, there is some social discrimination levelled at Syrians in Jordan; but it is muted compared with that expressed in Lebanon. The majority of Syrians in Irbid and in Amman, for example, are tied in real rather than fictive kinship, and thus negative social attitudes among these hosts tend to be kept closer to the chest. This may be associated with tribal custom and general conceptual concerns related to the requirement of hospitality to tribal kin and strangers or guests. But over time, even the guest can outstay his welcome. Many skilled Syrian workers in Jordan whose work is in demand in the informal market are pushing to have their skills recognized so that they can 'give something back' and so that they can leave the liminality of irregular and illegal work. One proposal—for Syrians to train Jordanians—that is gaining credence in 2017 was first articulated by a group of Syrian carpenters in 2014. Perhaps also playing out in Jordan and muting expressions of negativity towards Syrians is the fact that government and policymakers are known to appreciate the benefit accruing to the country from hosting large refugee populations, as was the case during the Lebanese civil war between 1975 and 1989; the First Gulf War and the flight of nearly 400,000 Palestinians from Kuwait, largely to Jordan; the massive influx of refugees from Iraq in 2006–7; and now Syrians post-2012. International and bilateral aid to help Jordan deal with these large mass influxes of displaced people have for many decades helped the country balance its national 'budget'. The Jordanian Compact agreed in February 2016 in London continues this same tradition of economic support.

THE UNMAKING OF A STATE AS SYRIANS FLEE

Syrians Seeking Refuge in Turkey

Syrians fleeing into Turkey initially crossed the border between the two countries unhindered. They were greeted as guests and provided with sanctuary—largely along the southern border with Syria, but also in Istanbul and in the central Anatolian region of Ankara, where some of the Syrian Circassian community had ties. A general sentiment of recognizing the needs of Syria's refugees was widely articulated, although over time the welcome started to wear thin and local host communities, especially in Kurdish neighbourhoods, began to express concerns. Many thought that refugees from Syria were being given salaries by the Turkish government; others felt that Syrians were working for lower wages (their Turkish employers did not have to pay taxes) and this was driving out the unskilled Turkish workers who had no safety net like that given to refugees from Syria when they lost their jobs. This lack of communication and understanding of the Syrians' situation led to demonstrations, arrests, and a dozen or so deaths in October 2014; many felt that more transparency on the part of the government in terms of just what Syrians were entitled to would relieve the critical situation and growing discriminatory attitudes. The third sector in Turkey—the charitable organizations and religious associations, including the Sufi—was quick to develop assistance and support programmes. Neighbourhood public kitchens providing free meals and bread to poor Turks as well as Syrian refugees resident in the area were common in Istanbul and in Gaziantep.

> My husband came first and then I joined him eight months later with our baby. At first we went to Mersin, but my husband couldn't find a job. When we ran out of money we came to Gaziantep, because the Syrian Interim Government was here. We thought there would be more jobs here. So we came here and two months later we met this nice man who found a job for my husband and rented us these two rooms. Our neighbours gave us some mattress and a TV to watch Syrian television. There is also a mosque nearby where I go and people give me diapers for the baby, bread and daily hot meals as well as supplies of sugar, pasta and oil.

(Hala, Gaziantep, 2014)

Lack of a common language may have been a problem in other times, but in the present crisis language seems to be less significant. Many poor and semi-skilled Syrians are finding some support from the

241

numerous NGOs and religiously motivated charities that have long existed in Turkey to work with the poor. For professionals and skilled workers the situation is more painful, as the language barrier has prevented them from being able to follow their professions (especially physicians, engineers, and lawyers).

> *I am from Homs where I ran a successful business, a family business importing furniture from China and Turkey. Before the crisis my income was good. I lived a happy life. I had the best of food, luxurious restaurants, and clothes brands. I didn't have to worry about anything. Our house was right in the centre of the clashes between the armed opposition and Syrian security forces. After the massacre in al-Khalidiyah on 4 February 2012, I was at a funeral for one of the martyrs and I got shot by security forces and was taken to my uncle's house. I was moved from one house to another for many weeks. Finally I decided to go to Damascus where I met a doctor who was trying to help a homeless family from Homs. As our business in Homs had been shut down I decided to stay in Damascus and work as a focal point providing logistical support and medicine for Homs. I did this for six months until professional relief organizations took over this work.*

> *I was afraid of being arrested and so decided to go to Turkey to help my cousin who was working with the Free Syrian Army. After four months I brought my wife and two children out in the back of an empty ambulance. At first we were in Reyhanli but then we decide to move to Istanbul. My son was coming of school age and there were no good schools in Reyhanli. In Reyhanli, there were many Syrians especially from Idlib and Aleppo as it is a border village. Here in Istanbul, the number of Syrians is less. The compound here where we live has many Syrians. We have Syrian neighbours from Aleppo across the street. We became friends, but they do not make up for our friends and loved ones in Syria and Homs. Here we have to find our way by exchanging experience with other Syrians about life in Istanbul. For example, if I want to have a residence permit, Syrians here tell you how to do it exactly, same thing happens when you want to rent a house. There are no centres to provide orientation and guidance on how to cope here. But we manage. We see Turkish people on the street, on buses, in cars, on the lifts, we say hi to them. They try to communicate with us to express their sympathy with our situation, but no more than that. We would certainly go back to Syria once the heavy fighting ends. Europe is completely out of my concern. I think there was a suggestion about forming a buffer zone inside Syria. If that happened, I would be the first to go there.*

> (Mahmoud, Istanbul, October 2014)

With nearly 3 million registered Syrians in Turkey by 2017, it is not surprising that relationships with the host community have changed over time, and national policy has also fluctuated. At times Turkey has maintained open borders and at others times closed them. Although Turkey has not requested large-scale assistance from the UNHCR, it has sought advice, and in the last few years allowed an increasing number of international and national NGOs to set up programmes and projects to provide assistance to Syrians, especially along its southern border. Of all the neighbouring countries, Turkey has enacted its own domestic asylum laws to provide Syrians with identification papers (as Syrians and not as 'refugees'), basic health care, and access to education. The country's well-established NGO sector, and its growing local community efforts to assist Syrians—set up by Turks and Syrians alike—is very much based on the notion of the duty to be generous (*karam*). However, not all Syrians in Turkey are aware of these provisions, or avail themselves of these opportunities. Poor communications, miscommunications, and confusion over government pronouncements regarding protracted residence or secondary citizenship mean that most Syrians in Turkey take each day as it comes. Sustainable livelihoods, or, at the bare minimum, survival in dignity, trump all other considerations.

Conclusion: Local Accommodation and an Eye on Return

The Syrian response to the Arab Spring in 2011 and ensuing armed conflict between non-state actors and the regime rapidly descended into a proxy war by 2014–15 which saw the displacement and dispossession of more than half of its population of 23 million. Although European states expressed alarm at what they saw as a massive influx of refugees to southern European shores, the numbers of Syrians reaching Europe and applying for asylum still had not reached a million by March 2017 (UNHCR 2017). The majority of Syrians have remained close to home in the neighbouring states of Lebanon, Jordan, and Turkey. Neither Lebanon nor Jordan has signed the 1951 Convention on the Status of Refugees, while Turkey restricts its interpretation to mean only refugees from Europe. Thus all three states have no obligations, under international law, to provide protection. Yet in all three, the duty to be generous, to provide sanctuary to the stranger, has manifested itself as the pervasive response to Syrians, whether as kinsmen, business partners, or just fellow humans. Certainly the response is not evenly delivered, and nor are all Syrians who have sought sanctuary in these host countries living in adequate shelter or free from hunger. What is most striking in reflecting on this exile is the agency, energy, and engagement of Syrians with their hosts at the local and regional level. Less than 10 per cent of all these Syrians are in refugee camps receiving basic shelter, food, and assistance from the UNHCR and its partner agencies.

Most Syrians are self-settled, and are increasingly engaged in the formal and informal economy of their host country. Some were able to take their businesses with them or already had established networks prior to the explosion of the civil war in Syria. Many of these well-off and middle-class Syrians, as they have re-established themselves in exile, have turned to each other to work together to create local projects and activities for the less fortunate Syrians in their midst. These joint projects are particularly widespread in Lebanon and Turkey. Many of these local and national initiatives are now focusing on education, taking up the UN slogan first articulated in 2012 that there be 'No Lost Generation'. The less well-off have sought work in the very large informal economies of all three neighbouring states. Their efforts to survive in dignity are strenuous and require greater assistance. Both Jordan and Turkey have recently agreed to permit the issuing of limited numbers of work permits for Syrians. However, the uptake of applications has been very slow, as many employers prefer the Syrians to remain in the informal economy—as do many Syrians themselves.

Numerous international organizations have begun to address the education, employment, and health concerns of Syrians in exile in these neighbouring countries, and plans are being drawn up at both international and national level to address, for example, the provision of education for school-age children. Recent surveys have confirmed that more than 60 per cent of school-age Syrian children in Lebanon and Turkey are not receiving education; the figures for Turkey are not much better (Chatty et al. 2014). The desire of Syrian parents to see their children back in education fuelled the huge spike in unaccompanied Syrian youth arriving in Europe in 2015. Now, with a concerted internationally funded drive in Turkey, Lebanon, and Jordan to provide education opportunities for Syria's youth, greater opportunity and access will make onward migration less attractive. The greater the expression and articulation of *karam* in providing for Syrians in their exile in neighbouring countries, the greater the likelihood of voluntary return one day—when conditions permit. It will be a return to a devastated land crying out for rebuilding. That challenge will be best met by bilateral, regional, and international efforts among Syrians, Jordanians, Lebanese, and Turks working together with the international community in an effort to revive the Syrian economy and society. Syria, whose strong society was imbued with a great sense of duty to the stranger and provided sanctuary to their neighbours over many decades, would be finally rewarded with a return gift. It was Marcel Mauss, in his seminal *Essay on the Gift*, who first articulated that the duty to provide a gift (hospitality) brings with it an obligation to return a gift (Mauss 2016 [1925]).

The historical legacy of providing refuge to numerous groups of dispossessed and displaced peoples over the past 150 years has not been forgotten either by the Syrians who are currently displaced or those who have received sanctuary in the past. The final decades of the Ottoman Empire saw many forced migrant groups enter Greater Syria and receive sanctuary and support. With the imposition of British and French Mandates in the inter-war years Greater Syria was dismembered, and the modern nation-states of Lebanon, Syria, Iraq, and Palestine came into being. Each of these states has also received forced migrants. However, after independence in 1946, it was the rump modern state of Syria that continued to receive significant mass influxes of dispossessed and displaced migrants: Palestinians in the 1940s and 1960s; Kurds throughout the second half of the twentieth century; Lebanese in the 1970s and 1980s during their civil war, and again in 2006; and Iraqis in the 2000s. These population movements became embedded in the psyche of the modern Syrian state, creating an even greater tolerance for movement, mobility, and migration. Large networks of families, lineages, and tribes, as well as significant social and economic capital, across the frontiers and borders of the Levant, came to characterize modern Syrian engagements. Thus when the country descended into armed conflict and violent war, considerations of such capital, as well as kinship networks and alliances developed and celebrated over the previous century and a half, became significant when Syrians came to decide whether to flee their homes and neighbourhoods but remain in Syria or whether to cross national borders in the search for sanctuary and safety. The previous centuries' tolerance of the 'Other' and the local conviviality that accompanied it as exemplified by the Ottoman *millet* system also meant that being hosted in the neighbouring states which had once been part of the Ottoman Empire and Greater Syria was somehow familiar. In addition, notions of duty, hospitality, and refuge operated at the individual and community level not only in Syria but also in the neighbouring states—and not because of an international rights-based humanitarian template or government decree. The granting of hospitality among Syrians and among the hosting societies in its neighbouring states was seen not only as a public good but also an act which enhanced the host's reputation. These social and ethical norms underpinned the success of Syrian self-settlement and local community hosting in the neighbouring countries of Lebanon, Jordan, and Turkey despite the enormous burden which the neighbouring states had to bear. As we enter the seventh year of the Syrian displacement crisis, it appears that the lessons learned from the late Ottoman reforms with regard to accommodation and integrating of forced migrants continue to hold true in the region once known as Greater Syria, and perhaps offer the West some salutary lessons.

NOTES

1. FORCED MIGRATION AND REFUGE IN LATE OTTOMAN SYRIA

1. Zolberg (1982) estimates that nearly three-quarters of the 200,000 Iberians banished from Catholic Spain were Jews. Some made their way clandestinely into neighbouring France (from which Jews had been officially expelled at the turn of the fourteenth century); others moved to the 'Low Countries'; still others moved to Portugal, whose sovereign saw an opportunity for economic gain. But most scattered among the Muslim states of North Africa and the Middle East, where they joined established communities of their co-religionists and where they were welcomed for the wealth and skills they brought with them.
2. There were 77 Muslims, 44 Christians, and 4 Jews in the first Parliament of 1876. The rapid changes in the composition of the empire are reflected in the 1908 parliament, where there were 234 Muslims (147 Turks, 60 Arabs, and 27 Albanians), 50 Christians, and 4 Jews (see Shaw and Shaw 1977: 278).
3. In 1866 Prince Karl of Hohenzollern-Sigmaringen became the leader of this semi-independent state. In 1881 Romania was declared an independent kingdom, with Karl taking the title King Carol I.
4. The Circassians, who had earlier been expelled with great brutality and mortality from their homelands by the Russians, were especially violent, and resisted Ottoman orders to stop.

2. THE CIRCASSIANS, CHECHNYANS, AND OTHER CAUCASIAN FORCED MIGRANTS REIMAGINING A HOMELAND

1. See FO 195–1184, Calvert to Blunt, Philippopolis, March 1878.
2. Marjeh used to be on the outskirts of the Old City in the nineteenth century. In the early twentieth century it became the locus of Ottoman

and then French Mandate administration. Now it is a central square in the middle of the commercial district of the city.

3. Most of the details regarding the arrival of Circassian refugees were drawn from reports of British consuls or consular officials in Syria and in Cyprus (FO 195/1201 and 11202 and FO 78/2847 and 2848). See also Karpat 1979.

4. The Hijaz railway was begun at Damascus in 1900. By 1908 it reached Medina in the Hijaz. It was built to a very high standard at very low costs in one of the fastest such projects ever completed in the Ottoman Empire. It was built faster and for less money than any other railway ever built (Rogan 1999: 66).

5. FO 424/210, Lloyd, Constantinople, 16 April 1906.

6. Diwaniyya district of Damascus was settled by mainly Kosovar and Albanian refugees throughout the twentieth century.

7. The Fadl, one of the oldest sheep-raising Bedouin tribes in Syria with a pedigree going back centuries, became a refugee tribe along with the Circassians after the June 1967 War. Some of the tribe made their way to Lebanon where they occupied the Bekaa Valley and Anti-Lebanon mountains.

8. Damascus consular reports 1883, 1895–6 195/1886 and 195/1932, and also Schumacher 1888: 57, 87.

9. FO 424, vol. 70, pp. 359–60. Confidential report 585/600 (Layard to Salisbury), 10 May 1878.

10. FO 424, vol. 210, pp. 27–8 (O'Connor to Grey). Enclosure No. 28, 16 April 1906.

11. An excellent ethnography of a Circassian community was conducted by Seteney Shami in her Ph.D. dissertation 'Ethnicity and Leadership: The Circassians in Jordan' (Shami 1982).

12. Shami's estimates are far more conservative than those of the Syrian Circassian community leaders, who claim that there are around 135,000 Circassians in Syria (Adel, personal communications, 2005).

3. THE ARMENIANS AND OTHER CHRISTIANS SEEK REFUGE IN GREATER SYRIA

1. See for example the contrasting positions of Shaw and Shaw 1977; Davison 1954; Walker 1997; Hovannisian 1997a; McCarthy 2001; Dadrian 1997; and Rogan 2015.

2. Melson (1996: 23) uses the UN definition of genocide to guide his work. This widely accepted definition formulated in 1948 takes genocide to mean actions 'committed with intent to destroy in whole or in part a national, ethnic, racial or religious group as such'. This defini-

tion clearly places the Armenian massacres in the category of genocide: either genocide-in-part or genocide-in-whole.

3. Arnold Toynbee had been sent out to the Ottoman Empire to set up an independent inquiry as to the Armenian massacres. His work is part of the Bryce Report (Toynbee 1916). Toynbee's analysis stops with the spring of 1916. It does not take into account three further massacres that occurred after 1916: one at Ra's al-'Ayn of 70,000, another at Intilli where 50,000 were killed, and a third at Dayr al-Zor where some 200,000 were reported killed (Aram Andonian, quoted in Dadrian 1986).

4. This was as a result of significant European and American missionary activity during this period, mainly by Presbyterian and Congregationalist groups. The American Board of Commissioners for Foreign Missions sent its first missionaries to the Middle East in 1819. After finding no success with Muslims and Jews, and little with Orthodox Christians, they turned their attention to Armenians, who were more willing to accept Protestantism despite strong opposition from the Armenian Gregorian Church. Missionaries from the American board of Congregationalists grew from twelve in 1819 to 209 in 1913. In that same year American missions were educating 26,000 students in 450 schools, mainly Armenians from Anatolia. See McCarthy 2001.

5. The Nestorian Church originated from the Nestorian controversy about the nature of Christ. A fourth-century bishop of Constantinople, Nestorius, regarded Christ as having a dual nature, one human and one divine. Nestorius was condemned by the Council of Ephesus in 431 CE. Those who refused to acknowledge his condemnation are referred to as Nestorians. See also Nisan 1991 and Arberry 1969.

6. The Armenakan Party was founded in Van in 1885. Its revolutionary programme stressed the need for nationalist organization and arming its adherents. The Hunchaks were founded in Geneva in 1887 by students and émigrés and then exported to Anatolia. The founders were Russian Armenians. None had lived in the Ottoman Empire. Their programme called for the assassination of both Ottoman Turks and Armenians who stood against the nationalist cause. From Europe, Hunchak organizers were sent first to Constantinople and then to the cities in the east. Their main recruits were young, educated Armenians. The third revolutionary party was the Dashnaks, founded in 1890 in Tiflis, and operating in Moscow, St Petersburg, and cities in Transcaucasia where there were Armenian students. Its programme was dedicated to the importation of arms and men into the Ottoman Empire, the use of terror, and the looting and destruction of Ottoman government installations. See Nalbandian 1963.

7. The Ottoman historians describe the events leading up to the Sasun massacres from a different perspective. They see the Sasunite attacks on the Ottoman tax collectors in 1894 as most significant. The Ottoman government is then credited with sending its army to pursue the Armenian guerrilla bands which were attacking Muslim inhabitants of villages along the withdrawal path. The Ottoman forces, along with the Kurdish 'Hamidiyye' semi-regular forces, then slaughtered the Armenian guerrillas as well as all the Armenian villagers who had sheltered them or resisted the Ottoman army. See McCarthy 2001.

8. According to Walker (1997), the Armenians in the Ottoman armies numbered as many as 100,000.

9. A number of the eyewitness accounts held in the Zoryan Institute in Toronto recount how some survivors were 'adopted' by Bedouin families and spent several years in the Syrian Jazireh herding sheep until British forces took over the region and demanded the release of these boys. Interviews with residents in Aleppo in 2005 also reveal that an underground network organized by a Muslim physician, who had daily contact with the Armenian refugees, was operating to identify adolescent Armenian girls and arrange for them to be moved out of the internment camps and married off to Muslims in order to save them from rape and death. See Zoryan Institute, Audio and video library of testimonies of survivors of the Armenian genocide.

10. See the recommendations over Syria in the King–Crane Commission (quoted in Hovannisian 1997b; United States 1943).

11. Hovannisian (1987) gives another justification for this attack on Armenia. It was derived from Atatürk's recognition of the menace that an expanded Armenia—as determined by the Treaty of Sèvres— posed to his efforts to create a Turkish republic. He needed to establish a border with Armenia which did not eat into eastern Anatolia. Thus the armies loyal to Atatürk breached the frontier with Armenia in October 1920 and forced the Armenian government to repudiate the terms of the Treaty of Sèvres, renouncing all claims to Turkish Armenia.

12. The First World War saw the greatest humanitarian effort in American history unfold. Near East Relief was the sole agency incorporated by Congress to aid refugees 'in biblical Lands'. Americans contributed to Armenian relief by building refugee camps and hospitals and by distributing food and clothing to hundreds of thousands of the destitute and orphaned. Most first-generation Armenian Americans owe their survival to Near East Relief.

4. THE KURDS SEEKING FREEDOM OF ETHNIC IDENTITY EXPRESSION

1. An estimate made by van Bruinessen (1992).
2. In January 1946 a Kurdish Republic of Mahabad was declared in the remote mountainous northern corner of Iran. In September that year Archie Roosevelt Jr, then assistant US military attaché in Tehran, visited the Kurdish Republic at Mahabad (Roosevelt 1947). These Kurds sought American government support for their national aspirations. By December 1946 the Kurdish state had collapsed and those Kurds involved took refuge in the Soviet Union and in Iraq.
3. The Kurds are predominantly Sunni Muslim, as are the majority of the populations of Turkey and Syria. In Iraq they are part of a sizeable Sunni minority (40–45 per cent) and in Iran they are a clear minority. See McDowall 2004.
4. *Bidoon* is a term in Arabic meaning 'without [citizenship]'. It is largely used to refer to those who are not recognized as citizens of the state in which they reside.
5. Another reason the struggle to define borders dissecting Kurdistan became important after the First World War was related to oil. No government—and its mandated authority—was willing to give up control of its oilfields in the Kurdish region: Rumaylan (Syria), Batman and Silvan (Turkey), or Kirkuk and Khaniqin (Iraq): see McDowall 2004.
6. In some cases a tribe may be no more than a ruling family that has attracted a large number of clients. The Barzani family in the nineteenth century attracted a large following of non-tribal peasantry escaping the repressive regime of neighbouring tribes. (McDowall 2004: 16).
7. Children of Kurdish and Arab tribal leaders from as far as the Hijaz were sent to these schools. They often became important government functionaries as well as the leaders of the various movements for independence and self-determination. For more details see Rogan 1996.
8. The Council of the League of Nations later gave Mosul to British-Mandated Iraq. See the decision of the 37th session of the Council of the League of Nations, 16 December 1925 (Vanly 1992: 161–2).
9. This was the Anglo-Iraqi Joint Declaration communicated to the Council of the League of Nations on 24 December 1922.
10. The Islamic Caliphate is a form of government representing the political unity and leadership of the Muslim world. From the time of Muhammad until 1924 successive Caliphates were held by the Umayyad, the Abbasid, and finally the Ottoman dynasties.

11. FO 371/164413. Report on the Census Taken in the Province of al Hassakah, 8 November 1962.

12. Öcalan founded this Marxist–Leninist Kurdish national liberation movement in 1975. Operating largely from the frontier regions, PKK activities are reported to have led to an estimated 12,000 deaths between 1984 and 1994. In response, the Turkish government admitted to emptying out 2,000 Kurdish villages in an attempt to undermine and defeat the PKK (McDowall 2004: 420).

13. 'Kurds Protest outside Syrian Parliament against Discrimination', Agence France Presse, 10 December 2002.

14. In the summer of 2005 the Syrian government announced that it was considering awarding nationality to 120,000 Kurds. There were reports of officials visiting *ajanib* Kurds and carrying out a census in preparation for this. In 2012, a year into the violent demonstrations that fanned across Syria, the Asad government offered to return citizenship to Kurdish *ajanib* and others.

5. PALESTINIANS RETURN TO THEIR 'MOTHERLAND'

1. The recognition was informal. To the Ottoman leadership, the Treaty of Paris marked a turning point in diplomacy: the courteous recognition that the nations of Europe accorded to the laws of the Ottoman state.

2. Ottoman Archives, F.M. (I), 47646/183, quoted in Karpat 1974.

3. As early as 1877 the Jewish colony at Jaffa as well as at St Jean d'Acre had aroused the concern of the Ottomans for the way in which the inhabitants had isolated themselves 'religiously and ethnically' from the local population (Ottoman Archives, F.M. (I), 36, 46.374/33, 1 February 1877, quoted in Karpat 1974: 71).

4. For example Dr Alfred Nossig of the Jewish Committee in Berlin made a request for an ambitious resettlement scheme in Palestine. The Ottoman authorities replied that at present they were occupied with resettling large groups of Muslims from Russia. Afterwards if land was left they would also take on the care of the Russian Jews (Ottoman Archives, F.M. (I), 587, 99125/39, quoted in Karpat 1974: 68).

5. In medieval times Jews had formed a very small portion of Jerusalem's population. Their numbers gradually increased over the centuries. By the middle of the nineteenth century Jews represented about half the total population of the city. By the end of the century Zionist immigration from Eastern Europe had produced a Jewish majority in Jerusalem (Kerr 1971: 355).

6. These are figures which Karpat derives from a number of sources including Margolis and Marx 1969 and Margalith 1957.
7. The commission estimated that a force of at least 50,000 would be needed initially in order to set up the proposed Jewish state.
8. See Antonius 1938.
9. In 1935 72,000 Jews arrived in Palestine. With a total population of just over a million, this was a very significant immigration. The total number of Jewish immigrants by this time is contested, with Khalidi (1971) indicating a figure near 300,000 and Farsoun and Zacharia (1997) a figure nearer to 150,000.
10. Hagana Archives, file 0014, 19 June 1938, quoted in Pappé 2006: 16.
11. Mayors of most Arab cities, the Arab National Guard, the Arab police, 137 Arab senior officials in the Mandate government, and 1,200 other Arab officials in government all publicly supported these demands and the strike (Zogby 1974: 109).
12. The legal status of Palestinian refugees in Syria is regulated by the Syrian Arab Republic Law no. 260 of 1957. The law stipulates that Palestinians living in Syria have the same duties and responsibilities as Syrian citizens other than nationality and political rights. In 1960 President Jamal Abdel Nasser (then president of the UAR) issued Decree no. 28 granting Palestinian travel documents to Palestinians in Syria.
13. Abridged Palestinian narrative history from Chatty and Lewando Hundt 2005: 69–70.
14. Abridged Palestinian narrative history from Chatty and Lewando Hundt 2005: 65.

6. THE MAKING OF A COSMOPOLITAN QUARTER: SHA'LAAN IN THE TWENTIETH AND TWENTY-FIRST CENTURIES

1. In 2001 the French Institute in Damascus (IFPO), in collaboration with the Maison de l'Orient de la Méditerranée/Université de Lyon 2 (GREMMO), and the Faculty of Architecture and Geography at the University of Damascus, began a multidisciplinary study of Damascus which undertook to examine the architecture and the socio-economic development of the Sha'laan Quarter of the city. In June 2006, with the assistance of Dr Françoise Metral, some of the notable families of this quarter were identified and interviewed. My role in the project was to contribute to the ethnographic history of the quarter through the personal testimonies of its inhabitants. With the support of a grant from the Council for British Research in the Levant (CBRL), I made three research trips to Damascus between May 2008 and April 2009

seeking out a representative sample of the oldest living residents of the quarter. I engaged a research associate, Jihad Darwaza, who ably sought out and negotiated informed consent with potential interviewees. Over three two-week periods I conducted a total of twenty-two interviews with a wide range of current and former residents in the quarter, from the grandson of Amir Nuri Sha'laan to a retired geography-teacher-turned-bookseller.

2. This quarter just outside the walls of the old city is today known as the Hariqa (fire) district.

3. The Sibki family came from Egypt with the campaign of Ibrahim Pasha in the mid-1800s. According to one Sibki informant, the grandfather had come as the campaign supply manager and was probably awarded this large tract of orchards and farmland as a reward for his service to the state.

4. The Midani family are generally understood to have built the two hybrid Franco/Arab two-storey houses in the orchards of Rawda just north of the Sibki farms.

7. IRAQIS AND SECOND-WAVE ASSYRIANS AS TEMPORARY GUESTS

1. Michel Aflaq, the Syrian political philosopher who was a major player in the founding of the Ba'th Party of Syria, went into exile to Iraq in the mid-1960s and became an important figure in the Iraqi Ba'th Party.

2. The reference here is to the Anglo-American invasion of Iraq in 2003, which was, in the minds of many Iraqis, unprovoked. The search for weapons of mass destruction was a Western construction later shown to be an empty goal.

3. In much the same way, advisers to US president George Bush and British prime minister Tony Blair had expected the Iraqi people to welcome British and American troops with flowers and sweets in 2003.

4. Hoffmann clearly articulates this dilemma in her description of how the first few international humanitarian aid organizations permitted to enter Syria in the mid-2000s regarded Iraqi refugees. The International Rescue Committee (IRC) saw Iraqis in Syria as troubled, victims of sexual violence, and in desperate need of trauma counselling. The Danish Refugee Council, furthermore, regarded the Iraqis in Syria as struggling due to their illegal status, where criminality and prostitution of their young women had created resentment with local hosting community. These assumptions were just that; they were not derived from any empirical studies. Rather, they emerged from the imaginings of the international humanitarian aid workers. See Hoffmann 2016: 103–5.

8. THE UNMAKING OF A STATE AS SYRIANS FLEE

1. Paul Bremer was the administrator of the Coalition Provisional Authority of Iraq between May 2003 and June 2004. He ruled by decree; his first order was banning the Ba'th Party and his second was dismantling the Iraqi army.

2. In 1920 the Covenant of the League of Nations endorsed the borders demarcated by Sir Mark Sykes between Syria and Turkey, Syria and Iraq, and Syria and Palestine/Transjordan. It also legitimized the French Mandatory authority over Syria and Greater Lebanon. This historic drawing exercise resulted in the division of many of the natural social groups of the Ottoman *Bilad al-Sham* across new nation-state borders.

BIBLIOGRAPHY

Abboud, Samer. 2016. *Syria*. Maiden, MA: Polity.

Agamben, Giorgio. 1998. *Homo Sacer: Sovereign Power and Bare Life*. Trans. D. Herrer-Roazen. Stanford: Stanford University Press.

Ahmad, Kamal Madhar. 1994. *Kurdistan during the First World War*. Trans. A. M. Ibrahim. London: Saqi.

Allsopp, Harriet. 2015. *The Kurds of Syria: Political Parties and Identity in the Middle East*. London: I. B. Tauris.

Amnesty International. 2008. *Iraq, Rhetoric and Reality: The Iraqi Refugee Crisis*, available at https://www.amnesty.org/en/documents/MDE14/011/2008/en/

Antonius, George. 1938. *The Arab Awakening: The Story of the Arab National Movement*. London: Hamish Hamilton.

Arberry, Arthur. 1969. *Religion in the Middle East*. Cambridge: Cambridge University Press.

Barbir, Karl. 1980. *Ottoman Rule in Damascus, 1708–1758*. Princeton: Princeton University Press.

Barbour, Neville. 1969. *Nisi Dominus*. Beirut: Institute for Palestine Studies.

Barkey, Karen, and Mark von Hagen, eds. 1997. *After Empire: Multiethnic Societies and Nation-Building: The Soviet Union and the Russian, Ottoman, and Habsburg Empires*. Boulder, CO: Westview.

Barsoumian, Hagop. 1997. 'The Eastern Question and the Tanzimat era'. In *The Armenian People from Ancient to Modern Times*, vol. II: *Foreign Dominion to Statehood: The Fifteenth Century to the Twentieth Century*, ed. R. G. Hovannisian, pp. 175–202. London: Macmillan.

Baum, Wilhelm, and Dietmar Winkler. 2003. *The Church of the East: A Concise History*. London: Routledge Curzon.

Bhabha, Homi. 1989. 'Location, intervention, incommensurability: a conversation with Homi Bhabha'. *Emergencies* 1: 63–88.

Bloxham, Donald. 2007. *The Great Game of Genocide*. London: Oxford University Press.

Bocco, Riccardo, Ronald Jaubert, and Françoise Métral, eds. 1993. *Steppes d'Arabies, états, pasteurs, agriculteurs et commerçants: le devenir des zones sèches*. Paris: Presses universitaires de France.

Brand, Laurie. 1988. 'Palestinians in Syria: the politics of integration'. *Middle East Journal* 4: 621–37.

Brandell, Inga, and Annika Rabo. 2003. 'Nations and nationalism: dangers and virtues of transgressing disciplines'. *Orientalia Suecana* 51–52: 35–46.

Brubaker, Rogers. 1995. 'Aftermaths of empire and the unmixing of peoples: historical and comparative perspectives'. *Ethnic and Racial Studies* 18 (2): 189–218.

Burgouyne, Elizabeth, ed. 1961. *Gertrude Bell, From her Personal Papers*, vol. II: *1914–1926*. London: Ernest Benn.

Chatelard, Géraldine. 2011. 'The politics of population movements in contemporary Iraq: a research agenda'. In *Writing the History of Iraq: Historiographical and Political Challenges*, ed. R. Bocco, J. Tejet, and P. Sluglett, pp. 359–65. London: World Scientific Publishers/Imperial College.

Chatty, Dawn. 2003. '"Operation Iraqi Freedom" and its phantom 1 million Iraqi refugees'. *Forced Migration Review* 18: 51.

———. 2007. 'Researching refugee youth in the Middle East: reflections on the importance of comparative research'. *Journal of Refugee Studies* 20 (2): 265–80.

———. 2010a. 'The Bedouin in contemporary Syria: the persistence of tribal authority and control'. *Middle East Journal* 64 (1): 29–49.

———. 2010b. *Dispossession and Displacement in the Modern Middle East*. Cambridge: Cambridge University Press.

———. 2013a [1986]. *From Camel to Truck: Bedouin in the Modern World*. 2nd edn. Cambridge: White Horse Press [New York: Vantage Press, 1986].

———. 2013b. 'Guests and hosts'. *Cairo Review* 9: 76–85.

———. 2014. 'The making of a cosmopolitan quarter: Sha'laan in the twentieth century'. *Syria Studies* 6 (2): 29–54.

Chatty, Dawn, and Roland Jaubert. 2002. 'Alternative perceptions of authority and control: the desert and the Ma'moura of Syria'. *Arab World Geographer* 5 (2): 71–3.

Chatty, Dawn, and Gillian Lewando Hundt, eds. 2005. *Children of Palestine: Experiencing Forced Migration in the Middle East*. Oxford: Berghahn Books.

Chatty, Dawn, and Nisrine Mansour. 2012. 'Displaced Iraqis: predicaments and perceptions in exile in the Middle East'. *Refuge* 28 (1): 97–107.

Chatty, Dawn, et al. 2014. 'Ensuring quality education for refugee youth from Syria (12–25 years): a mapping exercise'. University of Oxford, Refugee Studies Centre, 88 pp.

Colson, Elizabeth. 2003 'Forced migration and the anthropological response'. *Journal of Refugee Studies* 16 (1): 1–16.

Dadrian, Vahakn. 1986. 'The Naim–Andonian Documents on the World War I destruction of Armenians: the anatomy of a genocide'. *International Journal of Middle East Studies* 18: 311–60.

BIBLIOGRAPHY

————. 1997. *The History of the Armenian Genocide: Ethnic Conflict from the Balkans to Anatolia to the Caucasus*. Providence, RI: Berghahn.

Davison, Roderic H. 1954. 'Turkish attitudes concerning Christian–Muslim equality in the nineteenth century'. *American Historical Review* 59 (4): 844–64.

Derrida, Jacques. 2000. 'Hostipitality'. *Agnelaki* 5 (3): 3–18.

Dodge, Toby. 2003. *Inventing Iraq: The Failure of Nation-Building and a History Denied*. London: Hurst.

————. 2006. 'Iraq: the contradictions of exogenous state-building in historical perspective'. *Third World Quarterly* 27 (1): 187–200.

Eagleton, William, Jr. 1963. *The Kurdish Republic of 1946*. London: Oxford University Press.

ECHO. 2015. *Refugee Crisis in Europe. European Civil Protection and Humanitarian Aid Operations*. Brussels: European Commission Humanitarian Aid and Civil Protection Department.

Farsoun, Samih K., and Christina E. Zacharia. 1997. *Palestine and the Palestinians*. Boulder, CO: Westview.

Fernández, Eva, et al. 2014. 'Ancient DNA Analysis of 8000 BC Near Eastern Farmers Supports an Early Neolithic Pioneer Maritime Colonization of Mainland Europe through Cyprus and the Aegean Islands'. PLOS Genetics, available at http://journals.plos.org/plosgenetics/article?id=10.1371/journal.pgen.1004401

Fletcher, R. A. 1992. *Moorish Spain*. London: Weidenfeld & Nicolson.

Gambill, Gary. 2004. 'The Kurdish reawakening in Syria'. *Middle East Intelligence Bulletin* 6 (4): 1–8.

Gelvin, James L. 1998. *Divided Loyalties: Nationalism and Mass Politics in Syria at the Close of Empire*. Berkeley: University of California Press.

Gaunt, David. 2009. 'The Assyrian Genocide of 1915'. Assyrian Genocide Research Center, available at http://www.seyfocenter.com/english/38/

Gorgas, Jordi. 2007. 'La jeunesse Kurde entre rupture et engagement militant'. In *La Syria au présent: reflets d'une société*, ed. B. Dupret, Z. Ghazzal, Y. Courbage, and M. al-Dbiyat, pp. 269–76. Paris: Actes Sud.

Grabill, Joseph. 1971. *Protestant Diplomacy and the Near East*. Minneapolis: University of Minnesota Press.

Great Britain. 1896. Parliament, House of Commons. Sessional Papers, vol. 109, Turkey no. 1, C. 7894.

Gunter, Michael. 2014. *Out of Nowhere: The Kurds of Syria in Peace and War*. London: Hurst.

Hacker, Jane. 1960. 'Modern 'Amman: A Social Study'. Department of Geography Research Papers Series no. 3, University of Durham.

Hannerz, Ulf. 1996. *Transnational Connections: Cultures, People, Places*. London: Routledge.

Harper, Andrew. 2008. 'Iraq's refugees: ignored and unwanted'. *International Review of the Red Cross* 90 (869): 169–90.

Harvey, L. P. 1990. *Islamic Spain, 1250–1500*. Chicago: University of Chicago Press.

———. 1992. 'The political, social and cultural history of the Moriscos'. In *The Legacy of Muslim Spain*, ed. S. K. Jayyusi and M. Marâin, pp. 201–34. Handbuch der Orientalistik. Erste Abteilung, Nahe und der Mittlere Osten 12. Leiden: Brill.

Helms, Christina. 1981. *The Cohesion of Saudi Arabia*. London: Croom Helm.

Herzl, Theodor. 1896. *Der Judenstaat*. Trans. S. D'Avigdor as *The Jewish State*. New York: American Zionist Emergency Council.

Hirschon, Renée. 2001. 'Surpassing Nostalgia: Personhood and the Experience of Displacement'. Colson Lecture, University of Oxford, Refugee Studies Centre [unpublished].

Hobsbawm, Eric J. 1962. *The Age of Revolution: Europe, 1789–1848*. London: Weidenfeld & Nicolson.

———. 1997. 'The end of empires'. In *After Empire: Multiethnic Societies and Nation-Building: The Soviet Union and the Russian, Ottoman, and Habsburg Empires*, ed. K. Barkey and M. von Hagen, pp. 12–16. Boulder, CO: Westview.

Hoffmann, Sophia. 2016. *Iraqi Migrants in Syria: The Crisis before the Storm*. Syracuse: Syracuse University Press.

Hovannisian, Richard G. 1967. *Armenia on the Road to Independence, 1918*. Berkeley: University of California Press.

———. 1983. 'Causasian Armenia between imperial and Soviet rule: the interlude of national independence'. In *Transcaucasia: Nationalism and Socialism*, ed. R.G. Suny, pp. 277–92. Ann Arbor: University of Michigan Press.

———., ed. 1987. *The Armenian Genocide in Perspective*. New Brunswick, NJ and Oxford: Transaction.

———. 1997a. 'The Armenian question in the Ottoman Empire 1876 to 1914'. In *The Armenian People from Ancient to Modern Times*, vol. II: *Foreign Dominion to Statehood: The Fifteenth Century to the Twentieth Century*, ed. R. G. Hovannisian, pp. 203–38. London: Macmillan.

———. 1997b. 'The Republic of Armenia'. In *The Armenian People from Ancient to Modern Times*, vol. II: *Foreign Dominion to Statehood: The Fifteenth Century to the Twentieth Century*, ed. R. G. Hovannisian, pp. 303–46. London: Macmillan.

Humphreys, R. Stephen. 1999. *Between Memory and Desire: The Middle East in a Troubled Age*. Berkeley: University of California Press.

BIBLIOGRAPHY

Hütteroth, Wolfgang, and Kamal Abdelfattah. 1977. *Historical Geography of Palestine, Transjordan and Southern Syria in the Late Sixteenth Century*. Nuremberg: Junge & Sons.

International Crisis Group. 2008. *Failed Responsibility: Iraqi Refugees in Syria, Jordan and Lebanon*. Middle East Report No. 77. Brussels: ICG.

———. 2013. *Blurring the Borders: Syrian Spillover Risks for Turkey*. Europe Report No. 225. Antakya/Ankara/Istanbul/Brussels: ICG.

Johns, Jeremy. 1994. 'The *longue durée*: state and settlement strategies in southern Transjordan across the Islamic centuries'. In *Village, Steppe and State: The Social Origins of Modern Jordan*, ed. E. Rogan and T. Tell, pp. 1–31. London: British Academic Press.

Kalkas, Barbara. 1971. 'The revolt of 1936: a chronicle of events'. In *The Transformation of Palestine: Essays on the Origin and Development of the Arab–Israeli Conflict*, ed. I. Abu-Lughod, pp. 237–74. Evanston, IL: Northwestern University Press.

Kanafani, Ghassan. 1972. *The 1936–39 Revolt in Palestine*. New York: Committee for a Democratic Palestine.

Karal, Enver Ziya. 1982. 'Non-Muslim representatives in the first constitutional assembly 1876–1877'. In *Christians and Jews in the Ottoman Empire*, ed. B. Braude and B. Lewis, pp. 387–401. New York: Holmes & Meier.

Karpat, Kemal H. 1974. 'Ottoman immigration policies and settlement in Palestine'. In *Settler Regimes in Africa and the Arab World: The Illusion of Endurance*, ed. I. Abu-Lughod and B. Abu Laban, pp. 57–72. Wilmette, IL: Medina University Press International.

———. 1979. 'The status of the Muslims under European rule: the eviction and settlement of the Cerkes'. *Journal of the Institute of Muslim Minority Affairs (JIMMA)* 1: 7–27.

———. 1985. *Ottoman Population 1830–1914: Demographic and Social Characteristics*. Madison: University of Wisconsin Press.

Kedourie, Elie. 1984. 'Minorities and majorities in the Middle East'. *European Journal of Sociology* 25 (2): 276–82.

Kendal [Nezan]. 1980. 'The Kurds under the Ottoman Empire'. In *A People without a Country: The Kurds and Kurdistan*, ed. G. Chaliand, pp. 11–37. London: Zed.

Kerr, Malcolm H. 1971. 'The changing political status of Jerusalem'. In *The Transformation of Palestine: Essays on the Origin and Development of the Arab–Israeli Conflict*, ed. I. Abu-Lughod, pp. 344–78. Evanston, IL: Northwestern University Press.

Khairallah, Shereen. 1991. *Railways in the Middle East 1856–1948: Political and Economic Background*. Beirut: Librarie du Liban.

———. 1998. 'Railway networks of the Middle East to 1948'. In *The Syrian Land: Processes of Integration and Fragmentation: Bilad al-Sham from the*

Eighteenth to the Twentieth Century, ed. T. Philipp and B. Schaebler, pp. 000–00. Stuttgart: Franz Steiner Verlag.

al-Khalidi, A., S. Hoffman, and V. Tanner. 2007. *Iraqi Refugees in the Syrian Arab Republic: A Field-Based Snapshot*. Washington, DC: Brookings Institute/University of Bern Project on Internal Displacement.

Khalidi, Rashid. 1997. *Palestinian Identity: The Construction of Modern National Consciousness*. New York: Columbia University Press.

———. 2001. 'The Palestinians and 1948: the underlying causes of failure'. In *The War for Palestine: Rewriting the History of 1948*, ed. E. L. Rogan and A. Shlaim, pp. 12–36. Cambridge Middle East Studies 15. Cambridge: Cambridge University Press.

Khalidi, Walid, ed. 1971. *From Haven to Conquest: Readings in Zionism and the Palestine Problem until 1948*. Beirut: Institute for Palestine Studies.

Khoury, Philip S. 1983. *Urban Notables and Arab Nationalism*. Cambridge: Cambridge University Press.

Kirisci, Kemal. 2013. 'Syrian Humanitarian Crisis: The Fundamental Difficulties Facing Turkey'. Brookings Institution, available at https://www.brookings.edu/articles/syrian-humanitarian-crisis-the-fundamental-difficulties-facing-turkey/

Lancaster, William, and Fidelity Lancaster. 1995. 'Land use and population in the area north of Karak'. *Levant* 27: 103–24.

Lepsius, Johannes. 1897. *Armenia and Europe: An Indictment*. London: Hodder & Stoughton.

Lerner, Daniel, Lucille W. Pevsner, and David Riesman. 1958. *The Passing of Traditional Society: Modernizing the Middle East*. New York: Free Press/Collier-Macmillan.

Levy, Avigdor, ed. 2002. *Jews, Turks, Ottomans: A Shared History, Fifteenth through the Twentieth Century*. Syracuse, NY: Syracuse University Press.

Levy, Gideon. 2002. 'Education under Occupation: The Other Children of the War'. *Ha'aretz*, 1 September.

Lewis, Bernard. 1954. 'Studies in the Ottoman Archives, No. 1'. *Bulletin of the School of Oriental and African Studies* 16: 479–501.

Lewis, Norman. 1987. *Nomads and Settlers in Syria and Jordan, 1800–1980*. Cambridge: Cambridge University Press.

Lewis, Reina. 2004. *Rethinking Orientalism: Women, Travel, and the Ottoman Harem*. London: I. B. Tauris.

Lindholm, Charles. 2002. *The Islamic Middle East: Tradition and Change*. Oxford: Blackwell.

Loizos, Peter. 1999. 'Ottoman half-lives: long-term perspectives on particular forced migrations'. *Journal of Refugee Studies* 12 (3): 237–63.

BIBLIOGRAPHY

Lowe, Robert. 2006. *The Syrian Kurds: A People Discovered*. London: Chatham House.

Mackay, Angus. 1992. 'The Jews in Spain during the Middle Ages'. In *Spain and the Jews: The Sephardi Experience 1492 and after*, ed. E. Kedourie, pp. 33–50. London: Thames & Hudson.

Malkki, Liisa H. 1995. *Purity and Exile: Violence, Memory, and National Cosmology among Hutu Refugees in Tanzania*. Chicago: University of Chicago Press.

Marfleet, Philip. 2007. 'Iraq's refguees: "exit" from the state'. *International Journal of Contemporary Iraqi Studies* 1 (3): 397–419.

Marfleet, Philip, and Dawn Chatty. 2009. 'Iraq's Refugees—beyond "Tolerance"', *Forced Migration Policy Briefings* 5. University of Oxford, Refugee Studies Centre at the University of Oxford.

Margalith, Israel. 1957. *Le Baron de Rothschild et la colonisation juive en Palestine*. Paris: Libraire M. Riviere.

Margolis, Max, and Alexander Marx. 1969. *History of the Jewish People*. New York: Atheneum.

Mauss, Marcel. 2016 [1925]. *The Gift Expanded Edition*. Trans. Jane Guyer. Chicago: Hau Books.

McCarthy, Justin. 1983. *Muslims and Minorities: The Population of Ottoman Anatolia and the End of the Empire*. New York: New York University Press.

————. 1995. *Death and Exile: The Ethnic Cleansing of Ottoman Muslims, 1821–1922*. Princeton: Darwin Press.

————. 2001. *The Ottoman Peoples and the End of Empire*. London: Arnold.

McDowall, David. 2004. *A Modern History of the Kurds*. London: I. B. Tauris.

Melson, Robert. 1996. *Revolution and Genocide: On the Origins of the Armenian Genocide and Holocaust*: Chicago: University of Chicago Press.

Migliorino, Nicola. 2006. '"Kulna Suriyyin"? The Armenian community and the state in contemporary Syria'. *Revue des mondes musulmans et de la Méditerranée* 115–16 (special issue on La Syrie au quotidien: cultures et pratiques du changement): 97–115.

————. 2007. *(Re)constructing Armenia in Lebanon and Syria: Ethno-Cultural Diversity and the State in the Aftermath of a Refugee Crisis*. Oxford: Berghahn.

Montgomery, Harriet. 2005. *The Kurds of Syria: An Existence Denied*. Berlin: Europäisches Zentrum für Kurdische Studien.

Morris, Benny. 1987. *The Birth of the Palestinian Refugee Problem, 1947–1949*. Cambridge: Cambridge University Press.

————. 1992. *The Routes of Appeasement*. London: Routledge.

Nalbandian, Louise. 1963. *The Armenian Revolutionary Movement*. Berkeley and Los Angeles: University of California Press.

Nazdar, Mustafa. 1993. 'The Kurds in Syria'. *In People without a Country: The Kurds and Kurdistan*, ed. G. Chaliand, pp. 198–201. London: Zed Books.

BIBLIOGRAPHY

Niles, Emory, and Arthur Sutherland. 1919. 'The Report of Captain Emory H. Niles and Mr. Arthur E. Sutherland, Jr. on Trip of Investigation through Eastern Turkish Vilayets' [Niles and Sutherland Report]. US National Archives, 184.021/175.

Nisan, Mordechai. 1991. 'Assyrians: an ancient people, a perennial struggle'. In *Minorities of the Middle East: A History of Struggle and Self-Expression*, pp. 180–94. Jefferson, NC: McFarland.

Oliphant, Laurence. 1880. *The Land of Gilead*. London and Edinburgh: Blackwood & Sons.

Papikian, Hakob. 1919. Adanayi Yegherne. 'Teghekagir' [The Adana Calamity. 'Report']. Self-published report.

Pappé, Ilan. 2006. *The Ethnic Cleansing of Palestine*. Oxford: Oneworld.

Pierret, Thomas. 2013. *Religion and State in Syria: The Sunni Ulama from Coup to Revolution*. Cambridge: Cambridge University Press.

Pinson, Mark. 1972. 'Ottoman colonization of the Circassians in Rumili after the Crimean War'. *Etudes Balkaniques* 3: 71–85.

Pinto, Paulo G. 2007, 'Les Kurdes en Syrie'. In *La Syrie au présent: reflets d'une société*, ed. B. Dupret, Z. Ghazzal, Y. Courbage, and M. al-Dbiyat, pp. 259–68. Paris: Actes Sud.

Provence, Michael. 2005. *The Great Syrian Revolt and the Rise of Arab Nationalism*. Austin: University of Texas Press.

Quataert, Donald. 2000. *The Ottoman Empire, 1700–1922*. Cambridge: Cambridge University Press.

Al-Rasheed, Madawi. 1994. 'The myth of return: Iraqi Arab and Assyrian refugees in London'. *Journal of Refugee Studies* 7 (2/3): 199–219.

Richter, Julius. 1910. *A History of Protestant Missions in the Near East*. Edinburgh: Oliphant, Anderson & Ferrier.

Rogan, Eugene. 1996. 'Aşiret Mektebi: Abdulhamid II's School for Tribes 1892–1907'. *International Journal of Middle East Studies* 28: 83–107.

———. 1999. *Frontiers of the State in the Late Ottoman Empire*. Cambridge: Cambridge University Press.

———. 2009. *The Arabs: A History*. London: Allen Lane.

———. 2015. *The Fall of the Ottomans: The Great War in the Middle East, 1914–1920*. London: Penguin, Random House.

Rogan, Eugene, and Tariq Tell, eds. 1994. *Village, Steppe and State: The Social Origins of Modern Jordan*. London: British Academy Press.

Roosevelt, Archibald Bulloch, Jr. 1947. 'The Kurdish Republic of Mahabad'. *Middle East Journal* 1: 247–69.

Sassoon, Joseph. 2009. *The Iraqi Refugees: The New Crisis in the Middle East*. London: I. B. Tauris.

Schumacher, Gottlieb. 1888. *The Jaulan*. London: Palestinian Exploration Fund.

BIBLIOGRAPHY

Shafir, Gershon. 1999. 'Zionism and colonialism: a comparative approach'. In *The Israel/Palestine Question: Rewriting Histories*, ed. I. Pappé, pp. 81–96. London: Routledge.

Shami, Seteney. 1982. 'Ethnicity and Leadership: The Circassians in Jordan'. Ph.D. thesis, University of California, Berkeley.

———. 1995. 'Disjuncture in ethnicity: negotiating Circassian identity in Jordan, Turkey and the Caucasus'. *New Perspectives on Turkey* 12: 79–95.

Shaw, Stanford J., and Ezel Kural Shaw. 1977. *History of the Ottoman Empire and Modern Turkey*, 2 vols. Vol. II. Cambridge: Cambridge University Press.

Shlaim, Avi. 1988. *Collusion across the Jordan: King Abdullah, the Zionist Movement, and the Partition of Palestine*. Oxford: Oxford University Press.

Singer, J. David, and Melvin Small. 1972. *The Wages of War 1816–1965: A Statistical Handbook*. New York: John Wiley & Sons.

Slim, Hugo, and Lorenzo Trombetta. 2014. 'Syria Crisis Common Context Analysis'. Report for the Inter-Agency Standing Committee. New York: United Nations.

Snell, John. 1954. 'Wilson on Germany and the Fourteen Points'. *Journal of Modern History* 26 (4): 364–9.

Tannous, Izzat. 1988. *The Palestinians: Eyewitness History of Palestine under the British Mandate*. New York: IGT Company.

Tekeli, Ilhan. 1994. 'Involuntary displacement and the problem of resettlement in Turkey from the Ottoman Empire to the present'. In *Population Displacement and Resettlement: Development and Conflict in the Middle East*, ed. S. Shami, pp. 202–26. New York: Centre for Migration Studies.

Temperley, Harold. 1936. *England and the Near East: The Crimea*. London: Longmans, Green.

Thompson, Elizabeth. 2000. *Colonial Citizens: Republican Rights, Paternal Privilege, and Gender in French Syria and Lebanon*. New York: Columbia University Press.

Toledano, E. R. 1982. *The Ottoman Slave Trade and its Suppression: 1840–1890*. Princeton: Princeton University Press.

Toynbee, Arnold. 1916. *The Treatment of Armenians in the Ottoman Empire*. London: HMSO [part of the Bryce Report].

UNHCR. 2005. 'Self-Study Module 1: An Introduction to International Protection. Protecting Persons of Concern to UNHCR', available at http://www.unhcr.org/publications/legal/3ae6bd5a0/self-study-module-1-introduction-international-protection-protecting-persons.html

———. 2009a. 'Report on Asylum Levels and Trends in Industrialized Countries', available at http://www.unhcr.org/statistics/unhcrstats/4ba7341a9/asylum-levels-trends-industrialized-countries-2009-statistical-overview.html

———. 2009b. 'UNHCR Policy on Refugee Protection and Solutions in

Urban Areas, September 2009', available at http://www.unhcr.org/protection/hcdialogue%20/4ab356ab6/unhcr-policy-refugee-protection-solutions-urban-areas.html

———. 2014. 'Country Operation Profile 2014: Syrian Arab Republic', available at http://www.unhcr.org/pages/49e486a76.html

———. 2017. Europe: Syrian Asylum Applications, available at http://data.unhcr.org/syrianrefugees/asylum.php

United States. 1943. *Papers Relating to the Foreign Relations of the United States, 1919:The Paris Peace Conference*, ed. Joseph V. Fuller, vols. III-2, VI. Department of State. Washington DC: Government Printing Office.

UNRWA. 1992. *Basic Data on Palestine Refugees and UNRWA*. Vienna: United Nations Relief and Works Agency for Palestine Refugees in the Near East.

———. 2017. *UNRWA in Figures 2016*. UNRWA Communications Division, available at https://www.unrwa.org/resources/about-unrwa/unrwa-figures-2016

van Bruinessen, Martin. 1992. *Agha, Shaikh, and State: The Social and Political Structures of Kurdistan*. London: Zed.

Vanly, Ismet Sheriff. 1992. 'Kurdistan in Iraq'. In *People without a Country: The Kurds and Kurdistan*, ed. G. Chaliand, pp. 153–90. London: Zed.

Waines, David. 1971a. 'The failure of the nationalist resistance'. In *The Transformation of Palestine: Essays on the Origin and Development of the Arab–Israeli Conflict*, ed. I. Abu-Lughod, pp. 207–36. Evanston, IL: Northwestern University Press.

———. 1971b. *The Unholy War: Israel and Palestine, 1897–1971*. Wilmette, IL: Medina University Press International.

Walker, Christopher J. 1980. *Armenia: The Survival of a Nation*. London: Croom Helm.

———. 1997. 'World War I and the Armenian genocide'. In *The Armenian People from Ancient to Modern Times*, vol. II: *Foreign Dominion to Statehood: The Fifteenth Century to the Twentieth Century*, ed. R. G. Hovannisian, pp. 239–74. London: Macmillan.

Wedeen, Lisa. 1999. *Ambiguities of Domination: Politics, Rhetoric and Symbols in Contemporary Syria*. Chicago: University of Chicago Press.

White, Ben, Simone Haysom, and Eleanor Davey. 2013. 'Refugees, host states, and displacement in the Middle East: an enduring challenge'. *Humanitarian Exchange HPN* 59: 20–2.

Wilkinson, John. 1983. 'Traditional concepts of territory in south east Arabia'. *Geographical Journal* 149 (3): 201–315.

Yassin-Kassab, Robin, and Leila al-Shami. 2016. *Burning Country: Syrians in the Revolution and War*. London: Pluto.

Zaman, Tahir. 2016. *Islamic Traditions of Refuge in the Crises of Iraq and Syria*. London: Palgrave Macmillan.

BIBLIOGRAPHY

Zogby, James. 1974. 'The Palestinian Revolt of the 1930s'. In *Settler Regimes in Africa and the Arab World: The Illusion of Endurance*, ed. I. Abu-Lughod and B. Abu-Laban, eds., pp. 94–115. Wilmette, IL: Medina University Press.

Zolberg, Aristide R. 1982. 'State Formation and its Victims: Refugee Movements in Early Modern Europe'. Verhaegen Lecture, Erasmus University, Rotterdam.

Zoryan Institute. Audio and video library of testimonies of survivors of the Armenian genocide. Zoryan Institute, Toronto.

Interviews

Abdul-Salam, 2005.
Abu Alaa, 2006.
Abu Wadi, 2008.
Adel, 2006.
Adnan, 2001, 2005, 2006, 2011.
Afaf, 2009.
Barakat, 2005.
Bedros, 2009.
Fatima, 2008.
Fayez, 2008.
Hala, 2014.
Josephine, 2000.
Maha, 2011.
Mahmoud, 2011.
Mahmoud, 2014.
Mansour, 2006.
Marwan, 2014.
Mohammed, 2006.
Muna, 2011.
Amir Nawwaf, 2009.
Nazek, 2009.
Qahtan, 2006.
Ra'isa, 2005.
Rana, 2015.
Reem, 2015.
Sa'ada, 2001.
Samira, 2011.
Sarkis, 2005.
Suheil, 2009.
Umaymah, 2009.
Um Luqman, 2006.
Usama, 2008.

BIBLIOGRAPHY

Vahan, 2005.
Varukan, 2005.
Watfa, 2008.
Yusuf, 2006.
Ziyad, 2008.
Zuheir, 2008.

INDEX

269

INDEX

al-Asad, Bashar, 139, 140, 216, 221–3, 231, 233, 234, 252
al-Asad, Hafez, 140, 220
al-Askari Mosque, 201
Assyrians, 7, 8, 16, 40, 42, 44, 92, 122, 212, 232
  Adana massacre (1909), 98
  Aramaic, 92, 109
  Church of the East [Nestorian], 8, 12, 90, 92, 117, 200, 201, 202, 204, 232, 249
  in Iraq, 41, 129, 200, 201, 202, 204
  in Kurdistan, 116
  massacres (1894–6), 98
  genocide (1914–20), 92, 98, 109
  millet, 92
Atassi, Jamal, 191, 193
Atatürk, Kemal [Mustafa Kemal], 99, 128–31, 250
Attar family, 191
Austro-Hungarian Empire (1867–1918), 8, 18, 20, 29, 33, 95
Azerbaijan, 93, 99
Azeris, 50

B'eira, Rashid, 191
Ba'th Party, 188, 225, 254, 255
Babylon, 3, 16
Badia, 9, 68, 184
Badr Khan, Prince Jaladat, 134
Baggara tribal confederation, 234
Baghdad, 3, 71, 127, 206
  Abbasid Caliphate (750–1258), 16
  British Mandate (1920–32), 180, 203, 204
  First World War (1914–18), 125
  Kurds, 114, 115, 121, 127
  US-led War (2003–11), 206, 209
al-Baghdadi, Abu Bakr, 232
Bakdash, Khalid, 136, 138

Baksheesh, 217
Balaclava, battle of (1854), 55
Balfour, James, 155
Balfour Declaration (1917), 155–6, 163
Balkan wars (1912–13), 19, 60, 64, 73
Barada river, 13
  Yazid tributary, 181, 185
Barzan, 132
Barzani, Mustafa, 132, 137
Barzani family, 251
Barzani tribal confederation, 119
Basel, 154
Basra, 124, 203, 204
basterma (pastrami), 190
Batman, 251
Battle of Balaclava (1854), 55
Battle of Basra (1914), 124
Battle of Navarino (1827), 30
Battle of Sarikamish (1914–15), 97
Battle of Shu'aiba (1915), 124
Battle of Sinope (1853), 31
Batum, 153
Bayazit, 97
Bedouin, 9, 11, 40, 114, 115, 117, 119, 121, 122
  Aneza, 72, 119, 177
  Armenians, relations with, 250
  Beni Khalid, 233
  and Circassians, 62, 68, 69, 72–3, 75, 77, 80
  Al Fadl, 74, 75, 80, 248
  Hadidiyin, 233
  Al Hassanna, 233, 234
  in Iraq, 203, 204
  Kurds, relations with, 118, 133
  Mawali, 233–4
  in Palestine, 149, 150
  Shammar, 70, 118, 119
  and Syrian war (2011–), 228, 233–4

271

INDEX

INDEX

INDEX

INDEX